PORTFOLIO

LEADING FROM THE TOP

With more than half a century of work experience, 'Bala' has a unique blend of exposure to industry and academia that is not easy to come by. Three and a half decades of senior- and board-level responsibilities in companies such as Imperial Chemical Industries, Britannia, and Wipro are complemented by teaching and research activities at the Indian Institutes of Management Ahmedabad and Bangalore over the last two decades, and still counting. A non-practising chartered accountant with a PhD in business finance, his interests span corporate governance, business ethics and responsibility, and board-level counselling.

He has been on statutory and advisory boards of listed companies as well as early-to-midterm start-ups. He has served as a member of National Advisory Committee on Accounting Standards, CII's National Council on Corporate Governance, the advisory committee of National Stock Exchange's Centre for Excellence in Corporate Governance as well as a government committee on corporate excellence through governance, many of whose far-seeing recommendations have found their way into corporate legislation. He serves on the editorial and advisory boards of some Indian and International scholarly journals. He has designed and delivered training programmes for several hundred incumbent directors of public- and private-sector corporations, and taught courses to many management students and executives. He has authored and/or edited several books and research papers. *Leading from the Top* is his seventh book.

Bala lives with his wife, son, daughter-in-law and a charming granddaughter in Thane, near Mumbai.

INDIA'S BESTSELLING BUSINESS BOOKS SERIES

IIM
AHMEDABAD
BUSINESS BOOKS

LEADING
FROM THE TOP

Directors Who Make the Difference

N. BALASUBRAMANIAN

PORTFOLIO
PENGUIN

An imprint of Penguin Random House

PORTFOLIO

USA | Canada | UK | Ireland | Australia
New Zealand | India | South Africa | China | Singapore

Portfolio is part of the Penguin Random House group of companies
whose addresses can be found at global.penguinrandomhouse.com

Published by Penguin Random House India Pvt. Ltd
4th Floor, Capital Tower 1, MG Road,
Gurugram 122 002, Haryana, India

Penguin
Random House
India

First published by Random House India in 2013
Published in Portfolio by Penguin Random House India 2018

ISBN 9788184003161

Typeset in Sabon by Saanvi Graphics, Noida

Printed at Manipal Technologies Limited, India

www.penguin.co.in

MIX
Paper | Supporting
responsible forestry
FSC® C043100

This is a legitimate digitally printed version of the book and therefore might not
have certain extra finishing on the cover.

To
the Generation Next
Madhu, Rashmi, and Anannya

CONTENTS

Case Summaries

PREFACE

There was a time when we used to read about the corporate failures in the UK, the US, and elsewhere in the developed world and feel relieved that Indian corporate sector had kept itself by and large free from such developments. Of course, there were occasional capital market upheavals such as the Harshad Mehta securities scam and the Unit Trust debacle in the 1990s but these were taken in the stride as serious but relatively rare exceptions. Maybe many corporate misdemeanours were not detected and exposed. But the new millennium started with an unprecedented corporate fraud (Satyam Computers: although surfacing only in 2009, its origins went back to 2002); and as the years passed by, not a day has gone by without some report or the other about corporate dealings that don't seem right. Maybe our awareness of what is right and wrong in a corporate format had improved with the worldwide increase in corporate crime, maybe our reporting and investigative journalism had come of age, maybe the corporate sector was taking its cue from the scandals in government and political governance; whatever the cause, the striking fact is that much needs to be done to cleanse the corporate system to get it back on track of making business profitable through legitimate means, and ensuring the interests of all stakeholders, and especially absentee, shareholders.

There is need for greater appreciation of the basic ground rules in governing corporations. While the board is responsible for overseeing and ensuring good governance, it is equally also necessary for executive management and the ranks down the line to gain such appreciation so that they can perceive their role in the overall framework more precisely and discharge their assigned functions accordingly. This will not, of course, eliminate devious elements engaging in inappropriate activities for personal gain by design and intent; on the other hand, it would help those who wish to perform the right way but fail because of lack of proper understanding of the corporate format. I would like to believe this latter category represents a vast majority of the population, irrespective of their station in the corporate hierarchy, whether at the top at the board and executive levels or lower down in operational jobs. This short volume is addressed to those who while looking after their interests to the best of their ability, would also like to do so in the right way. After all, means are as important as the ends themselves.

Today's managers and professionals are tomorrow's directors and chief executives. A broader understanding of good governance and its consequences for themselves and the stakeholders they serve would help the boards of the future to better discharge their obligations in full measure. That will be a huge positive for the Indian corporate sector and concomitantly for the well-being of the country and its people.

If this volume helps and promotes better understanding and practice of good corporate governance among even a modest proportion of corporate directors, executives and managers, the students and others preparing for such positions, and the practitioners who advise, counsel and guide corporate officers, the book would have served its purpose.

FOREWORD

This book has been written by a person who deserves to be recognized as the father of corporate governance in India. He is undoubtedly one of the foremost thinkers in the field of corporate governance in the world. He has contributed enormously to improving corporate governance in India through his extensive research, numerous publications, teaching in academic and executive programes and participation in actual governance of corporations. This book, *Leading from the Top: Directors who make the Difference*, takes you through nuances of the entire gamut of issues involved in governing business organizations. The enormously rich experience of the author comes through in the lucidity of the language and the style of presentation. The highlight of the book is the extensive use of appropriate vignettes that capture the essence of ideas and concepts discussed. These provide the readers with anchors to navigate through the landscape of governance. Emphasizing the need for corporations to be ethical and observe the highest standards of probity, the author provides invaluable advice on how boards and individuals must conduct themselves to deliver on the expectations of stakeholders. The book is a mustread for all executives. While the relatively junior executives will get to unravel the fuzzy world of top management, the senior executives will learn about how they ought to conduct themselves in the near future when they are given the reigns of governance. Incumbent directors will also find the book useful as a guide to enhance their board contribution.

Samir K. Barua
Professor and Former Director
IIM Ahmedabad
October 2013

INTRODUCTION

Everyone remembers God when they are in trouble
No one remembers Him in good times
If you remembered Him in good times
Why will there be any bad times?

—Poet Saint Kabir

Satyam, Sahara, Sardha, SKS Microfinance, National Spot Exchange—just to mention a few corporations that made media headlines for all the wrong reasons: poor corporate governance, investor-inimical activities, regulatory circumvention, or even outright fraud on the companies and their shareholders. That India is not any exception and has been in august company elsewhere in the developed world is hardly a consolation for a country that is identified, with reason, as among the potential economic powerhouses of the future. And certainly not for its corporate sector which has shown entrepreneurial aggression not only within the country but also beyond its shores through a significant expansion of its footprint.

Why do companies, their promoters and executives with reputations and track records indulge in such misdemeanours despite the knowledge that long arms of truth and fair play are bound to catch up with them sooner or later? Is there something in the corporate DNA which, like Duryodhana's predicament in the Mahabharata, drives them towards the unethical even while knowing it to be wrong? And should this be happening despite constant reiterations of the need for mutually beneficial relationships between business and society? Peter Drucker, for example, wrote in 1946—that is some seven decades ago—after his study of *General Motors* in the US at the height of its importance and growth during the closing years of the second World War:

'Every institution has to be analysed in term of the beliefs and promises of the society which it serves. Does the institution strengthen the citizen's allegiance to his society by furthering the realization of society's ethical beliefs and promises? This is particularly important if we deal with an institution which is central to a society as by this very fact, its performance in the realization of the basic social beliefs and promises is regarded as indicative of the performance of society itself.'[1]

This was a remarkable analysis especially coming as it did from the country long considered the citadel of capitalism and free enterprise, where Adam Smith's *invisible hand* was allowed unrestricted reign to further personal profit and prosperity. But despite these underlying tenets of good corporate behaviour, corporations in the US and elsewhere including in India could not resist the temptations of travelling down prohibited paths to the detriment of their shareholders, other stakeholders, an even the society at large including the natural environment itself on which, business in the ultimate analysis depended for its inputs on a continuing basis.

Corporate growth in India since its political independence from British rule in 1947 has been significant. The publicly traded companies on the stock exchanges and the volume of trades have multiplied several-fold, although much of this activity is limited to possibly the top one hundred to two hundred companies. Legislation and regulation have been strengthened in line with global trends although the country is lagging behind in terms of rigorous enforcement and timely punishment for serious breaches. Many of the companies are listed overseas and several businesses are now truly multinational with global footprints. There is every reason to back up this impressive record with high standards of governance as well that would inspire investor trust and confidence, and grow acceptability of the country as a preferred investment destination.

The instruments for achieving this goal are corporate boards and an internalization of good governance practices based on conviction rather than as a measure of compliance. What is required is a drive towards greater appreciation of best practices and their rationale that would facilitate this very desirable transformation in the governance of corporate sector as a whole rather than, as at present, the preserve of a clutch of few companies that enjoy leadership positions in this field. This book is offered as an aid to accelerate this process.

Beginning with an overview of the subject in Chapter 1, the next five Chapters are devoted to the three pillars of governance, namely the shareholders, the board and the executive management including the dynamics of managing board effectiveness. Chapter 7 deals with the important topic of corporate reputation, ethics, and values. The concluding Chapter 8 seeks to dialogue with those aspiring to make a difference as directors on boards, whether they are already there or hoping to make it there.

Corporate governance, for all its theoretical richness, is essentially an applied discipline; all principles eventually have to help make better and more acceptable decisions in practice. Bearing this in view, the book has numerous case summaries of practical situations interspersed with the text which should assist in appreciating the underlying principles in their application. All the case summaries are based on real life examples though in some cases, the real names and case circumstances have been masked to protect their identity.

The book is offered in the hope it would serve its intended purpose of creating a much needed appreciation of the subject among incumbent directors and those knocking at the doors of board rooms as well as younger executives and professionals in practice with an eye on board positions as a career objective. It would also be useful to students in different disciplines and professions both at undergraduate and postgraduate levels to gain insights into the corporate form of business organizations. If this is achieved in some measure, it would have more than justified its publication.

CHAPTER 1

GOVERNING THE CORPORATION
An Overview

Two partners or brothers...united in the same trade and
behave as they should, will make greater profits than each
of them would separately.

—FRANCESCO DI MARCO DATINI, CA. 1400 AD[1]

I

Governance Leadership in Corporations

Why is it important to the government, to society and to investors to have corporations governed well more as a general rule rather than as enviable exceptions? If it is so essential, then why is it that we look to good governance only when major corporations turn up in distress and even failure but not otherwise, when the going had been good? Who is responsible for corporate scams and scandals—only the greedy managements, indifferent boards and directors, and the investors or also the regulators, independent auditors, and other reputational intermediaries in the system? Can excellence in governance leadership at individual corporations not only help them to steer clear of trouble zones but also lead to exemplary performance and success as judged in financial and societal terms? And how does one reach and sustain such levels of leadership in corporate governance? These are some of the questions that we now seek to address.

UNDERSTANDING CORPORATE GOVERNANCE

The case for good corporate governance thus seems quite strong. And yet, when the going is good, all the three constituents— the government, the society and businesses—do not appear unduly concerned about any observed gaps between the expected (normative) and the experienced (empirical) state of governance in the corporate sector. A proper understanding of what corporate governance encompasses is essential before a corporation can embark on a stable and sustainable pathway towards excellence and leadership in that arena. The following discussion articulates the meaning, offering a brief glimpse of

its internal and external dimensions, and its pay-off prospects—
whether all the effort is worthwhile after all.

MEANING OF CORPORATE GOVERNANCE

How should and how are business corporations run? What
is their purpose? For whose benefit are they created and
sustained? What costs are borne by society for allowing these
artificially created entities to serve their needs? And above all,
what processes need to be employed to ensure intended policy
objectives are translated into practice and achieved? These are
some of the concerns that corporate governance seeks to address.
Corporate governance is the field of study that encompasses the
interests of shareholders, employees, customers and vendors,
communities, financiers, and the government in the orderly and
balanced management of business corporations.

In short, corporate governance is about shareholder wealth
optimization with minimum undesirable costs to the community.
Corporate accountability is towards the shareholders of
the company with due consideration to, and management
of, other stakeholder interests. The emerging governance
framework integrating shareholder and stakeholder dimensions,
circumscribed by a legislative and regulatory environment, and
overseen by reputational agencies like independent auditors,
investigative press, institutional investors and so on, is depicted
graphically in Exhibit 1.1.

Exhibit 1.1: Corporate Governance Framework

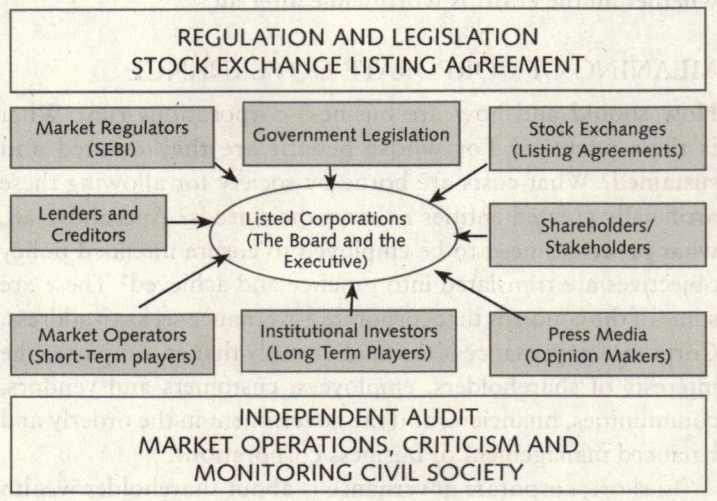

REGULATION AND LEGISLATION
STOCK EXCHANGE LISTING AGREEMENT

Market Regulators (SEBI)

Government Legislation

Stock Exchanges (Listing Agreements)

Lenders and Creditors

Listed Corporations (The Board and the Executive)

Shareholders/ Stakeholders

Market Operators (Short-Term players)

Institutional Investors (Long Term Players)

Press Media (Opinion Makers)

INDEPENDENT AUDIT
MARKET OPERATIONS, CRITICISM AND
MONITORING CIVIL SOCIETY

GOVERNMENT AND GOOD CORPORATE GOVERNANCE

In any country, especially in developing economies, business corporations constitute an invaluable component of their national wealth creation process. They provide employment opportunities and contribute significantly to direct and indirect tax revenues. They promote investment and growth contributing significantly to the GDP of their countries. Given these positives, it is in the country's interest to ensure a transparent and trustworthy ambience that is comforting and attractive to potential investors, both domestic and foreign. Just as it is the government's responsibility in a civilized nation to provide clean water and pure air, efficient communications, peaceful living conditions and so on, it is also its responsibility to provide for an orderly and transparent business environment that would inspire confidence on the part of domestic and international investors. Research suggests that overseas investors shy away from poorly governed companies in countries with relatively weak shareholder protection and related legal institutions since the investors' information and monitoring costs could be overly taxing.[2] Similarly, in countries with weak investor protection laws or their poor implementation, domestic investors may, if not constrained by local regulation, prefer to invest overseas in countries where corporate governance standards and the legal protection framework are perceived to be more favourable, unless domestic stock returns are so considerably attractive as to offset the costs of poor governance risks more than adequately. A good transparent corporate governance regime is therefore a major component of public policy to ensure continuous inflows of foreign investment while at the same time discouraging outflow of investible funds overseas at the expense of domestic investment opportunities.

There are further important reasons why governments would want to encourage good corporate governance regimes in their countries. Large scale business inevitably involves infusion of huge sums of money, some as risk-bearing equity and the rest as borrowings. Other than the controlling promoters' contributions, bulk of this funding is raised from the equity and debt security markets and other lenders, all of which, one way or another, involve *other peoples' monies*. There is thus nothing strictly private about public corporations to the extent that large proportions of their funding are sourced from external contributors. This is even more relevant in banks and financial institutions that operate on a small equity base and a very large deposits and borrowings portfolio and thus are very vulnerable to failure in case of loss of trust and confidence on the part of those lenders. The case of leading investment banks in the US during the 2008 financial meltdown is a striking example of how even a legendary firm like Lehman Brothers had to file for bankruptcy when that confidence was shaken. Corporate failures are by definition inevitable and the losses have to be borne by their risk-bearing equity holders; but their impact on the economy and their countries' reputation as safe investment destinations can often be disastrous. For example,in case of the global financial crisis of 2008–09, governments (and that means taxpayers) have had to infuse trillions of dollars to save their economies and the global financial systems. In India, when a company like Satyam Computers was distressed because of frauds perpetrated by the controlling promoters and their top management aides, government had to swiftly move in with damage control initiatives to preempt any serious erosion of the credibility and reputation of the country as well as the software industry which was (and continues to be) a significant foreign exchange earner and employer of millions of technical and other personnel directly and indirectly. That is the level of stake governments have in ensuring a sound corporate governance regime in the country.

SOCIETY AND GOOD CORPORATE GOVERNANCE

A well governed corporation is generally in a position to produce and deliver goods and services cost-effectively. It is also expected, in the process of its operations, to minimize external costs that it passes on to the society (such as degradation of the environment, excessive consumption of non-renewable resources, etc). Similarly, such a corporation may be expected not only to provide employment opportunities in communities where they have a presence but also to ensure working conditions that are free from work place discrimination, harassment, and other human rights violations. The communities may also hope to benefit from general improvements in their living conditions with better infrastructural, educational, and connectivity facilities as a result of increased commercial activity. Examples of such impact abound in every location that has seen such corporate concentrations. Bangalore in southern India is an illustrative case in point: what was essentially a sedate and sleepy city better known as a retirees' haven and for its salubrious climate and enchanting greenery till even the seventies and eighties has undergone a metamorphosis beyond recognition with the advent, among others, of information technology corporations like TCS, Infosys and Wipro. Its population has overtaken Kolkata's and Chennai's, its affluence has helped explosive growth in realty, hospitality, healthcare, education and various other service sectors. Bangalore (Urban) district reported a per capita GDP (at 1993–94 prices) of Rs 24,774 in 2001–02 compared to Rs 9,816 in 1991–92, moving up to number one rank within the state (number five in 1991–92); the percentage of population living below the poverty line in 1999–2000 was 9.9 percent, a significant improvement from the 31.4 percent reported in 1993–94.[3]

INVESTORS AND GOOD CORPORATE GOVERNANCE

The importance of good governance to those who actually put in their money as risk capital in a corporation is self-evident. In the corporate format (as will be discussed later) ownership of the firm is largely distanced from its control on day to day management, especially in case of publicly traded corporations. Where such share holding is largely dispersed as in the US and the UK, management control is entrusted to hired experts whose interests may not entirely be aligned with those of the shareholders. In virtually every other country including India, share holding is not widely dispersed but concentrated in the hands of sponsors or promoters who may also double up as executives managing the affairs of their corporation. Here again, the other shareholders (labelled *absentee shareholders* to reflect their absence in operational management control) have to contend with the potential non-congruence of their interests and the controlling shareholders'. Good governance entails processes and procedures designed to mitigate the negative impact of such divergence of interests and to deliver created value in the company to its rightful claimants, the shareholders without undue leakage in the transmission process. Such expropriation is an unavoidable risk that absentee shareholders accept and build in while pricing the company's equity securities in the market place. Better the perceived governance regime in a company, lower will be the governance risk premium investors will have to charge. Also, in case of corporate failures, it is the shareholders who bear the loss. Illustratively, while the US government pumped in billions to save companies like Freddie Mac and Fanny Mae of the sub-prime mortgage fame (or notoriety) in the 2008 financial meltdown, it was not to compensate the shareholders but to protect millions of Americans being thrown out of their mortgaged homes due to foreclosures. It is thus in the abiding interest of investors and shareholders to ensure the best possible governance structures and practices at the companies they invest in.

India still has miles to go before resting in terms of governance standards and practices. In 2012, India ranked 46th (33rd in 2007) among 183 worldwide in terms of investor protection, with a score of 6 out of 10 (same in 2007) across all countries considered. What is keeping it down, despite some promising steps already taken, are the legendary delays in the dispensation of justice and the weak enforcement and implementation of laws in the country, as has been noted in a 2004 World Bank review.[4]

THREE PILLARS OF CORPORATE GOVERNANCE

The governance edifice in corporations is built upon three key constituents: the shareholders, the board of directors, and the executive management in that hierarchical order. Shareholders as Principals 'elect' a board of directors charged with the responsibility of overseeing the business activities of the corporation and ensuring their interests are best served. The board in turn 'appoints' the chief executive and the management team to run the day to day operations efficiently and effectively in the ultimate interest of the shareholders, after duly addressing the interests of the stakeholders as well.

In this theoretical model, the three constituents are discreet and independent of each other. In practice though, variations are introduced. Some shareholders, the sponsoring or promoter category, get themselves elected to the board and also assume managerial positions in the company (Exhibit 1.2). In such cases,

Exhibit 1.2: Corporate Governance Hierarchy

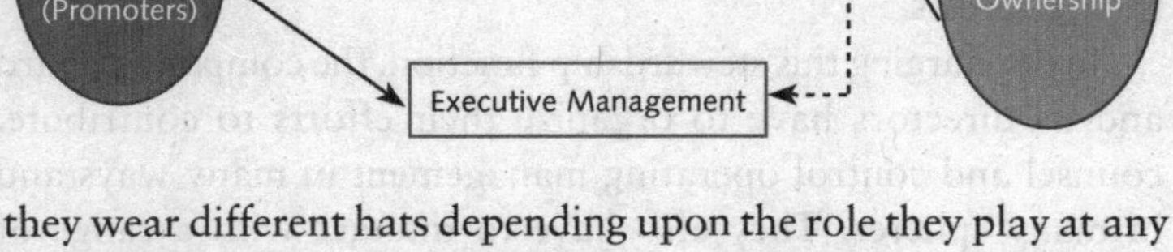

they wear different hats depending upon the role they play at any point of time and in particular circumstances. These situations may give rise to certain conflicts of interest which have to be addressed satisfactorily and in the best interests of shareholders as a whole group.

As a further measure of assurance to the shareholders that their 'agents' were running their company in accordance with their mandates under the supervision of the board, external independent auditors also report back to them on whether or not the financials prepared by the management reflect truly and fairly the financial state of affairs of their company.

These topics are discussed in greater detail later on but are briefly mentioned here to provide an overview of the structure of governance and the relative positioning of the constituents in this scheme.

FUNCTIONAL DIMENSIONS OF CORPORATE GOVERNANCE

Conscientious stewardship at the highest levels and running through the entire organization is an inseparable concomitant of good corporate governance. A steward is usually one who is entrusted with the task of looking after and managing the property, finances and other affairs with every due care and caution. In other words, a steward is akin to a trustee with *fiduciary* responsibilities for the care and control of another's funds, property, and so on to best protect and grow without any personal usurpation. In a corporate context, directors are fiduciaries for their shareholders and it is their duty to pursue their interests.

In discharging this stewardship function, the company's board and its directors have to organize their efforts to contribute, counsel and control operating management in many ways and in many spheres. They also have to interact with a range of relevant stakeholders, appropriately communicate internally and externally, ensure protection of the company's reputation and so on. These diverse tasks are generally grouped under internal and external dimensions of governance although in several matters there will be overlaps (Exhibit 1.3).

Exhibit 1.3: Dimensions of Corporate Governance

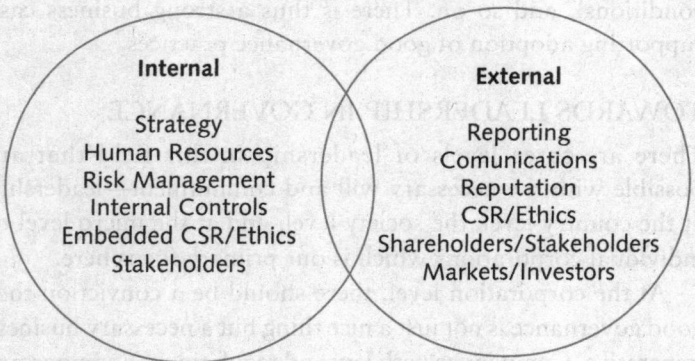

Internal

Strategy
Human Resources
Risk Management
Internal Controls
Embedded CSR/Ethics
Stakeholders

External

Reporting
Comunications
Reputation
CSR/Ethics
Shareholders/Stakeholders
Markets/Investors

DOES GOOD GOVERNANCE REALLY PAY?

The third element is the question whether good governance is just something of a feel-good exercise or are the cost and effort involved really worthwhile for the corporation.

Overall, research tends to support the conclusion that well-governed companies are more successful in the market place, their shareholder returns are such as to reduce their cost of capital (and hence financing costs), and their reputational status helps in opening up business opportunities as well as their standing in different markets. Illustratively, such companies are better able to attract and retain employees (thus lowering costs of employee hiring and turnover), banks and other financial institutions prefer to lend to them at sub-prime rates (thus reducing costs of financing), customers and vendors prefer to deal with them (thus improving brand loyalty and improved input costs and quality), business houses prefer to partner with them (thus opening up joint venture and other business opportunities), communities and states compete to have their presence among them (thus providing most advantageous locational and operational conditions), and so on. There is thus a strong business case supporting adoption of good governance practices.

TOWARDS LEADERSHIP IN GOVERNANCE

There are three levels of leadership in this field that are possible with the necessary will and commitment—leadership at the country level, the society level, and at the micro level of individual corporations which is our primary focus here.

At the corporation level, there should be a conviction that good governance is not just a nice thing but a necessary business imperative. Compliance with law and regulation is an important first step; those who wish to graduate from there and reach the commanding heights of leadership in the field will need to be inspired by the sheer ethical elegance of governance principles as guiding tenets of behaviour in every walk of business life. These have to be internalized not just at the board and top management levels but should flow through the organizational hierarchies down to the lowest level employees and especially those on the front lines in the market place because it is there that the external world has the opportunity to observe and experience their conduct and behaviour. It is there that corporate reputations are tested and proved.

Inherent values and beliefs in a corporation of course depend upon the tone at the top. So it is with leadership in governance. Directors and top management executives need to lead by example. Whether it is transparency in reporting or integrity in accounting; equitable dealing with employees or promises to customers and pledges to the community—the trust that the company and its employees evoke is usually a good measure of how well proclaimed policies have been internalized and practised on the ground. It is often said that with ownership and control of Indian companies largely in the hands of family groups of sponsors or promoters, the push for fully honest reporting of profits will be frustrated by the pressures of tunneling wealth to the controllers. This would of course change when promoters realize (as many do now) the financial impact of such practices on company valuations to their disadvantage.

A virtually complete absorption of good governance practices will be achieved only when every employee and manager in the firm appreciates that he is working for and on behalf of *all* shareholders of the corporation and not for the benefit of only the management, controlling shareholders, or the top management. This is difficult to internalize since the shareholders are an amorphous body of individuals and institutions usually unseen except at members' meetings once in a while, and then too only a few of them who turn up. On the other hand, the top management (including the controlling part owners) is very visible and involved on a day to day basis with the supervision, their career progression and so on. Top executives often compound the situation further by insisting upon employees' undivided loyalty to themselves. Given these circumstances, it is not surprising if the absentee shareholders of the company are farthest from the employees' thoughts while engaged in the daily chores of their jobs. If only they could understand the kind of trust that has been thrust upon them, there will be a marked change in their approach to their work. This is not to encourage indiscipline among the workforce or promote dissonance in the organization. Even simple measures like avoiding wastages and inefficiencies in processes, temptations towards self-dealing and corruption in normal transactions, and so on will begin to be viewed with discomfort. What earlier appeared to be insignificant and 'normal' perquisites of the job making small gains for self and the family would begin to look like major crimes. The thought of being a trustee of another being is a heady feeling and generally weighs heavily on one's conscience. And that is a first major step in adhering to ethical corporate governance principles at every level in the organization, from the board room and executive suites down to the factory floors and workstations. That also is the sign of the journey having begun towards the higher reaches of corporate governance leadership.

II

Setting Business in Context

Business does not operate in a vacuum. It does within the framework of a tripartite regime comprising of itself, the society and the government. It is licensed to produce and provide goods and services for the benefit of societal constituents fully complying with the relevant laws and regulations prescribed by the government. When business breaches any of the covenants underlying these arrangements, it is vulnerable to retributive disciplining by the society or the state as appropriate. Does this happen in reality? Indeed it does. Let us look at the churn in the annual Fortune 500 companies between say twenty five or thirty years ago and now—several top names of the earlier era no longer figure in that hallowed space. Either they have violated the laws of the land in some way or they have lost their societal license because their goods and services were no longer welcome or the societal costs of their operations outweighed the perceived benefits they offered. Maintaining such a delicate balance is the prime task of every business, even while earning a handsome reward for its entrepreneurs. This is especially so in case of corporations which seem to attract a natural antipathy from society, probably because of their perceived reach, influence, and private gains.

In a Utopian idealistic world, these three constituents of society exert equal and equitable pressure on each other such that a state of perfect equilibrium and complete social cohesion reign (Exhibit 1.4). This is hardly, if ever, achieved in reality. Very often business tends to push for that extra bit to earn more

Exhibit 1.4: Equilibrium State of Social Cohesion

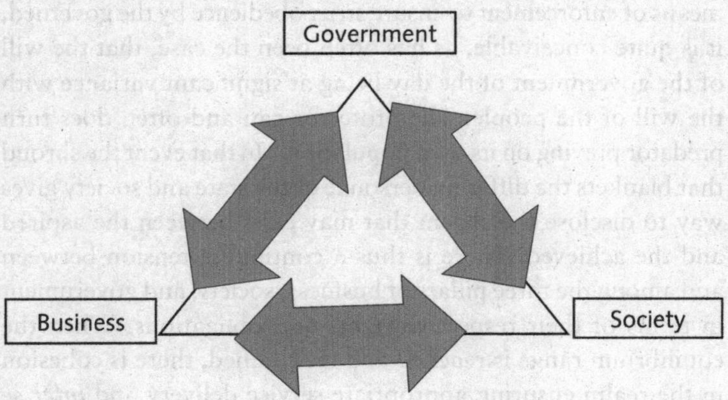

Government

Business

Society

profits for itself either by shortchanging societal expectations or by breaching the rules of the game laid down by the government of the day. History has shown that significant economic power wielded by business (or more correctly, certain sections of business) often facilitated by patronage and corruption is more than enough to influence government policies conferring profitable opportunities or condoning regulatory breaches. Such developments involving a collusion between two of the three constituents cannot but be inimical to the interests of the society or some of its subsets. Such aggression on their interests beyond tolerance limits would naturally lead to reactive initiatives by the civil society as have been frequently observed.

In discussing the tenuous equations between and among business, government and society, one will also have to reckon with the potential for mismatches between the aspirations of the people on one hand and on the other, the agenda of their elected representatives in a democracy or the powers that be in case of other forms of government. Having been entrusted with requisite executive authority to govern and the physical (often violent) means of enforcement to ensure strict obedience by the governed, it is quite conceivable, as has often been the case, that the will of the government of the day being at significant variance with the will of the people. The protector can and often does turn predator preying on its own population.[5] In that event the shroud that blankets the differing personae of the state and society gives way to disclose the chasm that may exist between the aspired and the achieved. There is thus a continuing tension between and among the three pillars of business, society, and government in terms of their respective rights and obligations. When the equilibrium range is reached and maintained, there is cohesion in the realm ensuring appropriate service delivery and *inter se* discipline with due regard to respective roles and restraints. The message is quite clear: society permitted businesses to freely operate to meet its needs at reasonable costs—monetary, social, and environmental—and was not averse to the entrepreneurial class making a profit for themselves in the process so long as it did not breach mandated requirements of the state made in public interest. If the State failed to reflect the interest of the people, society would not hesitate to step in to exert pressure both on the government and the business corporations to restore accepted norms of conduct. Business thrived when duly complying with or even excelling in the prescribed or desired regime; disaster or even demise would be the result otherwise.

Ensuring corporations do their business within socially accepted norms and in full compliance of the laws of the land is the task corporate directors and their executives are charged with. The processes and procedures that help them to do this are collectively labelled corporate governance. Excelling and exceeding these norms brings enhanced reputation to the corporations and in their own way help earn superior economic rewards for their owners. The rest of this volume is devoted to discussing ways and means that corporations adopt to achieve this objective, setting their business in this overall societal context.

III

Evolution of the Corporation

Corporations, or companies as they are called in India and many other countries, are so commonplace today that they seem to have always been around. The reality though is that incorporated companies (usually by government or royal charter) can only be traced to early seventeenth century and joint stock companies as we know them now were enabled in England in mid-nineteenth century. Of course, there were hybrid forms in earlier times that combined the features of partnerships and companies but traits such as limited liability and so on were certainly not among them.

EVOLUTION OF BUSINESS STRUCTURES

Ever since people began to exchange one product for another especially through the medium of money, the concept of *business* was in. Money represented wealth and was responsible for well-being and hence any spread of revenues over costs was keenly sought after. As long as it was limited to one's own agricultural produce or skilled services, the dominant business format was sole proprietorship, often with the support of the immediate family. These extended in course of time to include bought out items as well and associated services if there were skills available in the family or could be hired at reasonable cost. The scope of operations of these enterprises were always constrained by the resources they could mobilize on their own or from expensive money lenders, but the emphasis was not always on scaling up but to provide a reasonable income and assured self-employment for the family. At a conceptual level, this is a business model that was close to Mahatma Gandhi's heart as he was convinced that this would benefit India's millions in villages and would protect them from the perils of industrialization and urbanization that robbed people of their individualism and identities.[6]

The natural progression from sole proprietorship was towards partnerships where individuals pooled their interests, usually were actively involved in day to day operations, and shared profits in proportion to their investments. Such partnerships could be for pooling financial resources, skill sets, produce, or even geographical enhancements.

A forerunner to the modern day corporation began to take shape in Italy and northern Europe. Called *Compagnia*, signifying 'breaking bread together' in Latin, these firms were well knit associations of family and trustworthy friends—an important qualification since any failure leading to bankruptcy meant the partners going to jail and even servitude.[7] Then,

22

in due course of time, came the corporations that could undertake enterprises involving enormous resources and often great risks which individuals by themselves could not afford. Adam Smith[8] described three types of corporations in this context: those that were to attend to essential public works necessary for facilitating commerce in general such as roads, bridges, navigable canals, harbours and so on by the state; second, those which were chartered and regulated where members traded on their own capital stock and at their own risk, but subject to common regulations of the company that undertook on a monopolistic basis trade and commerce with overseas territories; and the third, joint stock companies where trading upon their joint capital stock with 'each member sharing in the common profit or loss in proportion to his share in this stock'. This is arguably the earliest recorded economic definition of a joint stock company as conceived in the eighteenth century.

SOME MILESTONES IN CORPORATE EVOLUTION

As noted earlier, corporate form of activity appears to have begun in early Middle Ages, with towns, universities, religious orders, and guilds of trades people being treated as distinct entities, quite separate from those comprising them. The oft-quoted British case, Salomon vs Salomon & Co., laid down in 1897 that the incorporated company was a separate distinct entity and had to be distinguished from the people who constituted that company. This distinction is important in that it shields the shareholders from any claims in respect of liabilities incurred by the company beyond their share of the entity's equity capital.

Limited liability as a concept was reportedly upheld in English courts by the fifteenth century but it was not until much later, in the mid-nineteenth century, that it evolved into the full-blown concept of limited liability for the shareholders in case of joint stock companies limited by shares.[9]

Bakan[10] quotes an English parliamentarian of that time as saying, 'the first and most natural principle of commercial legislation...that everyman was bound to pay the debts he had contracted, so long as he was able to do so' and that 'it [limited liability concept] would enable persons to embark in trade with a limited chance of loss, but with an unlimited chance of gain' and thus encourage 'a system of vicious and improvident speculation.' And yet, that was precisely the reason that was advocated in favour of the legislation—that it would open up new, risky adventures with potentially very high profits albeit with associated risks of failure. Nothing ventured, nothing gained! The eighteenth century Industrial Revolution in the UK signalled the advent of machines in manufacturing operations, including the ginning wheel and process technology, and the legendary steam engine which powered the growth of rail roads both in the United Kingdom and United States. All these ventures required finances beyond the reach of small groups of individuals, thus offering a fillip to the formation of joint stock corporations. Long before this of course, seafaring entrepreneurs and adventurers had set out for distant lands taking with them the produce and knowledge of their country, and bringing back valuable metals such as gold and silver, and commodities like silk from China and spices from India. All this required finances on a much larger scale than lone individual adventurers or small groups of partners could marshal. The substantial funds required to finance such expeditions had to necessarily be raised from the 'public' that went beyond kith and kin. In effect, the traditional concept that 'owners managed and managers owned' gave way to a situation where ownership of the business in varying proportions was held by a large number of people who had nothing to do with the management of the actual business. This was undertaken by the 'dominant' owners or, in later times, hired managers or professional executives with the requisite skills.

Major facilitators promoting the exponential growth of corporations in the US followed in the latter part of the twentieth century. New Jersey and Delaware[11] saw an opportunity to attract incorporations to their states by relaxing many inconvenient restrictions in company formation and operation. Most importantly, they also permitted a company to hold stock in another as a shareholder. It thus opened the doors for the development of the concept of corporate groups, with all its attendant potential for de-risking business ventures through separate but controlled legal entities, with the benefits of limited liability at each tier, but also exposing the economy to the perils of pyramiding, tunnelling, and a host of other potential abuses of related transactions.

Modern corporations are, and for quite some time have been, a significant part of peoples' lives. For sure they produce goods and services that enhance the wellbeing of the people but their single point agenda of profit and greed even at the cost of the people they profess to serve and the non-renewable earth resources they liberally draw upon are often matters of grave concern. As a product of economic freedom and entrepreneurial aggression, the modern corporations thus pose a continuing challenge to society's ability to harness their potential benefits while concomitantly attempting to contain their ill effects.

CORPORATE DEVELOPMENT IN INDIA

The corporate form of organization in India became a reality with the passing of an Act in 1850 'for registration of joint stock companies' although even prior to this companies under Charter of the British Crown, such as the East India Company had been in operation. Limited liability was introduced in 1857, and in 1860 the concept was extended to banking and insurance companies as well. The managing agency system, arguably unique to India,[12] blossomed during the years following. While the managing agency system suffered significant abuse in later decades and had to be abolished by law in 1969-70, the fact remains that its contribution to the growth of Indian industry and the corporate form of business organization was unequivocally impressive. Many of the modern day business groups in India inherited such companies and businesses when their British owners and managers returned home following India's political independence in 1947.

Growth of limited liability companies in India during the twentieth century and into the twenty-first has been exponential at over twenty five times in the last half a century alone.

CLASSIFICATION OF CORPORATIONS

Businesses can be structured in different formats, depending upon requirements unique to their circumstances. As noted earlier, sole proprietorships and partnerships are constrained by the resources they could raise for their business but their most important disadvantage is that, unlike in limited liability companies, their business liabilities can be recovered not only from their business assets but also from their personal estates. Further, the lifespan of their business is co-terminus with their own; thus businesses built over a long time necessarily get extinguished with the death of the proprietor or a partner and have to start virtually all over again under their successors.

Companies, on the other hand, once incorporated enjoy perpetual existence unless extinguished by due process of law; they have an identity that is unique to themselves and are independent of the persons comprising its membership; and in case of limited liability companies (which virtually all business corporations are) members' liability is limited to the nominal value of their shares or the amounts they have guaranteed to contribute in case of companies limited by guarantee.

Corporations can also be classified on the basis of different criteria (Exhibit 1.5); while all common characteristics apply equally to all corporations, there are certain unique traits that apply based on their classification (Exhibit1.6). These dictate decisions on how businesses will be structured to suit their particular circumstances.

Exhibit 1.5: Selected Modern Day Business Structures

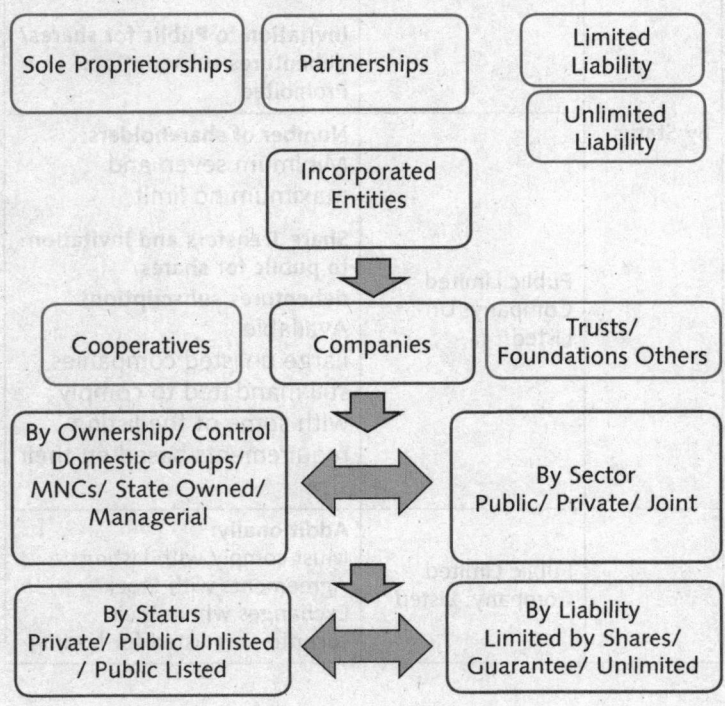

Exhibit 1.6: Classification and Characteristics of Companies

(Common Traits: Independent identity, Perpetual succession, Can sue and be sued)		
By Status	Private Limited Company	**Number of shareholders**: Minimum two and maximum two hundred (not including current employees, past employees with continuing holdings since before exit)
		Share Transfers: Restricted
		Invitation to Public for shares/ debentures subscription: Prohibited
	Public Limited Company: Un-Listed	**Number of shareholders:** Minimum seven and maximum no limit
		Share Transfers and Invitation to public for shares/ debentures subscription: Available Large unlisted companies still mandated to comply with some of the listing requirements based on their size
	Public Limited Company: Listed	**Additionally:** Must comply with Listing Agreements with Stock Exchanges where their securities are listed for trading

By Sectors	Public Sector	Any company in which not less than fifty-one per cent of the paid-up share capital is held by the Central Government, and/or by any State Governments, including subsidiaries of such a company Any company incorporated under an Act of Parliament or a State legislature
	Private Sector	Other than those in the public sector and joint sector
	Joint Sector	Where the Central or State governments partner with companies in the private sector
By Ownership and Control	Domestic Groups	Where domestic family or professional group owns a majority of voting rights or controls composition of the board, or has control over operations and management of the company
	Multi National Groups	Similar except that a foreign company or group has such ownership and/or control
	State Owned	Similar except that the Central or State government(s) has such ownership and/or control
	Unaffiliated	Companies where there is no identifiable promoter or sponsor and company is managed by executives

By Liability	Limited by Shares	Members' liability not to exceed face value of shareholding
	Limited by Guarantee	Members undertake to contribute in the event of winding up
	Unlimited	Members' liability unlimited and can extend to personal estate

Note: Companies Act 2013 has provisions also for One Person Companies that have only one member

IV

Corporate Accountability

Who are the corporation, its directors, and executive management accountable to? This is a question that has engaged scholars and practitioners alike over decades without reaching any measure of consensus or conclusion. Opinions have ranged between an exclusive accountability to the company's shareholders and responsibility to a spectrum of other stakeholders involved with the corporation.

The shareholders, initially the promoters or sponsors and later followed by others, create and operate the corporation under the laws of the country. As their brainchild, it is naturally accountable to their creators. Whether the initial sponsors continue their active association with the company in terms of managing its day to day operations or delegate that task to professional executives to be overseen by themselves or their elected representatives on their behalf, does not dilute the company's primary accountability to the shareholders. Anyone associated with the operations of the company thus derivatively becomes equally accountable to the shareholders at large essentially. As intermediaries between the shareholder population and executive management, the board and the directors are positioned in the role of trustees to the shareholders and are said to owe them a *fiduciary* obligation to look after and promote their interests.

And yet, in the course of doing its business for the benefit of its shareholders, the company must out of necessity interface with numerous other players. To begin with, it needs to deal with its executives and other employees. It has to engage with vendors and service providers who offer inputs for its operations. It should be concerned with its customers as without them, as Mahatma Gandhi famously said, there will be no need for its existence itself. Then there will be fund providers, the communities where it is sited and present, and last but not the least, the government on which it would have to depend for a conducive environment in which it can operate. Collectively, these constituents are referred to as stakeholders in the corporation (besides of course its shareholders).

ACCOUNTABILITY TO SHAREHOLDERS

The conventional model of corporate governance is based on a theory called *legal contractualism* in which two or more parties come together to make a pact to carry on commercial activity and such agreements are indeed the basis for the corporation. In effect, this theory supports the view that private enterprise should have the freedom to enter into entrepreneurial contracts in furtherance of legitimate business and private gain, and the regulatory role of the state to that extent ought to be circumscribed so long as the general requirements of the laws of the land regarding lawful objectives, fair competition and so on, are met. Indian law adopts this concept,[13] subject to certain requirements with regard to stakeholders.

In another categorization termed *economic contractualism,* a company is positioned as a voluntary association between shareholders rather than a creation of the state. Thus viewed, an incorporated company is fundamentally a *nexus of contracts.* Corporate constituents contract not with each other, but with the corporation. An employment agreement is a contract between the corporation and its workers, and not a contract with each individual shareholder of the corporation. If there is default in meeting the obligations under any contract entered into between the company and another party, it is the firm that will be sued, not its constituents, or those managers responsible for its performance. It is the entity that is under obligation to perform, with failure leading to penalties which will be paid out of the entity's resources rather than those of its shareholders or managers. The various constituencies thus are linked to the nexus that is the firm, and not to each other.

The major implication of the contractual theory is that it supports the status of shareholders as the owners of the corporation, with its concomitant obligation that the company, its board of directors and the executive are all accountable to the shareholders to the exclusion of any other constituencies or stakeholders (unless specifically provided for by law). The contractual theory of the corporation is also at the root of the hard position taken by many scholars ruling out any social responsibility being imposed on corporations.

Residual Claimants

Exclusive accountability to shareholders is also predicated upon the *Residual Claimant Theory* that broadly derives from the principles of private property along with the rights and risks attached to its ownership. In practical terms, equity shareholders pool their monies together to run the incorporated business, not unlike several partners getting together for the same purpose. Of course, the singular distinguishing factor is that unlike the analogous partners, these shareholders, because of the organizational structure and mode of operations do not manage the business themselves but let a group of executives or some of the other promoting shareholders operate it under the surveillance of an elected board of directors. The form of organization, by itself, should not make any difference in determining who the real owners are.

The residual claimants theory with reference to corporate governance reasons as follows: shareholders are residual claimants to the firm's income. Creditors have fixed claims and employees' remunerations are generally negotiated in advance of performance. The gains and losses from abnormally good or bad performance are the lot of shareholders, who stand last in the claims queue. As residual claimants, shareholders have the right to make discretionary decisions and bear their consequences. As such, shareholders do justify their claim, legally and morally, to be the *owners* of the business with important control rights. On this basis, a clear line of accountability to the shareholders, to the exclusion of any other stakeholders, is in full accord with all cannons of natural justice. Indian corporate law relating to claims also follows this line of reasoning.

CORPORATIONS AND THEIR STAKEHOLDERS

In contrast, the *Communitarian* theory is premised on the basic assumption that grant of company status by society as represented by the state, is not just a concession or privilege (especially with the added incentive of limited liability to the shareholders), but is essentially an instrument to be utilised by the State for public good. In this sense, it is positioned diametrically opposite the more individualist and *laissez faire* approach of contractualism models. In this view, the level of a corporation's utility to society is not judged on the basis of wealth created for its shareholders but on the criteria of whether it meets the requirements and contributes to the wellbeing of relevant societal constituents. This approach also lends credence to the oft-quoted sentiment that a corporation exists and operates within a society, with its sanction and license, which can be withdrawn or diluted if the societal expectations are not met. It is in this perspective that this model justifies state intervention in, and regulation of, corporate operations. This approach imposes corporate responsibility and accountability to the stakeholders and society at large, and likely acts as a sobering counter-weight to potential corporate abuses of power and inclinations towards unbridled greed. The difficulty of course is in determining which stakeholders are *relevant* to each company in its unique circumstances.

Who is a Stakeholder?

Narrowly defined, stakeholders would mean all groups, entities and individuals who are vital to the survival and growth of the corporation; a wider definition would embrace all groups, entities and individuals who can affect, or who are affected by the decisions of the corporation. It is under this latter categorization that six groups already mentioned are usually considered corporate stakeholders. In these days of cellular specialization and competitive advantage, it would be prudent to apply a liberal connotation to at least some of these descriptions. For example, suppliers may not just be of goods and infrastructural facilities directly acquired but may also include a variety of outsourced vendors and contractors, besides other technology, knowledge, and service providers. Employees will cover both the top management group including whole time directors and other blue, white and gold collared personnel. Communities may not be restricted to just the place where the company is headquartered but also extend to locations where its facilities are sited or its products and services are sold.

HEEDING THE WINDS OF CHANGE

There is an emerging trend that is clearly discernible in corporate governance frameworks across the world, particularly since the late nineteen nineties. There is increasing recognition that the shareholder primacy dictum and its wealth maximization goals could not, and should not, be pursued to the exclusion of the claims and interests of other stakeholders. Thus, for example:

- *OECD Principles of Corporate Governance* lays down that, 'the corporate governance framework should ensure...the board's accountability to the company and the shareholders,' but also postulates that the governance framework 'should recognize the rights of stakeholders established by law or through mutual agreements and encourage active cooperation between the corporations and stakeholders in creating wealth, jobs, and the sustainability of financially sound enterprises.'
- In the UK, the Companies Act 2006, even while stipulating that directors should act in the best interests of all shareholders, mandates that in doing so they should have due regard to 'the interests of the company's employees, the need to foster the company's business relationships with suppliers, customers and others, and the impact of the company's operations on the community and the environment.'

- The *King Report-III on Governance for South Africa* emphasises the inclusive approach of governance that calls upon boards of directors to also consider the legitimate interests and expectations of stakeholders other than shareholders.
- In Japan, the *Corporate Governance Principles* make a strong affirmative statement that, 'A company is not able to exist until it is able to secure transactions with each of its stakeholders. Given that this is so, a company can be thought of as something that belongs to everyone.' Creation of shareholder value is indeed the driving objective of corporations but this has to be achieved honouring this important social covenant.
- *The German Corporate Governance Code* charges the Management Board with responsibility for 'independently managing the enterprise in the interest of the enterprise, thus taking into account the interests of the shareholders, its employees and other stakeholders, with the objective of sustainable creation of value.'

In India, the Securities and Exchange Board of India's (Kumar Mangalam Birla) Committee's *Report on Corporate Governance* reiterated the fundamental objective of corporate governance as being the enhancement of shareholder value, *keeping in view the interests of other stakeholders*. The Companies Act 2013 stipulates, 'a director of a company shall act in good faith in order to promote the objects of the company for the benefit of its members as a whole, and in the best interests of the company, its employees, the shareholders, the community and for the protection of environment.' It is clear that India along with many other countries is moving towards a model of enlightened capitalism with shareholders co-existing with other stakeholders in the common pursuit of profit and wellbeing.

In his discourse on the duties of the king, Kautilya, the great Fourth century BC Indian political strategist postulated, 'In the happiness of his subjects lies his (king's) happiness; in their welfare, his welfare.'[14] Much of this ancient wisdom applies to the present day corporation as well. The *real* stakeholders including all the shareholders certainly constitute the population of the corporate kingdom.

Leadership corporations—by definition those who stand out from their peers—seem to have understood and practised these imperatives in their own spheres long before regulation and legislation began to close in on them. The significant growth in the number of companies that publish sustainability reports in recent years is arguably one demonstrable measure of the recognition and importance that corporations attach to a range of stakeholders they identify as relevant and unique to their business operations. It is imperative that corporations steer a middle course that would protect and enhance shareholders' wealth while satisfactorily 'managing' the real stakeholders' aspirations without compromising shareholders' interests. Such an integrated model that seamlessly combines the interests, expectations and aspirations of all stakeholders including shareholders would seem to be the most viable governance model for the decades ahead.

CHAPTER 2

SHAREHOLDERS
The Risk-bearing Investors

Everyone was in the stocks now ... needy clerks, poor
tradesman's apprentices, discarded service men and
bankrupts—all have entered the ranks of the great monied
interest.

—*THE ECONOMIST*, Ca. 1850

I

Shareholder Primacy

Shareholders are the touchstone of corporations. They create them, sustain them, and hope to benefit from them. They can be a manageable size as in the case of private companies, many more in public companies, and in multitudes in large listed companies.[1] Large proportions of these shareholders are usually *absentee shareholders*—not having any role in the day to day operations of their companies. These day to day operations are delegated to the executive management under the supervision of a board of directors who are elected by the shareholders. The power of the shareholders is enormous as has been witnessed now and then[2] in case of extortionary abuse. As corporations seek to understand and accommodate product markets to meet their needs and profit from their custom, they need also to understand and delight the investors who constitute their market for risk capital; if customer is king in the product/service market place, then shareholders and investors are indeed the kings in the capital market arena.

CATEGORIES OF SHAREHOLDERS

While it is customary to refer to shareholders generically, in practice they come in different shapes and sizes! Broadly:

- The primary classification is on the basis of the nature of shares investors hold in the company, whether they are equity shareholders or preference shareholders. Preference shares carry rights as to dividends and/or return of capital in the event of winding up of the company prior to their redemption on expiry of their term. In the pecking order they stand ahead of the equity shareholders who are

40

the last in the queue. Equity shareholders are in fact the full risk-bearing entrepreneurs and as such they stand to gain wholly (after meeting prior commitments) or lose wholly in case of business failure. When we talk of investor protection, shareholder primacy and so on, it is this category of equity shareholders that we refer to.

- Shareholders are also classified on the basis of their nature or status—as promoter shareholders who sponsor the corporation and generally are also in operational control; as institutional shareholders who hold relatively large blocks of shares in companies and because of their expertise and size have an influential position opposite company boards and managements; and small or retail shareholders, whose holdings being small, do not generally have the expertise or the inclination to effectively participate in meetings and matters that are brought up in members' meetings.

- Shareholders can also be classified on the basis of their investment horizons—as long term shareholders (which may mean holding the shares for two years or more), short term investors (who may comprise of a range of people and institutions with trading objectives that may span a few months or even a single trading session on a stock exchange). The question that has often been raised is which shareholder group's interests the company and its board should promote and protect; the balance of view generally tends to lean more towards long-term shareholders than the short-term investors.

- The next classification is based on the participation levels of shareholders—those who are passive (most of the small retail investors will fall in this category), active-passive (some institutional shareholders who may actively

41

influence management decisions or actively participate in voting and attendance at members' meetings but not both), and active players (who actively participate in influencing company policies and practices from outside and also exercise their franchise on matters coming up before members' meetings).

- Most importantly, shareholders are identified as controlling or promoter groups or absentee shareholders (having nothing to do with the company's operations). A *promoter* (or controlling shareholder) is defined as one, (a) who is named as such in a prospectus or is identified by the company as such; or (b) who has control over the affairs of the company, directly or indirectly whether as a shareholder, director or otherwise; or (c) in accordance with whose advice, directions or instructions the board of directors of the company is accustomed to act.[3] Controlling promoters may not always have a majority of voting rights but can and do survive on the premise that the absentee majority is so dispersed as not to be able to put up any united opposition effectively.

- A further classification of the shareholders within the controlling category will identify family or domestic groups, multinational groups, and state-owned public sector group. Each of these groups will have unique characteristics, principally owing allegiance to their affiliation interests that often may not coincide with the interests of other absentee shareholders.

RIGHTS OF SHAREHOLDERS

Although most small and retail shareholders in large publicly listed companies understandably evince little interest in company matters apart perhaps from dividends declared, it is important for them to know that both law and good practice bestow on them a series of valuable rights which they can exercise if they choose to. The OECD Principles for example enumerate the following non-exhaustive basic rights:

- Secure methods of ownership registration and conveyance, respecting the sanctity of the concept of 'property' and reserving their entitlement to have their ownership duly recorded and recognized together with their freedom to dispose their shares by selling and transferring in their absolute discretion (except as mutually agreed, or as restrained by law)
- Obtain relevant and material information on a timely and regular basis, so that they can be duly informed
- Participate and vote in general shareholder meetings and elect and remove members of the board
- Share in the profits of the corporation after duly meeting prior claims

Many of these rights are, of course, subject to board decisions in the interests of the company. For example, the board may refuse to register a share transfer if it felt that such a transfer may prejudicially affect the stability or interests of the corporation as a whole (as in a case of potential takeover of the management of the company or any of its businesses). Legal recourse is available to aggrieved shareholders. Indian company law provides for judicial review and redressal in case a sufficient number of shareholders believe the company is being mismanaged or the minority shareholders are being oppressed. These are extreme situations but shareholders can take heart that their interests would be reasonably protected. Of course, small retail shareholders can hardly take on the might of the large companies in terms of financial resources and available expertise to fight a prolonged battle especially in a judicial environment of inordinate delays. In suitable cases, such actions if at all will have to be choreographed by shareholder collectives and large block holders who may have the requisite resources.

DIMENSIONS OF SHAREHOLDER PRIMACY

There are three perspectives in which the question of primacy could be explored—shareholder primacy over other stakeholders in the company, shareholder primacy over the board and executive management, and shareholder primacy over other shareholder groups from among themselves. We have already noted, while discussing corporate accountability, the directional trends around the world including in India towards an increasing recognition of corporate responsibility towards other stakeholders, and how as a result the exclusive accountability to shareholders has been circumscribed. We now turn to a discussion of the other two dimensions.

SHAREHOLDERS AND THE BOARD

The hierarchical relationship between the shareholders and the corporate board, while on the surface apparently unambiguous, has been the subject of on-going debates among the legal fraternity. Simply stated, the board is a collective designation for all the directors; directors are elected by the shareholders at members' meetings as their representatives to oversee business operations of their company, and the shareholders may also countermand their election (subject to some exceptions) and remove them, if they in sufficiently large numbers wish to do so. The board is expected to report to the shareholders annually in general meetings on the company's performance and other matters, or at other intervals if required to seek shareholders' approvals on specific initiatives. All this would seem to indicate the primacy of the shareholders over their boards but in reality it has been argued that the situation may not be so open and shut.

In the last decade, divergent views have been expressed on this issue by legal scholars[4] building upon similar debates since the 1930s[5] especially with reference to the US, more specifically the State of Delaware where major corporations are incorporated because of its business-friendly regime. It is obvious that in case of large publicly traded corporations, shareholders running into millions cannot possibly have a say in the day to day operations of their companies, and that this task is best delegated to executive management under the watchful oversight and guidance of the board. But the question is: to what extent should and could shareholders have a voice in shaping not only the policies but also the people who will conceptualize and consummate those policies? The relationship between the shareholders and their delegated or constituted attorney, namely the board, in a trusteeship principal-agent equation itself has often been questioned in some of these arguments. For example it has been argued that the board, having been elected, is a self-regulating and self-regenerating instrument whose primary objective is to protect the interests of the corporation, its survival and sustainable growth and prosperity. It is in this context that shareholder primacy over the board has been diluted to a level where boards and corporations have been assigned the status of bodies virtually independent of the shareholders.

The Indian position is way ahead of many other developed countries on several aspects of explicit shareholder empowerment. For example,

- Shareholders elect their directors individually, not as a slate as in the US

- Shareholders vote on directorial remuneration individually unlike in the US where it is only in recent times that the 'say-in-pay' movement has been gaining ground
- In case of material related party transactions, the other shareholders have the right to approve or reject the proposals by a super majority among themselves
- Small shareholders may elect their representative as a director
- Shareholders may exercise their voting rights through postal ballot on certain key issues
- There are express mandates on what the boards cannot do without shareholder approval

There are two major weaknesses in the Indian regime though—there is very little institutional investor activism and there is relatively poor regulatory implementation, monitoring, and disciplining routines in practice.

The efficacy of these valuable enablers of shareholder primacy is wholly dependent on the level of participation by the shareholders in company meetings and resolutions, which is not easy to come by and hence may remain theoretical unless institutional shareholders, with their expertise and material stakes, take it upon themselves to judiciously exercise their franchise on important issues involving investor protection.

SHAREHOLDERS OVER OTHER SHAREHOLDERS

In a discussion on shareholder primacy, it may sound odd that there could be situations where among themselves some shareholders may seek and defend their primacy against their other co-shareholders but in reality such situations do abound. This is particularly so when a group of shareholders—usually the controlling or sponsoring promoters—enter into transactions with the company where they are concerned or tend to benefit to the exclusion of other shareholders. Related party transactions involving matters such as group company mergers and divestitures, preferential share issues, setting up competing subsidiaries and other entities, transferring favourable corporate opportunities to other group companies or unfavourable opportunities from other group entities to the disadvantage of the other shareholders, and executive compensation of promoter managers are some of the issues that may fall under this category. The remedy in such instances is not to reject wholesale such proposals but to have them put up for approval of the other shareholders. Indian law now requires approval by more than 75 percent of the shareholders excluding those interested in such transactions.[6]

Do Shareholders owe any fiduciary responsibility to other Shareholders?

In general, shareholders do not owe any fiduciary or other obligations either to the company or to other shareholders. The position is premised on the ground that when shareholders act, they do so as principals and owners rather than in any delegated or representative capacity. It is also a well-established principle that as owners, shareholders can certainly act (and vote) in their own best interests without reference to the impact of their decisions on the company or other shareholders. Controlling shareholders, though, stand on a different footing depending upon the level of dominance or influence that the controlling individual or entity exercises upon a corporation's directors and officers who may be their nominees or appointees. This is the basis of the provisions in the Companies Act.

These principles could have a far-reaching impact on controlling shareholders' actions with regard to their implications for subsidiary or affiliate companies. For example:

- If a parent has (or plans) more than one subsidiary in the same or similar lines of business, how would the parental action impact—either directly or through its nominees on the subsidiary board and executive management—the interests of the non-controlling shareholders in those subsidiaries? [**Case summary 2.1: Pfizer India**]

- In case of listed joint ventures and technical collaborations, if one or more of the participating partners were to exit for whatever reason, should its block holdings in the company be privately sold to the surviving partner (often leading to stronger control and entrenchment) or should they be offered proportionately to all the remaining shareholders? Especially if the sale is negotiated at less-than-prevailing market-prices, such transactions assume ethical and fiduciary overtones of the dominant shareholders sequestering for themselves benefits that would seem to belong to all shareholders in proportion to their holdings. [**Case summary 2.2: Hero Honda**]

- Controlling shareholders may prefer, for a variety of reasons,[7] to de-list from the stock exchanges and take their companies private, a status that may[8] offer them greater freedom and privacy from public glare. While this is a legitimate option available to companies, it may have to be done with due consideration for the absentee shareholders who have been with the promoters when they needed them. It is also possible that some of the shareholders may decide to stay on despite delisting albeit without the liquidity and other advantages foregone, and in that case it may not always be possible for the promoters to forcibly exit them. [**Case summary 2.3: Sterlite**]

- Executive compensation, especially to promoters and their nominees is another area amenable to such abuse. Although directorial remuneration is to be approved individually by the shareholders at their meetings, nothing stopped the promoters from voting in favour of their compensation packages with the support of their boards. With their voting rights now restricted on such resolutions, other shareholders now have the option of either supporting or rejecting such proposals as deemed reasonable by them. (**Case summary 2.4: Jindal Steel and Power**)

II

Ownership and Control

Shareholders in joint stock companies are often loosely referred to as owners of the company. This is particularly true in the context of family controlled entities where it is not unusual to refer to them as family *owned* or simply as 'their' company; this is further compounded by the families themselves when the patriarch, on his impending age-or-health-related retirement or to forestall family infighting, decides to distribute 'his' companies among different siblings and other claimants, as if the subject companies were his personal property. Nothing can be farther from the truth. It is only the operational and management control of these corporations that was being bequeathed to his chosen heirs, along with his ownership rights of share holdings in the respective companies. The key point is that incorporated companies own their assets and other rights, not their shareholders who only own their shares in those companies.

Some eighty years ago, two academics in the US[9] highlighted this obvious but often misunderstood phenomenon in their path-breaking study of US corporations underscoring the changed concept of property ownership with the advent of the corporate format of modern organizations. A multitude of shareholders owned fractions of their equity capital and, with very few exceptions, had little involvement in their resource allocation and decision making processes. These 'changed corporate relationships have unquestionably involved an essential alteration in the character of property', which was now split into *passive property* of the shareholders with neither control nor accountability, and *active property* consisting of relationships under which an individual or a few individuals held power over the enterprise virtually without any effectively enforceable duties.[10] These developments in effect established managerial independence of decision making and business conduct, and also lead to concerns over excessive corporate and executive power and its potential abuse.

Five types of corporate control have been identified as follows:

- Absolute control through complete ownership. Wholly owned subsidiaries of corporations will fall under this category. Individuals can also own 100 percent of a business. In these cases there will be no shares to be sold or traded on the stock exchange
- Control by an individual or small group, through a straightforward majority in the company's voting stock
- Control without such complete or majority ownership of capital but through legal devices. Four such methods were identified, namely, pyramiding, with the help of a chain of companies which one dominates even though the net investment in the company at the end of the chain is small; issuing non-voting stock; issuing some controlling shares with excessive voting powers; or creating a voting trust

- Minority control, where any individual or small group, even though not controlling a majority of votes, was able to dominate. This would be achieved by retaining power to appoint a majority of directors on the board, or by mutual covenants between partners in joint venture through shareholders' agreements and so on
- Management control, where the ownership was so widely spread that no individual or small group had even a minority interest large enough to influence company affairs. In the Indian context, even large block holders like domestic financial institutions may not have the power to influence the controlling managers for reasons we have already noted

Indian law defines 'control' as including the right to appoint a majority of the directors to control the management or policy decisions exercisable by persons acting individually or in concert, directly or indirectly, including by virtue of their shareholding or management rights or shareholder agreements or voting agreements or in any other manner.[11] As will be seen, this comprehensive description covers virtually every possible mechanism for exercise of power over the affairs of a company.

There is a second and perhaps even more important dimension to voting power in relation to corporate control. Shareholders' voting rights (democratic or plutocratic) can only be exercised at members' meetings either in person or by proxy (and by postal ballot when so required or authorized). Given the dispersal of shareholders across geographies in case of international corporations and even within countries otherwise, it is virtually impossible (and perhaps not worthwhile in case of small holdings) for a vast majority of absentee shareholders to attend and participate in such general meetings. Natural lethargy and indifference would also rule out significant participation in case of voting by postal ballot. In developed markets, proxy voting mitigates this problem to some extent but in India this system is as yet not adequately developed. The result is that while shareholders have the right, it rarely translates into effective exercise. This makes the task of controlling shareholders quite easy in getting the kind of resolutions they wish to be approved at these meetings, especially if the companies could also persuade any block holders like financial institutions either to support their resolutions or abstain from voting on them.

INTER-CORPORATE HOLDINGS

A game changer in terms of corporate development and growth with their concomitant, power was the acceptance that corporations can hold shares in another corporation. In this context, reference is usually made to the American Constitution that promised 'life, liberty, and property' to every white male citizen of the new Nation. Corporations as creations by law are entitled to the same property rights as individual citizens and thus have been allowed to hold shares in other corporations. The Indian situation is no different and thus there is no bar to inter-corporate shareholdings.

The ramifications of this innocuously straightforward principle are indeed far reaching. This paved the way for the formation of large groups of corporations with a controlling holding corporation and also the genesis for the development and growth of multinational corporations spread around the world but subject to overall direction and control of the holding company in the home country. Since only a reasonably substantial shareholding was required to control the subsidiaries and affiliates, it was possible for an individual, family or even a corporation to have access to disproportionately vast corporate

Shareholders

assets and resources (control rights) far in excess of their equity investments (cash flow rights) in the overall business edifice. In Exhibit 2.1, it can be seen for example, that although the ultimate holding company has cash flow rights of only 177.03

Exhibit 2.1: Corporate Groups—Control Rights to Cash Flow Rights Escalation

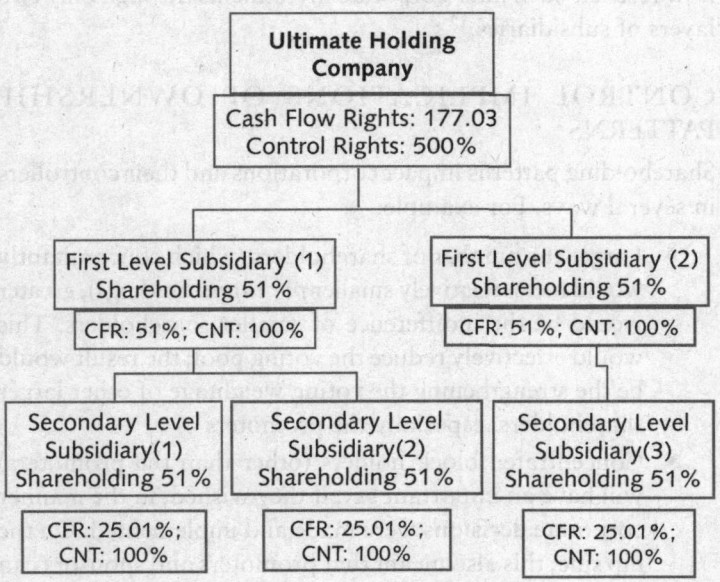

percent from its five two-level subsidiaries, it has control over 500 percent of the resources of the five subsidiaries put together. This is a simplified illustration; in practice, there can be many more subsidiaries and any such subsidiary may also have shareholdings in other subsidiaries at a peer level or above or below in the hierarchical tree of entities; other business formats could also be introduced, such as trusts partnerships etc. Overall depending upon the maze created, the multiple of control rights over cash flow rights could indeed be astronomical! Linked to the freedom and power of the corporation and its management we have already referred to, this can be and often is a lethal prescription for as potential abuse of such authority. Recognizing the abusive potential of such uninhibited pyramiding, Indian law now restricts such inter-corporate investments through only two layers of subsidiaries.[12]

CONTROL IMPLICATIONS OF OWNERSHIP PATTERNS

Shareholding patterns impact corporations and their controllers in several ways. For example:

- Larger the number of shareholders (which concomitantly would mean relatively smaller *per capita* holdings), greater would be the indifference of smaller shareholders. This would effectively reduce the voting pool; the result would be the strengthening the voting weightage of other larger shareholders, especially the promoters

- Concentrated block holders (other than the promoters) will have an important say, if they wished, in the manner corporate decisions were made and implemented. On the flip side, this also meant that promoters and sponsors can more easily negotiate with fewer large block holders to go along with their decisions

- In case of large investors owned or controlled by the State, promoters could more easily enlist the support of the political establishment to instruct their controlled institutions to fall in line with management initiatives by absenting from meetings, abstaining from voting, or actively supporting relevant resolutions at shareholders' meetings

- Given the growing complexities of corporate investments, individual investors around the world chose to route their investments through institutional investors like mutual funds, pension and insurance outfits and so on. During the first decade of this millennium in India, in case of private sector domestic groups, most of their retail investor holdings were largely absorbed by their promoters to strengthen their entrenchment in their companies, partly as a defence against hostile takeover bids. In case of management controlled companies (with no identified promoters), such retail holdings largely migrated to institutional shareholders. (Exhibit 2.2)

Exhibit 2.2: Median Shareholdings in NSE *Nifty, Junior Nifty and 100* **(in %)**

(Companies figuring in the respective indices at 31 December, 2001 and 2011)

Domestic Private Sector Companies

Category	NSE Nifty		NSE Junior Nifty		NSE 100	
	2001	2011	2001	2011	2001	2011
Promoters	28.50	46.80	36.67	45.98	32.08	46.75
Institutional	33.04	30.77	15.25	28.07	26.46	30.57
Non-Institutional Retail	33.09	19.34	40.65	20.08	35.95	19.54

Management Controlled Companies

Category	NSE Nifty		NSE Junior Nifty		NSE 100	
	2001	2011	2001	2011	2001	2011
Institutional	46.43	53.25	28.89	42.42	45.98	51.09
Non-Institutional Retail	46.02	32.69	32.59	38.08	40.31	36.26

III

Groups, Parents, Subsidiaries and Affiliates

The most prominent feature of plutocratic voting regimes is the encouragement they offer to corporations to consolidate and considerably expand their control over assets and resources with often relatively small equity investments. There are several reasons why corporations would want to structure their businesses in to several related corporations.

- Each corporation is a distinct legal entity with limits on its shareholders' liability. This applies to corporate shareholders as well. Subsidiaries, even if 100 percent owned, offer a method of risk segregation and containment and can be used as part of an overall risk management strategy adopted by the corporation. In general, there are of course circumstances when this strategy may not work and the liabilities of the subsidiary may in fact devolve on the parent (known in legal parlance as lifting or piercing the *corporate veil*) but, given some reasonable precautions to keep the entities separated in terms of decision making, perceived parental influence and operational control, and so on the scheme may by and large work. The contentious case of Union Carbide Corporation initially and Dow Chemical later on following its acquisition of UCC with respect to the liabilities arising from the 1984 Bhopal gas tragedy at Union Carbide India, a subsidiary is an illustrative case in point.

- Especially in overseas operations, host country regulations might mandate a locally incorporated business entity, often with local participation as well. This might necessitate a subsidiary or affiliate format of organization but depending upon relative strengths, parents may be able to reserve for themselves control over composition of the local board of directors and also other key issues of technology, intellectual property and marketing turf to meet their requirements. Many of the joint venture vehicles (such as between General Electric and Wipro for medical systems and Godrej and Procter and Gamble for consumer products) fall under this category.[13]

- Currency and tax regimes in different countries vary significantly and parents may wish to move profits and cash resources to more advantageous countries or even route investments through subsidiaries located in such countries; special purpose vehicles incorporated as subsidiaries may serve this objective. Foreign direct investments in Indian companies routed through subsidiaries located in Mauritius (which has an investor-friendly tax treaty with India) are examples falling under this category.

- Corporatization of self-contained business segments (in preference to structuring them as strategic business units within the parent company) may be seen as conducive to improving focus and containing, especially labour costs with managements being rewarded disparately depending upon market and risk profiles of the businesses. Spinning off the non-IT businesses of Wipro in to separate companies is an example of this kind of corporatization in the hope that valuations of these independent businesses including IT would improve, uncluttered by the business profiles of each other. This case however went beyond this objective and led to a ownership change and exit from the listed market as well.

- Keeping acquired businesses separate may at times help the parent to avoid past-related liabilities; similarly, discreet business entities may help the parent in case of divestment or discontinuance without unduly affecting the parent or other group companies.

PARENT COMPANY AND THE HOST COUNTRY

Parents as shareholders in an overseas subsidiary have some onerous responsibilities. Multinational corporations largely have always been regarded with distrust and even hostility in most jurisdictions especially in the developing countries around the world. They are generally assumed to be indulging in bringing in outdated technology and products, profiteering with unconscionable end-product pricing, unreasonable transfer pricing for input materials and knocked-down kits for further local assembly or processing, royalty and know how fees, and in having little or no commitment to local markets and communities. Sometimes, they are also perceived to be exerting uncalled for political and policy influence in host countries. Almost all countries including India have regulatory regimes that seek to minimize and mitigate such abuses but thanks to some irresponsible instances such perceptions do persist. Often inappropriate overseas behaviour leads to impairment of the parent company's reputation in its home country itself requiring costly damage control actions to ensure speedy restoration. [**Case summary: 2.5 BHP Billiton**]

A major area of contention in the MNC arena is the transfer of outdated and sometimes even unproven technology and negligent safety measures for disaster prevention and recovery. Union Carbide's pesticides plant located in Bhopal has already been referred to in a different context. What safety precautions were deemed essential for a similar plant in the US were disregarded in its Indian counterpart; use of a hazardous intermediary based on its cost advantage, without ensuring requisite safety precautions and effective communication; and disregarding insistent internal alerts and warnings of a disaster waiting to happen; these were not the kind of responses expected of a responsible corporation, much less of an MNC from a developed country.

PARENT COMPANY EXPOSURE IN HOME COUNTRY

Some countries, for example the US, have stringent laws that seek to rein in their corporations from misbehaving overseas in their pursuit of business and profit. The Foreign Corrupt Practices Act is one such initiative that prohibits US companies from bribing government officials and others through their subsidiaries to gain business advantage. In a 2013 settlement case in the US, the SEC agreed to waive prosecution because the company had first on their own informed SEC of the corruption practised by its Argentinian subsidiary based on their internal investigations, cooperated in the ensuing investigations, and improved their internal control and compliance mechanisms following the event, and had even closed down its local operations. This example illustrates not only the practical difficulties of MNCs with operations far and wide in ensuring their corporate policies are fully complied with but also highlights the corrective measures they need to take in consequence and adopt a cooperative approach in the regulators' investigations, all of which would earn them regulatory approbation, some nominal fines notwithstanding.[14]

Breaching the discipline of strict neutrality in host country politics (and even a perception to that effect) can impair MNC reputations adversely, notwithstanding any good work they may do in the country or internationally. [**Case summary 2.6: Royal Dutch Petroleum in Nigeria**] As MNC shareholders, their best option would be to ensure both at policy formulation and practical implementation levels they remain vigilant and steer a carefully crafted course that keeps their host countries happy and their own shareholders satisfied and well protected.

IV

Institutional Shareholders

These are a special category of shareholders, not so much because of their financial muscle (which can be substantial) as due to their own accountability to their constituencies. In addition their role as large block holders in their investee companies vests them with a responsibility to ensure both their good governance and satisfactory performance in their investee companies. This category generally includes development banks, insurance and pension companies, mutual funds, unit trusts and other such institutions that channel funds from others to invest in company shares, debentures, and other instruments such as government securities and corporate bonds and so on. It is not surprising therefore that the OECD Principles suggest that 'the effectiveness and credibility of the entire corporate governance system and company oversight will...to a large extent depend on institutional investors that can make informed use of their shareholder rights and effectively exercise their ownership functions in companies in which they invest.'[15]

PREFERRED OBLIGATIONS OF MAJOR INSTITUTIONAL INVESTORS

Given their financial clout and shareholding size together with their expertise, institutional investors are in a position to influence and improve corporate governance in their investee companies, eventually to the benefit of their own constituencies. The Stewardship Code in the UK[16] succinctly enumerates (on a Comply or Explain basis) the desirable role of major institutional investors in the following seven principles, namely:

- Publicly disclose their policy on how they will discharge their stewardship responsibilities
- Have a publicly disclosed robust policy on managing conflicts of interest in relation to stewardship
- Monitor their investee companies
- Establish clear guidelines on when and how they will escalate their stewardship activities
- Be willing to act collectively with other investors where appropriate
- Have a clear policy on voting and disclosure of voting activity
- Report periodically on their stewardship and voting activities

These principles clearly recognize the power and accountability of such investors both in improving corporate governance and performance of their investee companies and their own constituent investors whose funds they have under management.

Unfortunately, India does not yet have any equivalent guidelines or mandates prescribed by regulators.[17] Their transparency and accountability in many cases may be compromised by the controlling owners of the institutions themselves. For example, the largest of the domestic institutional investors in India like Life Insurance Corporation of India, General Insurance Corporation of India and its subsidiaries (Oriental, National, New India and United India), Unit Trust of India, and some of the development banks are all owned and controlled by the government and as such may be susceptible to political and bureaucratic interventions that may not always in the best interests of their constituencies on whose behalf the investments are made. More than a decade ago, a government appointed committee had suggested:

> 'Institutional investors should also lead by example in terms of transparency and good governance in their own operations, and decisions on investee company proposals. Widely disseminating their position and justifications on company proposals (say by posting this on own or those of their investee companies' web sites) will enhance their image as objective and rational shareholders working for the benefit of all investors.'[18]

Like many of the Committee's other recommendations, this was also perhaps far ahead of its time. Hardly any disclosure is made by such institutions even now either of their policy or of their voting on specific resolutions of their investee companies on key resolutions impacting shareholder interests and their justification. There is apparently a strong case to improve disclosure practices of institutional investors with respect to their voting decisions on investee company resolutions.

INSTITUTIONAL INVESTOR ACTIVISM

Elsewhere in the developed world, coinciding with their growing share of the equity markets, institutional shareholders have made rapid strides in actively pursuing an activist agenda with regard to their investee corporations. A classic example in the US is the California Public Employees Retirement System (CalPERS) which sets (and follows up on) very high standards of corporate governance for the companies they invest in. For example, long before New York Stock Exchange and Nasdaq had prescribed independence criteria for directors, CalPERS had set much higher standards of independence for the directors of companies they were invested in. It is also customary for them to annually put non- or low-performing companies on notice to improve or else face change of management. Similar organizations exist in the UK and a few other countries but not so far in India to any appreciable extent. Many institutional investors though have shown resistance and opposition to management proposals not considered in general shareholder interest. Satyam Computers and Coal India are conspicuous examples of such action—in the firstcase, the company had to reverse an intra-group merger proposal that camouflaged transfer of cash to the controlling shareholders and the other involved government-dictated unfavourable pricing and other commercial terms leading to shareholder value erosion, which was resisted and led to the public sector company and its directors being sued for dereliction of duty towards shareholders. In both cases, the institutional investors were foreign-based; in contrast, perhaps not surprisingly, one had rarely witnessed such actions or resistance from Indian institutional investors in the recent past seeking to redress absentee shareholder-unfriendly management decisions.

V

State as a Shareholder

A distinguishing feature of the Indian corporate landscape is the significant presence of State owned Enterprises (SOE), many of them publicly listed for trading; as of March 2011, there were 22 of them on the NSE CNX 100 and ten on the NSE Nifty.

Government as a shareholder has two important responsibilities. First, to act as an enlightened dominant shareholder whose behaviour towards other absentee shareholders (in case of listed companies) is worthy of emulation by others; and second, to adopt good governance practices and excel them wherever possible to enhance both corporate performance and to transparent and timely communications to the shareholders and other stakeholders.

SOE SHARE OWNERSHIP—BEST PRACTICES AND INDIAN EXPERIENCE

Building upon their *Principles of Corporate Governance* generically applicable to all corporations, OECD's *Guidelines on Corporate Governance of State Owned Enterprises* (2005), specifically addresses governance issues in corporations in the public sector. Two of these six guidelines[19] are of special relevance to share ownership and dominance related matters:

Guideline II: State acting as an owner:

- The state should act as an informed and active owner and establish a clear and consistent ownership policy, ensuring that the governance of state owned enterprises is carried out in a transparent and accountable manner, with the necessary degree of professionalism and effectiveness

- The government should not be involved in the day-to-day management of the SOEs but should allow them full operational autonomy to achieve their defined objectives (sub-guideline B)
- The state should let SOE boards exercise their responsibilities and respect their independence (sub-guideline C)

Guideline III: Equitable Treatment of Shareholders:

- The state and the state owned enterprises should recognize the rights of all shareholders and in accordance with the OECD Principles of Corporate Governance ensure their equitable treatment and equal access to corporate information
- SOEs are required to develop an active policy of communication and consultation with all shareholders (sub-guideline C)
- SOEs are enjoined to facilitate participation of minority shareholders in shareholder meetings in order to allow them to take part in fundamental corporate decisions such as board election (sub-guideline D)

Transparency towards all shareholders is especially highlighted, as is also the need for the state to establish itself as an exemplary role model and follow best practices regarding the treatment of minority shareholders.[20]

There are many deviations from these salutary guidelines in many countries, India included. Problems of undue political interference, passive boards and inadequate transparency have been cited as causes prompting public concern, even while there is recognition of the complex issues and trade-offs facing governments in reconciling implementation of sound ownership practices and their practice within the State system.[21] Some countries have implemented these non-binding guidelines in respect of their SOEs. For example:

- In most OECD countries, minority shareholders' rights are recognized and in some cases, specifically protected. The state, as the dominant owner, 'ties its own hands' and adopts measures or general policies to prevent abuse of minority and non-controlling shareholders. Some of these measures include board representation for minority shareholders, decision-making powers at general meetings of members, and right to information about the company's situation

- In most OECD countries, minority shareholders of SOEs have no more rights than similar shareholders in other corporations. Some countries however, have provided for further measures. For example:

  ❖ In the Slovak Republic, in state majority owned SOEs, minority shareholders are given majority representation on their boards

  ❖ In Italy, minority shareholders of listed SOEs have special rights through the election system of the board: a cumulative voting type mechanism assigns disproportional voting rights in favour of the minority shareholders

  ❖ In Norway, minority shareholders are represented in the committee nominating directors on the board

  ❖ In Sweden, for listed companies a nomination committee of four or five largest shareholders discusses board nominations and remuneration

  ❖ Italy specifically requires that listed SOEs do not provide any information to the ownership entity that it does not also give their minority shareholders, so as to comply with the requirement of equitable treatment of all shareholders

The Indian experience is still far behind these best practices with respect to government shareholdings in publicly listed corporations. The government reserves to itself the right to issue directions to the SOEs on various issues to subserve public policy interests even if those were not in the interests of shareholders; a large proportion of directors on their boards are 'appointed' by the government without the need to have them approved by the other shareholders; in case of public sector banks, non-government shareholders do not even have the basic right of 'approving' the audited accounts but only 'note' them. The 2010 government guidelines on corporate governance applicable to central public sector enterprises make some improvements over earlier practices but still fall short of international best practices. Such gaps in good governance practices relating to minority or absentee shareholders introduce an often valid perception of high governance risk of investing in public sector enterprises in India and thus their shares are likely to trade in the market at a discount over their true value.

Case 2.1: Pfizer in India

Incorporated in 1950 as Dumex, a private limited company, it was taken over in 1958 by Pfizer of US and was rechristened as Pfizer Limited, with Pfizer US holding 60 percent of the equity. The rest was was held by the directors, employees and the public. In 1966 the company went public and was listed on Mumbai, and National Stock exchanges.

Pfizer India was into manufacturing and distribution of pharmaceuticals, agricultural and animal health products, pharmaceutical chemicals, nutritional products and items for personal, household, and industrial use.

In 1988, as part of regulatory compliance to reducing foreign equity holding in Pfizer India from 60 percent to 40 percent, Pfizer US offered for sale, 20 percent out of its 60 percent equity at a 200 percent premium over its face value to existing equity shareholders, employees, directors and to a subsidiary of Pfizer US.

A decade later, as part of a consolidation exercise, Pfizer US approached the Foreign Investment Promotion Board (FIPB) for permission to set up a 100 percent subsidiary, Pfizer Corporation Private Ltd, in India to manufacture high-tech formulations. FIPB approved the proposal.

This was not acceptable to the minority shareholders of Pfizer India who feared that the proposed wholly owned subsidiary would be preferred by the parent and all the benefits arising from new introductions, diversions of existing profitable products and the prospective patent law changes. In a representation to the FIPB, the Pfizer Minority Shareholder Association asked for protection for the minority shareholders. Fortunately for the minority shareholders, a key ministry of the government in charge of Chemicals and Fertilisers was against the proposal.

In the protracted litigation that ensued, it was also highlighted that under extant regulation (Press Note 18), an overseas investor had to obtain a 'no objection' clearance from a joint venture partner before starting another subsidiary in the same field of business and similarly Pfizer US should be asked to obtain the concurrence of the other shareholders of Pfizer India (in the absence of any identified local partner).

In the event, after protracted litigation, the minority shareholder lost their case, with the courts upholding the rights of the majority shareholder, Pfizer US to set up the 100 percent subsidiary as proposed, since all necessary approvals for the proposal had been granted by the government.

Case summary 2.2: Dominant Ownership Impact
Hero Honda

A joint venture between the Munjals-led Hero group and Honda of Japan, the company was incorporated in 1984 and over the years had risen to be India's largest two-wheeler producer. The partners decided to call off their association after some seventeen years. The Indian Promoter Group and Honda Motor Co. Ltd., Japan ('Honda') entered into a Share Transfer Agreement on January 22, 2011, with Honda agreeing to transfer its entire 26 percent holding to the Munjals, the Indian Promoters. The acquisition was completed on March 22, 2011 and the shares were transferred. Hero Honda was a listed company as of December 2010, with some 65,000 plus non-promoter shareholders. The shareholding pattern was: Munjals 26.21 percent, Honda Motors 26 percent, Institutions 38.04 percent and others, including small shareholders 9.75 percent. Post this private buy-out of Honda's shares, the remaining promoters, Munjals' holdings had gone up to 52 percent.

The negotiated price for the transferred shares reportedly carried a substantial discount on the ruling market price, a benefit that was sequestered by the Munjals, the surviving promoters, There were concerns that parts of this discount would probably be made up by increasing royalties to Honda, which will be borne by the company and hence by all its shareholders. Even otherwise, in fairness shouldn't Honda have offered their holdings to all the shareholders in proportion to their holdings? As joint promoters and directors, don't they have any fiduciary obligations to the absentee shareholders thus adversely impacted? Was it right for the Munjals to have acquired Honda's holdings to the exclusion of all other shareholders?

Case summary 2.3: Sterlite Industries Minority Squeeze Out by Whatever Name

In corporate ownership structures, there are times when the dominant shareholders, either following an acquisition or even otherwise, seek to buy out the other shareholders, an operation generally labeled as squeeze out or freeze out of (usually) minority shareholders. There are of course ethical dimensions to these exercises as to whether it is equitable to thus jettison co-owners once deemed essential, even if they were to be fairly compensated financially but the legality of such operations have never been doubted. Given the problems of the squeeze out process in the Indian context however, companies have often resorted to less troublesome routes in law to achieve their objective. One of these is the capital reduction route where the dominant controllers seek to buy back the holdings of the 'external' shareholders, often with the funds of the company itself. And there can be several 'heads-I-win-tails-you-lose' variants as well. Here is a 2002 Indian example.

In 2002, Sterlite proposed, in a Scheme of Arrangement approved by the High Court of Bombay, to purchase from its shareholders approximately 50 percent of the company's equity excluding the Equity Shares of those Shareholders from whom the Company receives a written intimation (in a prescribed form) within the stipulation period of their intention to continue holding the Equity Shares. This was rather unusual where silence was being deemed as acceptance by the concerned shareholders leading to their shares being bought back, eventually leading to reduction of the share capital of the company. The controlling shareholders conveying their intention of not selling their holdings were thus in a happy position of their holdings being increased substantially as a percentage of the reduced equity capital of the company.

The purchase consideration was paid partly in cash and partly in non-convertible debentures; those not desirous of surrendering their shares (or who serendipitously overlooked to exercise the written option to express their intent of not surrendering their shares) just had to accept the cash payment sent along with the offer; and quite helpfully, the company had also arranged with HDFC Bank to buy the non-convertible debentures at a pre-negotiated price from the shareholders who just had to return an attached form.

Securities and Exchange Board of India (Sebi) and the Indian government took the matter to court on the ground that this procedure was in the nature of a squeeze out of minority shareholders without offering them the applicable rights; instead, the company used the provisions of the Companies Act (as it stood then) relating to reduction of capital and in the process substantially eliminating a large proportion of the company's institutional and retail equity holders. The Bombay High Court which heard this plaint did not find anything illegal in the entire process since the law did not prohibit the route adopted by the company and in any event the company had complied with all the required conditions. In fact, Sebi's right to maintain its plaint was also rejected (This led to a change in the requirements under the Listing Agreements concerning squeeze outs but these could only apply prospectively).

Source: Court Judgments—Sebi Vs Sterlite, SCL 478 BOM

Case summary 2.4: Overruling Negatively Impacted Shareholder Votes Jindal Steel and Power (JSP)

JSP is a large listed company in the steel and power space with consolidated annual revenues and post-tax profits for the year ended March 2012 respectively of some Rs 132 billion and Rs 40 billion. The promoters, Jindal family and their associates held 58.97 percent of the equity (including 2.87 percent pledged or otherwise encumbered), with the balance being held by Institutional Investors (28.2 percent), small shareholdings (7.58 percent—124,059 holders) and others (5.25 percent). By all accounts, the company's growth and profit performance was excellent.

Naveen Jindal, the company's chairman and managing director, youngest son of the founding patriarch who was a parliamentarian and power minister of the northern state of Haryana, and himself an incumbent member of parliament, has been credited with turning around the company and taking it to its current commanding heights in the industry. He is also reputed to be among the top earning CEOs in the country at around Rs 73 crore in 2012.

Among the items proposed for approval at the company's annual general meeting in September 2012, there was one that sought to authorise the chairman and managing director to '... revise, from time to time, remuneration of Wholetime Directors of the Company, by whatever designation they are called, by way of annual increments or otherwise. Resolved further that the increase in remuneration in case of each such Wholetime Director, at every time, should not exceed 100 percent of their respective Cost to Company (CTC) immediately before the revision...' This wording could arguably cover the remuneration of the managing director as well since he would also qualify as a whole time director, especially with the explanatory phrase in the resolution 'by whatever designation.' Fixing one's own pay in a public company was against all canons of equity and fairness; in any case, executive compensation was a board responsibility in the absence of a compensation committee of the board (JSP didn't have one) which in terms of its supervisory and oversight functions, the board could ill afford to delegate to its executive chairman.

At the meeting, this resolution was approved by majority since the promoter group which piloted the resolution through the board earlier voted in favour. The institutional and other shareholders not in operational control were poorly represented at the meeting with less than 40 percent of the institutional shareholdings of 28.2 percent in the company being voted; and expectedly, small retail shareholders hardly bothered to attend or vote by proxy. The net result was that an interested shareholder group with its voting power had succeeded in overruling the concerns and objections of the absentee shareholders, turning the entire voting exercise into a predictable legal farce.

Case summary 2.5: BHP Billiton

BHP Billiton, once affectionately named *The Big Australian*, was the darling of investors, with a consistent record of profits and growth ever since it was founded as Broken Hill Proprietary Company in the eighteen eighties in New South Wales in southern Australia. A century later, its footprint covered some forty countries across the world, figuring among the topmost mining companies. With its exclusive focus on profits and wealth creation for its shareholders, BHP did not particularly care if it violated environmental and safety standards in its operations. It was undoubtedly emboldened by the fact that the company was a significant contributor to national exports and revenue; often its writ ran large on the political scene with the country, irrespective of the parties in power, keen to legislate to protect its interests. And the company ensured on its part it left no stone unturned in its effort to seek and obtain broad spectrum political patronage.

Although its record of skirmishes with regulators was long and well known, its cavalier behaviour in operating a gold and copper mine in the Star mountains of Papua New Guinea (PNG) near the Ok Tedi river basin in the late nineteen eighties and nineties turned out to be its nemesis. Its local operating subsidiary with government participation began to dump its mining waste (after extraction of most of the copper content) into the river Ok Tedi without building a Tailings Dam (to arrest flow through of residual copper and other sediments) as originally conceived. The effects of this irresponsible action (with the government unwilling to act stringently for fear of losing its substantial revenues from the operations) was the predictable damage to the flora and fauna of the basin and ruining of the livelihoods and property of several hundreds of thousands of poor farmers downstream several hundred miles towards the Gulf of Papua.

In legal actions that followed, the company was obliged to agree to compensate the farmers but as usual in such cases involving developing countries, the money was painfully inadequate and protests continued. In addition, the company was afraid of the mind boggling future liabilities that might devolve on it and some face saving way to contain if not obviate such liabilities had to be found; and it was.

But the impact on the company's reputation was staggering. Shareholders who were once delirious supporters turned antagonistic and took the company to task for such irrational behaviour. Even as the company belatedly tried to mend its ways and retrieve its lost reputation, the stigma wouldn't go away. Years later, when the Michigan University's Graham Environmental Sustainability Institute appointed the company to its Advisory Board, critics inside the University and outside pilloried the authorities for conferring on the company an image of respectability it did not deserve! Back home in Australia, the *Big Australian* was desperately looking to forget the past and trying to position itself as the *Global Australian*. Indiscretions overseas have a knack of haunting the parent at home, often indelibly.

Case summary 2.6: Royal Dutch Petroleum in Nigeria

The paradox of Nigeria, the western African country ranked eleventh largest oil producer in the world, is despite its natural wealth 70 percent of its population has to eke out livelihoods in abject poverty. Internecine violence among the diverse tribal communities and regions that comprised the State and the unbridled corruption as a way of life, undoubtedly compounded by multinational greed for products and profits were the main contributing factors to the dismal state of affairs in the country.

All the oil majors were in Nigeria to claim their share of action. Shell, the largest oil group in the world naturally was also there and wittingly or otherwise got embroiled in the local politics. Despite its Nigerian vision to be among the world's leading oil producing countries contributing to the sustained development of the country and its people, the company was perceived to be supportive of violent suppressions of protests by locals. As complainants argued before the US Supreme Court, after concerned residents of Ogoniland [where its operations were based] began protesting the environmental effects of Shell's practices, the company was alleged to have enlisted the Nigerian Government to violently suppress the burgeoning demonstrations. Throughout the early ninetes, Nigerian military and police forces attacked Ogoni villages, beating, raping, killing, and arresting residents and destroying or looting property. It was claimed that the company aided and abetted these atrocities by, among other things, providing the Nigerian forces withfood, transportation, and compensation, as well as by allowing the Nigerian military to use its property as a staging ground for attacks.

In June 2004, a Shell-commissioned report claimed that Shell admitted that it had inadvertently fed conflict, poverty, and corruption through its oil activities in Nigeria. But the company was prepared to help and join in any government or society initiated programme for reforms. Shell became a favourite target for both physical and verbal attack of otherwise warring critics who chose to unite for this purpose. In 2004, Shell's operations had to be suspended and doubts were expressed if they were ever likely to be resumed. The damage to its global reputation was immense.

Nigeria is a country that Shell cannot afford to leave nor can it manage to operate in peacefully. Steering a safe and non-controversial course without being seen as politically incorrect would appear to be its only option.

Source: US Supreme Court Opinion in Esther Kiobel et al vs Royal Dutch Shell et al, 569 US 10-1491 (2013), April 17, 2013; Shell Reports; and Shell Websites

CHAPTER 3

BOARDS AND DIRECTORS
Stewards and Monitors

The board of directors is an amiable entity, meeting with
self-approval and fraternal respect but fully subordinate
to the real powers of the managers.

—JOHN KENNETH GALBRAITH[1]

I

Board Primacy

For a company, its board is the supreme authority, subject only to its own charter documents and the laws of the land. All powers in respect of the company reside in the board. It is elected by the shareholders and hence primarily accountable to them but having been so elected, the task of running the business of the corporation is vested in the board and through it, executive management. Corporate powers can be exercised only when properly delegated by the board or as provided for in the Articles of Association of the company.

PRIMACY OVER THE EXECUTIVE

The primacy of the board, in theory, over executive management is quite clearly established around the world although in general its exercise seems to be relatively rare, and even then, only when the corporation was in dire straits. It is also closely linked to corporate ownership structures. For example, in countries with dispersed ownership like the US boards have tended to assert themselves more readily (Vikram Pandit, the Citibank CEO being replaced in 2012 despite the popular perception of his having seen the bank safely through troubled times after the global financial meltdown in 2008-09 is a case in point) than in countries like India with concentrated ownership in the hands of family groups. Even in case of comparable management controlled companies in India, CEO separations at the instance of their boards is a rare phenomenon indeed. Company law in India is quite categorical—although the managing director of a company is entrusted with the executive control over the whole or substantially the whole of its business he is nevertheless subordinated to the board of directors. Usually, the managing directors' contracts provide for a wide array of powers and authority to enable him to effectively manage the affairs of the company. If some extraordinary action is required to be taken which is not covered by these delegated powers, specific approvals of the board will need to be obtained generally prior to the transaction or decision but in special circumstances by subsequent ratification.

Virtually every country code of corporate governance is premised on board supremacy over the executive. The supervisory, oversight, and control roles of the board over the executive are the constant themes running through all of them.[2]

In practice though there is a perception that boards are a passive, necessary embellishment and are often seen as powerless. Partly this is due to the greater visibility of the CEO and his or her executive team as the 'doers'; partly this is due to the position of CEO and board chair being combined, thus blurring the roles played by an individual in that dual position. The CEO being in the limelight of market attention is indeed justified since he represents the executive responsible and accountable for the company's performance. The board is mostly in the background but nevertheless charged with the responsibility of overseeing the successful delivery of sustainable profits and growth to the shareholders. Not unlike Cicero's description of the person steering a ship, 'He that governs sits quietly at the stern and scarce is seen to stir,'[3] the purposeful board may not be seen or heard in the normal course and need 'not necessarily be heavy-handed, and should be able to keep the corporate ship on course with a minimum use of the tiller.' And yet, as has been observed time and again, there have been compelling circumstances when some boards have had to, and to their credit, did indeed, act with a 'heavy hand' and have done themselves and their companies proud.[4]

PRIMACY OVER SHAREHOLDERS

We have considered in the earlier chapter issues relating to shareholder primacy including over the board; as noted, this topic has been a subject of continuing debate. Three of the arguments advanced in support of board primacy are summarized below.

- Given the large number of shareholders in publicly traded corporations, organizational structures based on *consensus* and *authority*[5] opting for consensus from shareholders in management decision making would be impossible; hence, a duly elected board with unfettered authority (subject only to limitations mandated by law or the shareholders themselves through their Articles of Association or resolutions) is the only feasible alternative to effectively carry on the business of the corporation.[6]

- Enhanced empowerment of shareholders would undermine managerial flexibility and likely lead to more power and clout in the hands of institutional intermediaries with little or no accountability to the company or its shareholders at large.[7] Enabling boards to act independently for the benefit of the company is therefore the preferred option.

- Shareholders are one of the several stakeholders in the company, providing risk capital. According exclusive primacy to that amorphous group (which by definition ought to be heterogeneous in terms of investment goals, time horizons and so on) would militate against the sustainable interest of the company and the shareholders themselves. Shareholders therefore need to assure other stakeholders that all of them are together in creating value and this is best done by ceding control to a board of directors. The company as an independent entity is better driven and monitored by a manageable group of directors vested with the authority to do so.[8]

Indian law seems to tilt the balance in favour of the shareholders to a greater extent than for example in the US. A number of decisions including election of directors individually, their compensation, approval of increases in, and further issue of, capital, and so on require shareholder approval, but overall, 'the board is entitled to exercise all such powers, and do all such acts and things, the company is authorized to exercise and do.'[9] As long as the board operates within this eminently broad mandate and keeps within the law of the land, its primacy is absolute; where not so covered, shareholders have the right to approve or reject board proposals. This distribution of powers between the shareholders and the board offers a reasonable scheme of checks and balances on their respective domains of primacy.

There is, however, a major caveat threatening board primacy in case of oppression and mismanagement of the company. In such cases the government on its own initiative or on application by eligible members, can approach the Company Law Tribunal for a direction to remove and replace any offending persons like the managing director, other directors, or even the entire board.[10] It was on this basis that in 2009 the incumbent board of Satyam Computers was superseded and replaced with new directors nominated by the government. These are salutary provisions to protect the interests of the company, its shareholders, and even those of an entire industry or the country. The erring board forfeits its authority and primacy in such situations.

II

Role and Responsibility

The stewardship role of the board has already been noted. Being positioned at the centre stage of the governance regime (as graphically displayed in Exhibit 1.1), the board and the directors have a major trusteeship responsibility to the company and all its (and especially absentee) shareholders on the one hand, and on the other to direct and oversee the executive in setting and achieving business objectives in shareholder interest. In carrying out this obligation, the board will need to ensure the company and its executive management pursue practices in line and conformity with board policies and regulatory prescriptions, and manage relationships with other relevant stakeholders in a manner conducive to the company's long term sustainable performance and growth.

CONTRIBUTING, COUNSELLING, AND CONTROLLING

Given that the board does not normally[11] engage in direct executive functions but is required to 'get things done' on the basis of its approved policies, three distinct dimensions of board role can be identified in its interface with the executive. These are the contributing, counselling, and controlling roles. In the *contributing* dimension, individual directors bring to bear on the discussions the weight of their expertise and experience, aimed at protecting and enhancing the company's wealth-creating capabilities; in the *counselling* dimension, directors assume mentoring responsibilities and counsel on the approaches the executive plans to adopt in respect of specific initiatives, such that the wealth-creating processes are smooth and within the value-frame laid down; and in the *controlling* dimension, the board exercises its surveillance functions to ensure that created wealth passes to the rightful claimants without undue leakage in the process. The challenge, perhaps, is in achieving clarity among all the directors, as to which dimension of board responsibility was in play at any given time. The board or committee chairs are probably the best persons to drive the discussion in the right direction consistent with the relevant dimension.

While all the three dimensions are equally important, it is highly unlikely that every board member will have all the three competencies in equal measure. Some will have more of domain knowledge and operating experience that would help in their contributing role but not have the requisite skills in exercising the control role to the same extent. This is generally the case with technology experts and academics in specialised fields of management and operations. On the other hand, directors with an accounting, audit, finance, or legal background may be well equipped to excel in the controlling role but perhaps not to the same extent in the other dimensions. There are directors who excel in all three dimensions because of their breadth of experience, depth of domain skills, and innate or acquired business acumen gathered over decades of hands-on exposure to a variety of industries, situations and circumstances, but such combinations are relatively rare, highly prized and sought after. Shareholders and the executive who have boards with such members should consider themselves truly blessed and fortunate. For the rest, it is a matter of complementing each other such that the aggregate skill sets of the board in these three dimensions are roughly equal or tilted in favour of one or the other dimensions as the circumstance of the company may require, with members contributing in different proportions to reach the desired balance. This is a key consideration in the composition of boards.

The key challenge is to determine the disparate mix of board resources among the three dimensions depending upon each company's requirements. Strategy formulation and performance monitoring would normally receive the highest priority in most corporations and the board's contributing role in this field could come into full play. It is also important to recognise that domain expertise need not necessarily be limited to the business requirements of the company; it could well relate to other associated fields of expertise: for example, a technology-driven company may need advice and contribution not only in their field but also in the area of patents law and practice; a company whose business model is based substantially on inorganic growth may need help in the fields of mergers and acquisition, taxation and accounting, valuation and so on. Where board level expertise in such fields is not available or easy to come by, boards should supplement their skill sets by hiring external help to bridge the gap and reach the right balance.

The counselling role is best played by those who have 'been there, done that' and hence in a position to share insights on how to achieve the desired goals without succumbing to the pitfalls inherent in the process. Such wisdom is usually the result of years of hands-on exposure to similar situations and internalising lessons learnt both in success and failure. This is the primary reason that explains the older age profile of directors on corporate boards. Falling in this category would also be expatriate directors on domestic boards of companies with global business footprints or aspirations. They bring their wisdom gleaned from their home country as well as from other countries they had been involved with in their career. The controlling role of the board would largely cover the area of systems and processes in the organization that even while facilitating operations ensure that adequate and appropriate control measures were in place and being followed. From an agency theory viewpoint, this would also include appropriate oversight and surveillance by the board to ensure that corporate objectives set by the board are achieved operating within the prescribed value framework, that created wealth as well as wealth creating assets are adequately protected and duly distributed or held in trust for the shareholders, and that the financial accounting, auditing and reporting practices were robust and transparent. Initially this would call for substantial time and resource investments by the board and its committees until reasonable systems are in place, and the board gets periodical reassurance through internal audit and assurance mechanisms. Once a relatively stable state is reached, the board and the committees could consider tempering their resource allocation to this role. There is of course no room for complacency at any time and the watch words in the context of control ought to be healthy skepticism and eternal vigilance.[12]

DIRECTORS' DUTIES

Within the framework of fiduciary obligations enjoined upon company directors, two broad categories—loyalty and care— have been identified.

- Duty of loyalty meaning that a director must demonstrate unyielding and undivided loyalty to the company's shareholders. At all times, the directors are required to put the company's and its shareholders' interests before their own; and also to eschew situations where their duties to one set of shareholders may conflict with those of another set of shareholders which will be the case when a director sits on boards of two or more companies competing in main lines of business or when they are involved in situations involving mergers, acquisitions or disinvestments

- Duty of Care meaning that a director must exercise due diligence in making decisions; discover as much information as possible both from within the company and from without so that he or she, with due application of mind and objective, unbiased reasoning, could come to an independent judgement on what is in the best interests of the company and its shareholders. This would also include the director allocating adequate time and effort to the company's affairs and matters coming up for decision, demonstrated by regular attendance and informed participation in board and committee meetings and discussions

These primary duties are often supplemented by other extensions, such as

- Duty of candour or disclosure which requires interested directors to disclose to the company, the board or the shareholders as the case may be, of material facts and circumstances relevant to conflicted transactions so that informed decisions may be possible
- Duty of good faith in support of fair dealing that involves acting in good faith in sharing all relevant details of the conflicted transaction with those charged with the responsibility of decision making on the matter and recusing oneself from the discussions as well as in voting on the resolutions so that the non-interested directors may take the decision without any direct or indirect pressures that may otherwise be there

Most related party transactions (between one or more directors and the company) have the potential risk of directors' fiduciary obligations being breached because of the inherent conflict of interest between the two contracting parties. Indian company law seeks to address these issues by incorporating these salutary principles while enumerating the duties of directors and also prescribing certain situations requiring interested directors' non-involvement in decisions.

Box. 3.1: Duties of Directors

A director of a company shall:

- Act in good faith in order to promote the objects of the company for the benefit of its members as a whole, and in the best interests of the company, its employees, the shareholders, the community and for the protection of environment
- Exercise his duties with due and reasonable care, skill and diligence and shall exercise independent judgement
- Not be involved in a situation in which he may have a direct or indirect interest that conflicts, or possibly may conflict, with the interest of the company
- Not achieve or attempt to achieve any undue gain or advantage either to himself or to his relatives, partners, or associates

Source: The Companies Act, 2013, Section 166

- Every director shall disclose to the company his concern or interest in any company or companies or bodies corporate, firms, or other association of individuals which shall include the shareholding
- Every director of a company who is in any way, whether directly or indirectly, concerned or interested in a contract or arrangement or proposed contract or arrangement entered into or to be entered into

---

- with a body corporate in which such director or such director in association with any other director, holds more than two percent shareholding of that body corporate, or is a promoter, manager, CEO of that body corporate; or
- with a firm or other entity in which, such director is a partner, owner or member, as the case may be, shall disclose the nature of his concern or interest at the meeting of the Board in which the contract or arrangement is discussed and shall not participate in such meeting

Source: The Companies Act, 2013, Section 184

These fiduciary duties are derived both from common law as laid down by judicial pronouncements over time, and legislative or regulatory requirements that mandate certain dos and don'ts including disclosure requirements and non-participation by interested directors in board discussions and decision processes. Listing agreement provisions applicable to publicly traded companies and statutes such the Companies Act are examples of such interventions. Many of these requirements are designed to identify and pre-empt transactions that may involve conflicts of interest leading to a breach of fiduciary duties or to provide sufficient disclosure to assist informed decision-making by the other directors or, in case of members' meetings, the shareholders. A significant escalation in such regulatory initiatives has been noticeable in recent times, driven by large scale corporate frauds and misdemeanours. For example, in the US, the 2002 Sarbanes-Oxley legislation following the Enron collapse and other corporate scams and Dodd-Frank legislation in 2010 following the global meltdown of 2008-09, and the Walker Review of 2009 in the UK, to cite just a few. Legislative and regulatory reforms in India have also been preceded by stock market manipulations by Harshad Mehta in the early nineties; failures in the Unit Trust of India, the major fraud in Satyam Computers and so on have given a fillip to regulatory interventions.

III

Independence and Objectivity

An underlying assumption in the agency theory of corporate governance is the virtually inevitable non-congruence of goals between shareholders and executive management. In practice this translates in to an imperative need for surveillance of the executive to ensure that its self-serving initiatives do not unduly usurp what rightfully ought to be rendered to the shareholders. Effective execution of this task requires a set of people with independence of thought, objectivity of approach, and loyalty to the principals; and with no economic dependence or moral or other obligation to the executive that could impair due performance of their duties. Independent directors on company boards are expected to perform this task on behalf of the shareholders, in addition to their other contributions to the success of the company in the interest of the shareholders.

This is not to say that all non-independent directors on boards need not, or will not exercise similar discipline to ensure shareholder interests are well protected; in fact by virtue of being directors, it is equally their fiduciary responsibility as well to do best by their shareholders. There are several such directors who do so too; but human nature being what it is, '...primitive, universal, and insuppressible instinct that impels

[man] to satisfy his desires with the least possible pain',[13] the inclination towards expropriation, overtly or covertly, of what rightfully belongs to another ought to be expected unless proved otherwise in exceptional cases. And to preempt or mitigate such losses to the eventual legitimate beneficiary, the shareholders in this case, ought to be a major preoccupation for those who, being independent and non-aligned, have been chosen precisely to do that. Whether the institution of independent directors has been able to fully discharge that responsibility in all cases is another matter that will be explored presently.

To be functionally effective, both the board collectively and directors individually should be independent.

BOARD INDEPENDENCE

This is largely a function of board composition supplemented by its functioning processes. The general belief is that the larger the proportion of independent directors on the board, the stronger its independence quotient would be. This is the reason why governance codes and listing requirements around the world mandate a substantial proportion (often a majority) of independent directors on listed company boards. In India, at least one third of a listed company's board is required to be independent[14] (and one half if the positions of board chair and chief executive are combined in a single person[15]). In practice though, even a single such director, depending upon his or her stature and persuasive capabilities, could be effective and carry conviction to the rest on the board.[16] A particularly significant insight into the power and potential of *independence* is available in the Gandhian concept of *satyagraha*,[17] where the individual, 'wants nothing for himself', and therefore is able to enter into any 'conflict for the sake of those around him, without hostility, without resentment, without resorting even to violent words.' In such a *satyagraha*, 'it is never the numbers that count; it is always the quality, more so when the forces of violence are uppermost.' Extrapolated to the more materialistic world of corporate boards and directors, there can be no more appropriate description of the power and potential of the concept of *independence* in directors. In ancient Indian tradition, Bhartrihari wrote an inspiring verse that bears a strikingly analogous modern day comparison: 'As the Sun alone illuminates the entire world with his brilliant rays, a single warrior by himself can conquer the entire world with his extraordinary valour.'[18] Very few codes or regulations around the world are able to capture this essence of director independence in such simple and yet so powerful a connotation.

Board independence however is not just a sum of its parts alone. Other factors also impact upon it. One such factor is the issue of board chair—CEO duality: an independent chair can bring to bear upon the deliberations a greater degree of objectivity on decision making than would be the case if the chair were also the chief executive. Another contributory to board independence and objectivity is the freedom and flexibility of the board chair to set the agenda for the meetings. Providing adequate support material well in advance of the meeting allows non-executive directors the opportunity to be well prepared for discussions; an independent chair can certainly facilitate purposeful discussions and draw in all directors to elicit their views on matters so that the board can reach well informed decisions. Equally important is the facility to have dissenting views recorded in the minutes in case of strong and material differences of opinion among directors on any matter under discussion. While a majority will always prevail, this practice, when routinely followed, helps independent directors to offer their views freely and without any inhibition of being singled out as a difficult colleague. Absence or inadequacy of these rather fundamental components of board processes can seriously erode board independence.

DIRECTOR INDEPENDENCE

At a personal level, independence is an attitude of the mind and reflective of the strength of character. Directors who take their trusteeship obligations seriously will do justice to their jobs conscientiously, whether or not they meet all prescribed tests for establishing independence. Nevertheless, some broad guidelines on required criteria of independence are helpful in objectively verifying a person's independent status in relation to a company. In India, Clause 49 of the standard listing agreement between the stock exchanges and the listed companies prescribe these requirements (**Box 3.2**). Company legislation also, for the first time in India, mandates in case of all public limited companies not less than one third of the board to be independent directors satisfying laid down criteria (**Box 3.3**).

**Box 3.2: Criteria of Independence under Clause 49
of the Listing Agreement**

'Independent director' shall mean a non-executive director of the company who:

a. apart from receiving director's remuneration, does not have any material pecuniary relationships or transactions with the company, its promoters, its directors, its senior management or its holding company, its subsidiaries and associates which may affect independence of the director

b. is not related to promoters or persons occupying management positions at the board level or at one level below the board

c. has not been an executive of the company in the immediately preceding three financial years

---

d. is not a partner or an executive or was not partner or an executive during the preceding three years, of any of the following:

   i.   the statutory audit firm or the internal audit firm that is associated with the company, and

   ii. the legal firm(s) and consulting firm(s) that have a material association with the company

e. is not a material supplier, service provider or customer or a lessor or lessee of the company, which may affect independence of the director;

f. is not a substantial shareholder of the company i.e. owning two percent or more of the block of voting shares.

g. is not less than 21 years of age

Explanation for the purposes of the sub-clause (iii):

a. Associate shall mean a company which is an 'associate' as defined in Accounting Standard (AS) 23, 'Accounting for Investments in Associates in Consolidated Financial Statements', issued by the Institute of Chartered Accountants of India

b. 'Senior management' shall mean personnel of the company who are members of its core management team excluding Board of Directors. Normally, this would comprise all members of management one level below the executive directors, including all functional heads

c. 'Relative' shall mean 'relative' as defined in section 2(41) and section 6 read with Schedule IA of the Companies Act, 1956

d. Nominee directors appointed by an institution which has invested in or lent to the company shall be deemed to be independent directors

Explanation:

'Institution' for this purpose means a public financial institution as defined in Section 4A of the Companies Act, 1956 or a 'corresponding new bank' as defined in section 2(d) of the Banking Companies (Acquisition and Transfer of Undertakings) Act,1970 or the Banking Companies (Acquisition and Transfer of Undertakings) Act,1980 [both Acts].'

— Clause 49 A (iii), National Stock Exchange
(as of 31 October, 2013)

Box 3.3: Criteria of Independence under Companies Act 2013

Independent director in relation to a company, means a director other than a managing director or a whole-time director or a nominee director

a. who, in the opinion of the Board, is a person of integrity and possesses relevant expertise and experience

b. i. who is or was not a promoter of the company or its holding, subsidiary or associate company

   ii. who is not related to promoters or directors in the company, its holding, subsidiary or associate company

c. who has or had no pecuniary relationship with the company, its holding, subsidiary or associate company, or their promoters, or directors, during the two immediately preceding financial years or during the current financial year

d. none of whose relatives has or had pecuniary relationship or transaction with the company, its holding, subsidiary or associate company, or their promoters, or directors, amounting to two percent. or more of its gross turnover or total income or Rs 50 lakh or such higher amount as may be prescribed, whichever is lower, during the two imme-diately preceding financial years or during the current financial year

e. who, neither himself nor any of his relatives

    i.   holds or has held the position of a key managerial personnel or is or has been employee of the company or its holding, subsidiary or associate company in any of the three financial years immediately preceding the financial year in which he is proposed to be appointed

    ii. is or has been an employee or proprietor or a partner, in any of the three financial years immediately preceding the financial year in which he is proposed to be appointed, of

        a. a firm of auditors or company secretaries in practice or cost auditors of the company or its holding, subsidiary or associate company; or

        b. any legal or a consulting firm that has or had any transaction with the company, its holding, subsidiary or associate company amounting to ten per cent. or more of the gross turnover of such firm

    iii. holds together with his relatives two per cent. or more of the total voting power of the company; or

    iv. is a chief executive or director, by whatever name called, of any nonprofit organization that receives twenty-five percent or more of its receipts from the company, any of its promoters, directors or its holding, subsidiary or associate company or that holds two per cent. or more of the total voting power of the company; or

f. who possesses such other qualifications as may be prescribed

Section 149 (6) and (7)

The essence of director independence is threefold—economic or pecuniary, emotional or filial, and psychological or behavioural freedom from those whose actions (or inactions) are to be overseen, guided and controlled. Economic independence is sought to be established by ensuring the independent director is not in receipt of any pecuniary benefits (other than board fees) from the company or its controlling shareholders or executive management through any form of consulting, employment, or other means (such as material donations to charities the director is connected with) that would make them feel obligated. It is in this background that one should view independent directors' fees and other remuneration—it should be attractive enough to compensate for the time and expertise of the individuals and the value they bring to the company and its shareholders, but not be so disproportionately high to become a source of dependence for the directors. Emotional independence is concerned with any filial connections that might come in the way of objective judgement. Falling under this category are close relatives such as parents, grandparents, wives, sons, daughters, siblings, and their immediate relatives. Psychological independence is facilitated when the individual does not carry any hierarchical or other behavioural subservience to anyone else on the board. Theoretically, the touchstone of director independence is whether a person can evaluate an action or proposal on merits without fear or favour, restraint or inhibition in the company of other group members, irrespective of its consequences on the security and sustainability of his own position.

EMPOWERING BOARD AND DIRECTOR INDEPENDENCE

Although board independence has been identified as a major instrument of protection of absentee shareholder interests, its efficacy and effectiveness in practice has been a matter of debate. The general perception is that the institution of independent directors has not delivered up to its promise essentially because its constitution is flawed. It is the board and (in case of concentrated ownership as in the case of India) the controlling shareholders who 'appoint'[19] the independent directors charged with the task of policing executive actions. It is argued that this is to expect the directors 'to bite the hand that feeds', something quite difficult to do in the best of circumstances. While this is not an unreasonable argument, it is necessary to reiterate the fundamental trusteeship responsibility of the directors that militates against this rationalization; in fact, truly independent directors would prefer to exit such boards rather than compromise their conscience and reputation.

IV

Composition and Structure

Constituting an effective board of directors is an involved exercise, no less so than for example selecting members of a cricket team or a philharmonic orchestra. Numbers, skill sets, exposure and experience, domain knowledge and such other factors having to be considered to efficiently achieve the desired end result. It is not always possible to get the ideal group due to a variety of reasons including non-availability of a desired member, limitations imposed by constituency demands, plethora of people with the same or similar skill sets, and so on. As in everything else in life, companies tend to compromise and trade-off on available options eventually to end up with what at best could only be termed as sub-optimal choices.

Boards especially of large listed corporations will have a mixture of executive or whole time directors and non-executive part time directors, some of whom will be independent and others non-independent. Some will be nominated by certain constituencies such as financial institutions lending to the firm, or the government, or even other large block holders; some others may represent other constituencies such as employees and officers of the company, or shareholders with small holdings. Directors are to elect one among them as the chairman of the board who may be an non-independent executive such as the managing director of the company or a non-executive director; if, as is largely the case in the US and quite common in India, the positions of chairman and managing director are combined and occupied by the same individual, boards may elect a senior independent director as a lead director to bring about a measure of objectivity that may normally be difficult to expect from an executive chair. Exhibit 3.1 sets out a typical unitary board membership scheme.

UNITARY AND TWO-TIER BOARD MODELS

Most countries of the world including India have adopted a unitary board model where the corporation has at its apex a single board comprising of executive and non-executive directors. Most of our discussion is based on this model of board governance. Some countries though, especially in Continental Europe and predominantly in Germany, operate on a dual system of two-tiered boards—a management board comprising of executives only and a supervisory board with shareholders' and workmen's directors but no executive representation from within the company.

Considerations and constraints broadly similar to the unitary system discussed above apply to the composition of the

Exhibit 3.1: Typical Scheme of Board Membership

Board Composition

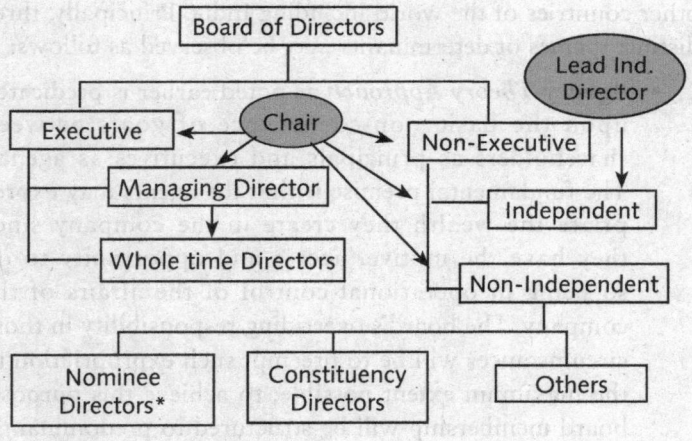

* Unless specified otherwise

supervisory boards also. Given the membership criteria of the two boards, the position of chairman in the two-tier boards can never be occupied by the same person and the question of a lead director therefore does not usually arise. Also, in Germany with its adoption of the principle of co-determination (which involves participation of worker representatives in the supervisory board), board composition has to reckon with inclusion of workmen representatives to maintain the prescribed balance between workmen directors and other directors.[20]

BOARD STRUCTURES

What kind of a board a company gets will largely depend upon the governance objective or approach it has adopted either of its own choice or by the socio-political environment of the country it operates in. It is also dependent up on the structure of corporate ownership, whether dispersed as largely in the case in the US and the UK, or concentrated and dominant as in most other countries of the world including India. Principally, three distinct themes of determinants may be observed as follows:

- *Agency Theory Approach* as noted earlier is predicated upon the basic non-congruence of goals between shareholders as principals and executives as agents. The fundamental premise is that the agents may expropriate the wealth they create in the company since they have the motive, access and opportunity to do so being in operational control of the affairs of the company. The board's overriding responsibility in those circumstances will be to preempt such expropriation to the maximum extent possible; to achieve this purpose, board membership will be structured to predominantly include independent and objective outside directors with little or no allegiance to the executive management who can dispassionately evaluate and decide on proposals and procedures that would favour shareholder interests and protect 'their' wealth and wealth-creating assets in the company. Board competencies in demand will largely include investigative and forensic skills, accounting and legal expertise, skill sets relating to procedural controls, risk management, financial communication and reporting, and so on

- *Stewardship Theory Approach* is built around the belief that managers are more than just rational, economic individuals focused exclusively on personal pecuniary benefits, and recognises that people could be motivated by non-pecuniary objectives and aspirations, for example, 'the need for achievement and recognition, the intrinsic satisfaction of successful performance, respect for authority and the work ethic.'[21] Pecuniary compensation need not be the main motivation of members of the technostructure. Identification and adaptation may be the driving forces. Above a certain level, these may operate independently of income[22]

This recognition negates the agency theory assumption of goal incongruence inherent in the separation of ownership and control. On the contrary, the stewardship approach finds virtue in the assumption of control by the executive, empowering them to maximize corporate wealth creation, endowed as it is with technical and managerial expertise, improved information access, and most importantly, a firm commitment to the corporate objectives and well-being. Such an approach would strongly suggest insider dominated boards, fewer, if any, outside, non-aligned, independent directors, and reduced focus on control with a concomitant increased emphasis on contribution to the firm's wealth creation efforts

- *Resource Dependence Approach* postulates that firms exert control over their environment by co-opting the resources needed to survive and grow.[23] The most direct method for controlling dependence is to control the source of that dependence but that may not always be possible or even worthwhile by acquisition and ownership. Linkages could be forged (except where they are proscribed by competition law or other such legislation) that could facilitate cross flow of information and leads from one to the other. The familiar question about a directorial candidate in such instances would be—what does he bring to the table?

Board membership in such situations would be dependent upon the benefits of inducting a member on to the board, such as the doors that can be opened, linkages to the external environment potentially helpful to business objectives, or even an activist or potential adversary whose presence inside on the board is preferable to leaving the person outside as an opponent. Interlocking boards is a common mechanism used in this approach.

While its appeal is fairly universal, countries like India and companies with concentrated ownership structures are particularly prone to adopt this approach. This also contributes to over boarding of elite directors in demand for any of these resources they bring to their boards.

COMPONENTS OF BOARD STRUCTURING

We now turn to a discussion of some of the key components of board structures set out in Exhibit 3.2.

Exhibit 3.2: Board Structures—A Conceptual Framework

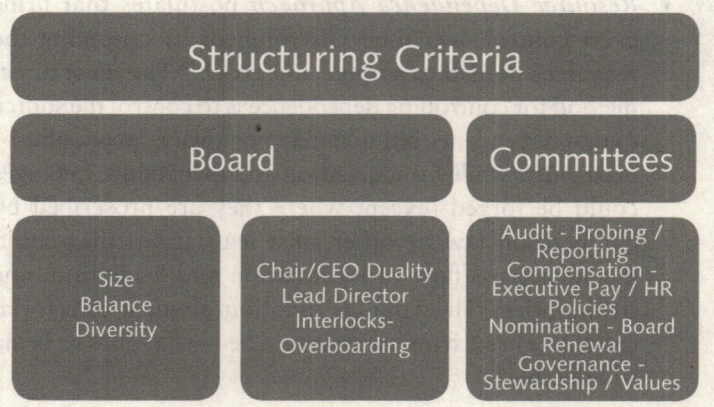

Structuring Criteria

Board

Committees

Size
Balance
Diversity

Chair/CEO Duality
Lead Director
Interlocks-
Overboarding

Audit - Probing /
Reporting
Compensation -
Executive Pay / HR
Policies
Nomination - Board
Renewal
Governance -
Stewardship / Values

Exhibit 3.3: Independent Directors—Surveillance in Action

Independent Validation Process

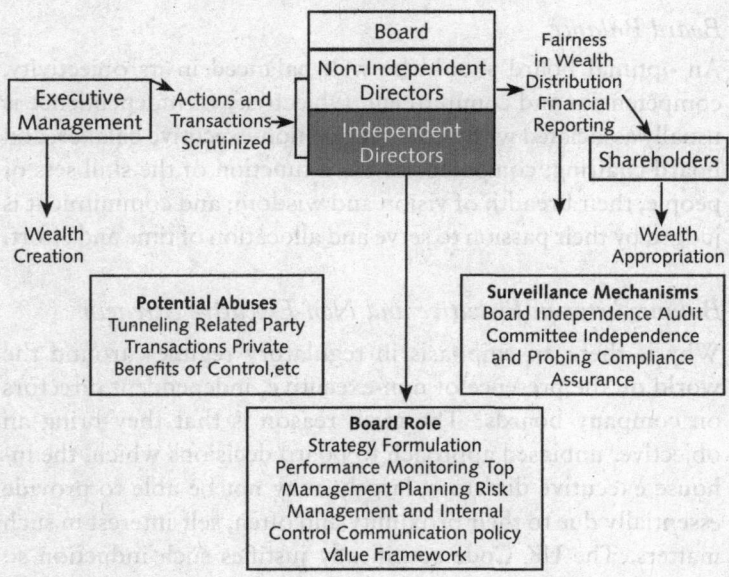

Board Size

There is no such thing as an ideal board size. It will depend upon perceived requirements (of both necessity and accommodation) in the circumstances of the company. As the UK Code (FRC 2012, B-1) proffers, 'The board should be of sufficient size that the requirements of the business can be met and that changes to the board's composition and that of its committees can be managed without undue disruption, and should not be so large as to be unwieldy.'

The average board size in India in 2012 was 11.03 (BSE 100); comparably, 10.7 in the US S&P 500 and 10.4 in the UK FTSE 100.[24]

Board Balance

An optimal board should be well balanced in its objectivity, competencies and commitment. Objectivity or independence is usually associated with executive and non-executive balance, and board chairing; competencies are a function of the skill sets of people, their breadth of vision and wisdom; and commitment is judged by their passion to serve and allocation of time and effort.

Balance between Executive and Non-Executive Strength

Why is there an emphasis in regulatory regimes around the world on the presence of non-executive, independent directors on company boards? The main reason is that they bring an objective, unbiased approach to board decisions which, the in-house executive directors, largely, may not be able to provide essentially due to their proximity and often, self-interest in such matters. The UK Code specifically justifies such induction so that 'no individual or small group of individuals can dominate the board's decision taking.'[25] Similar provisions and practices apply in the US as well where more than a majority of the board members are non-executive. In India, not less than a third of the board of listed companies and large unlisted public companies is required to comprise of independent directors.[26]

The incompatibility of the pure agency theory approach (which for example Indian regulators adopt while mandating non-executive independent directors) with the concentrated corporate ownership structures of corporations in India (which would tend to lean more towards the resource dependence approach) is one of the main reasons why the institution of independent directors is perceived to be ineffective in India.

Board Diversity

This relates to the demographics of the board as a contributor to board competencies and effectiveness. Does the board have the right balance of skills, breadth of experience and exposure, and socio-cultural variety of value to the company? In large transnational corporations, the international character of their board composition lends credibility and reassurance. Representation to ethnic minorities has assumed importance in developed countries, more to project the image of a broad-based corporation rather than to demonstrate allegiance to any specific constituency. Two issues are taken up here for discussion: first, how does such diversity help in decision making; and second, where do we stand especially on gender diversity on boards.

How does Diversity help in Decision Making?

Decisions on an issue by a group of persons is always considered to be better and more balanced than those by a single person, since they have the benefit of diverse perspectives of group members with different profiles of age, gender, tenure, functional and educational background, socio-cultural roots and so on. This explains why multiple judges hearing matters is preferred in courts to a single judge hearing them. This is also the reason for key institutions such as the Election Commission, Vigilance Commission, Competition Commission and various other regulatory bodies like the Securities and Exchange Board of India are constituted with several members. The same reasoning applies to Panchayats or the five-member group of village elders called upon to decide on disputes and other matters brought to them for judgement. Groups will yield such better results only if their members bring to the table a diverse range of skills and insights but not otherwise. Conceptually, these observations are based on the *Upper Echelon Theory* (from the behavioural-psychological arena) which suggests people with common echelon traits will tend to view matters from the same or very similar perspective, leading to a *false consensus effect* where decisions may not necessarily be the best under the circumstances. On the other hand, heterogeneous groups, while undoubtedly vulnerable to more protracted discussions and disagreements, have been observed to produce more balanced and better results. Although cohesion in groups is pleasant and more easily managed, it has been observed that too much cohesion may be dysfunctional in reaching balanced and better decisions.[27]

The same logic works for corporate boards as well since they are groups of people sitting together to control and guide executive management in achieving their set goals and looking after the interests of absentee shareholders. The greater the diversity of profiles of board members, the higher would be the probability of arriving at better decisions in the interest of the company and its shareholders and other stakeholders.

Overall, theoretical research postulates that diversity in board composition is conducive not only to improving shareholder returns (because of their favourable impact on the quality of strategic decision making and monitoring) but also, and perhaps more importantly, to enhancing stakeholder engagement and consequently, stabilizing and improving the potential for sustainable growth for the corporation.

Gender in Board Diversity

Women on boards have attracted discussion both from a contributory and inclusivity viewpoint.[28] It has been argued that women bring to board room discussions a different perspective based on their experience, are willing and able to offer more application and commitment, do not shy away from asking tough and probing questions, and are more attuned to handling social responsibility and environmental issues with greater sensitivity than men in general can.

These findings and observations apply even more strongly to emerging economies like India, as businesses have to cope with the twin challenges of operating profitably in a more competitive international environment and ordering their activities so that they are fully in accord with the more demanding societal expectations.

Other Dimensions of Board Diversity

Board diversity, of course, is not exclusively a gender-centric issue. Among the others many are country specific such as ethnic minorities such as African-Americans, Hispanics, Indians, Chinese and immigrants of other nationalities in the US, aborigines in Australia, and native Africans in post-apartheid South Africa.

Other avenues for board diversity include a range of other constituencies such as religious and ethnic minorities, economically backward communities, and civil society organizations. Diversity is also augmented by the inclusion of social scientists, academics, former bureaucrats and officers from armed forces, journalists, environmentalists, and other such specialists depending upon the nature of a company's business and the level of its interface with the societies in which it operates. Multinational companies may find induction of experts from host countries on to their local boards a useful means of diversity. Similar will be the case of expatriate directors on companies with a global footprint or aspirations. In a country of sub-continental dimensions and diversity such as India, boards may consider a broad based induction from different parts of the country as a demonstrable measure of their national stature.

BOARD CHAIR—CHIEF EXECUTIVE DUALITY AND LEAD DIRECTORS

Two of the three key pillars of corporate governance are the board and the executive (the third being the shareholders). In this bilateral relationship, the executive function is charged with the responsibility of implementing approved policies and programmes to achieve the set goals, while the board has a supervisory and overseeing role in monitoring executive performance. The chief executive officer heads the executive function while the chairman leads the board. Given their respective roles in the hierarchy, it is clear that the individuals in these positions have to be different as combining the *supervising* and the *supervised* roles will lead inherent incompatibilities and role obfuscation.

The second important reason for this preferred separation is the desire to build in checks and balances in the top hierarchy of company governance. No one individual should have unfettered powers of decision. There may be exceptional individuals who can do justice to both the jobs without any bias, but there is merit in the exhortation not to, 'lay their liberties at the feet of even a great man, or to trust him with powers which enable him to subvert their institutions.'[29]

Indian law requires these two positions to be separated in listed and other specified class of public companies but does not mandate board chairs to meet the independence criteria.[30]

Lead Independent Director

To mitigate the erosion in the effectiveness of the board in cases of a combined executive chairman or even a separate but non-independent board chair, the concept of a lead independent director has been evolved. Even where the board chair is different from the CEO, the lead director concept might be useful when discussing the chairman's own performance or other matters concerning the role and behaviour of the chair; in addition, this also provides the chairman a sounding board for eliciting alternative views on key board matters.[31]

CHAPTER 4

BOARD COMMITTEES
In-depth Oversight

Know that [Truth]...by constant questioning *Pariprasna*
—Bhagavad Gita[1]

I

Purpose and Scope of Committees

A board's agenda is generally a collection of diverse topics—some deal with statutory procedural requirements such as confirmation of minutes of previous meetings, others are more substantive like dealing with strategic issues or performance reviews and capital expenditure approvals. Some need relatively little time while others may call for detailed presentations and discussions. Some items such as consideration of financials require accounting and numeracy skills while others may call for general management expertise. Since board membership is usually a complementary collection of varied competencies, individual contribution to discussions will not be uniformly participative. For each of the items, some will be actively involved while many others may be passive listeners, leading to sub-optimal use of board's time collectively. Smaller sub-groups of directors with appropriate skills meeting in committees to discuss and convey to the full board their decisions (where empowered) or recommendations therefore is a more efficient and effective alternative.

In a sense, committee work may be compared to the detailed portions of any lengthy document or report; its final output may be seen as an executive summary of the report which can then be considered by the full board with the assurance and comfort that in-depth application of the mind and attention to detail required for an informed decision had already been contributed by directors at the committee level.

BOARD PRIMACY OVER COMMITTEES

Committees are creatures of the board, and as such they are hierarchically subordinate to the full board. Committees derive their authority from the powers delegated to them by the board (or in some instances by statutory or regulatory mandates). The board, on reviewing the recommendations of the committee may decide to accept the recommendations with or without modifications, or even reject them, though this would have to be under very unusual circumstances indeed. After all, the main purpose of the committee structure is to avail of the time and expertise of the committee members on the delegated matters, and it would hardly be sensible not to abide by their recommendation. On the other hand, where the committee is vested with decision-making powers, and accords its 'approval' in a matter within the terms of delegation, it will not be open to the board to rescind that approval with retrospective effect. Of course, this will not preempt the board from re-visiting the decision, and modifying or rescinding it prospectively, if in its wisdom such correctives are called for, subject to any statutory disclosure requirements.[2]

Committee Decisions and the Board

To what extent, if at all, the directors (other than committee members) are absolved of any personal responsibility in matters deliberated upon by the committees. To say the other directors have no responsibility at all will run counter to the concept of collective responsibility of the board; to hold them equally responsible without any exceptions would be inequitable as they would be held accountable for decisions or recommendations to which they had no opportunity of applying their mind. The answer to this practical question lies in ascertaining whether the board as a whole discharged its *duty of care* criterion adequately.

It is a ground reality that boards usually rely upon board committees, and in turn, committee members often rely on the advice of specialists and experts including those from within

113

the executive ranks. The key of course is to ensure that this reliance is well placed and justified, and also subject to any applicable legal or regulatory limitations. Care is evidenced by the directors committing time, by regularly attending meetings, by being adequately informed as to board decisions, and when circumstances suggest, by making appropriate inquiry into the operations of the business or into facts that will inform their decisions.[3] In case of committees and their recommendations, the board and the directors should be satisfied that the members chosen had adequate expertise, experience, and time commitment to discharge their committee responsibilities. Having appointed the committee members, the board as a whole and the non-committee directors in particular would be well advised to ascertain whether committee meetings were held as frequently as warranted in the circumstances of the company, whether the meetings were well attended especially by those with special skills and knowledge of particular topics under discussion, and whether there were any unrecorded dissent or reservations on their decisions or recommendations. By noting, approving or even simply ratifying committee decisions and recommendations, the board and the other directors may well be deemed to have endorsed those committee recommendations or decisions. If such inquiries had been made and duly recorded as part of the board proceedings, the non-committee members may have a reasonable defence of having exercised due care and applied their mind. Flowing from this, directors are entitled to rely on information provided by officers, board committees, legal counsel, public accountants, and so on, so long as they have assured themselves that the information or advice proffered is within the fields of their expertise and in case of delegated matters (such as to a board committee), their delegation is permissible according to the legal, regulatory and in-house charter frameworks.

Boards, Committees, and Information Flow

Some of the topics assigned to different committees may have overlapping dimensions. For example, human resources policies concerning payroll may be reviewed by the HR committee or compensation committee with respect to pay procedures and payment schedules; it may be reviewed by the audit committee as well from the viewpoint of adequacy of internal control measures or while reviewing internal audit reports covering pay roll procedures. At the full board levels too, some of the discussions may relate to a topic that had been reviewed by more than one committee. It is essential therefore that all directors keep themselves *informed* of the proceedings of all committees whether or not they are members of any of them. This is enabled by ensuring the following processes:

- Minutes of the proceedings and decisions of all committees are to be tabled at the following meeting of the full board for discussion and any action arising

- The draft minutes of the meeting approved by the Committee chairman after due circulation to committee members for comment, should be circulated to all directors as a routine agenda item well in advance of the board meeting

- The chair of each committee should brief the board at its following meeting on key decisions and recommendations and highlighting any dissent or reservations expressed by any committee member

- All directors, whether committee members or not, would do well to browse through the draft committee minutes and to carefully listen to the committee chairs' briefings; in case of any reported dissent, they may also seek to hear the views of the dissenting committee members so that they are able to arrive at an informed opinion for themselves

- If any director wishes to support any dissent, it would be in order to request a board discussion before the committee recommendations are accepted and actioned. As with other matters, directors not agreeing with the committees' majority decisions may also express their dissent and ensure their dissent is duly recorded in the board minutes

The key is to achieve to the fullest extent possible, complete, credible and timely information access to all board members on all matters of critical importance; turf protection is injurious to the well-being and effectiveness of board committees and consequently, of the boards and their companies.

COMMITTEES IN PRACTICE

While company boards may constitute as many committees as they deem necessary taking in to account the needs and circumstances in each case, some of them are virtually a constant in all companies. Company legislation and stock exchange listing requirements also mandate certain committees and lay down their minimum expected profiles and task responsibilities. The principal committees are:

- Audit (and Risk) Committee
- Compensation (or Remuneration)and Nominations Committee[4]
- Stakeholders Relationship Committee
- Corporate Social Responsibility Committee

While these are the committees mandatorily required in listed and other notified companies, boards can and do constitute other committees as well required in their circumstances. Thus, where board involvement or approval is frequently required, an executive or management committee, or a committee of directors may be constituted with delegated authority; banks and financial institutions typically use this mechanism to deal with numerous routine matters like approval of loans, guarantees, and so on. It is also customary for listed companies with large number of shareholders to create a share transfer committee to deal with such transfers and transmission requests. Besides these, companies may also constitute special or *ad hoc* committees to deal with different emerging situations. For example, in case of a serious fraud, a special committee may be formed to focus on all aspects of the issue and may include on the committee members of not only the audit and risk committee but also of other committees depending upon the nature of the fraud and the expertise required to unravel the situation and circumstances that allowed the fraud to be perpetrated. Similar will be the case for dealing with acquisitions where a small group of directors may be charged with the task of closely interacting with the negotiating executive team. The driving factor in all cases is the need to explore the subject in depth, the time commitment and expertise required, and the relative ease of getting a smaller group of directors together frequently as compared with the difficulty of assembling a larger number of directors if the full board were to do the job itself.

II

Audit (and Risk) Committee

Traditionally seen as the first among equals of board committees, largely by virtue of its important controlling and surveillance role over executives' decisions concerning related party transactions, financial accounting and reporting, risk management oversight, and interface and influence with external independent auditors, the audit committee's work load and demands on members' time are perhaps the most exacting. The American Bar Association[5] articulates the role and position of the audit committee in the following words:

'The audit committee is critical to the corporate governance structure, and its existence and some of its functions are legally mandated. It has general oversight responsibility for the company's financial reporting process and internal controls. It also has the exclusive responsibility for retaining and overseeing the performance and independence of the corporation's external auditor. When the external auditor audits the company's internal controls over financial reporting under Section 404 of the Sarbanes-Oxley Act, it will evaluate the committee's performance. The audit committee also increasingly serves as a forum in which the internal and external auditors, as well as the corporation's legal counsel and its compliance and ethics personnel, can candidly report and discuss issues relating to accounting, auditing, financial reporting, risk management, legal, compliance,and ethical matters.'

In India, the Companies Act 2013 and the listing agreements set out in detail the role and minimum scope of audit committees which are quite extensive and reflect their importance of and dependence upon this committee as a critical component of the governance structure in corporations.

Membership

Since 1978, companies listed on the New York Stock Exchange were required to constitute audit committees comprising 'solely of directors independent of management and free from any relationship that, in the opinion of its Board of Directors, would interfere with the exercise of independent judgement as a committee member. Directors who are affiliates of the company or its subsidiaries would not be qualified for audit committee membership.'[6]

Building upon the Cadbury prescription, the UK Corporate Governance Code[7] stipulates:

'The board should establish an audit committee of at least three, or in the case of smaller companies two, independent non-executive directors. In smaller companies the company chairman may be a member of, but not chair, the committee in addition to the independent non-executive directors, provided he or she was considered independent on appointment as chairman. The board should satisfy itself that at least one member of the audit committee has recent and relevant financial experience.'

In India, listed and other notified public companies are required to have audit committees consisting of a minimum of three members, with a majority of its membership including the committee chair qualifying as 'independent' and all members being able to 'read and understand' financial statements.[8] The stock exchange listing agreements with companies build on these basic mandates especially on a director's independence status.

Independence, Objectivity, and Confidentiality

In addition to its contributory role as exemplified by the expertise and experience generally required for its membership, the audit committee has a strong evaluation, surveillance, and judgement orientation within the corporate governance framework. While the contributory and oversight monitoring roles are commonly shared with the whole board, the audit committee's functions, conceptually, involve a necessarily probing approach, a

119

constructively skeptical attitude. It is indeed not for the audit committee to accept without questioning what is placed before it, but rather to satisfy itself that what is placed is fair, objective, and in the overall interest of the company and its investors. The committee's independence, expertise, and time availability will be severely tested when it is called upon to make judgement calls on critical issues like the appropriateness of accounting policies, fairness of related party transactions, or adequacy of internal control mechanisms.

Audit committee independence can often be vitiated in practice by exogenous circumstances. For example, if the chief executive or some of the other executive or promoter directors are present as 'invitees' at the committee deliberations, either as a matter of board courtesy or because they can provide background information, it may become virtually impossible for subordinate officers (barring a few courageous exceptions) to be candid in their submissions to the committee. The result will be that the committee will be denied potent inputs that may help them in discharging their responsibilities. With this in view, the UK Corporate Governance Code (2012, B) stipulates,

> 'No one other than the committee chairman and members is entitled to be present at a meeting of the nomination, audit or remuneration committee, but others may attend at the invitation of the committee.'

Although there are no similar injunctions in Indian law or regulation, this wholesome practice may well be adopted by companies with leadership aspirations. If the executive directors or their functionaries or specialists need to be consulted for their views or expertise, committees may find it more expedient to do so separately for specific agenda items so that they may reach objective and balanced conclusions, without denying themselves the opportunity of candid inputs from others. Indian law does confer a 'right to be heard' on the external auditors and other key managerial personnel when audit reports are discussed in the committee. The salient point is that non-members of such committees should not *impose* themselves on committee proceedings by their presence when not specifically invited. It is also up to the committee chairs to ensure that such invitations are extended sparingly, based purely on the committee's needs.[9]

While exercising their *independent* jurisdiction, audit committees should also be conscious of, and appropriately pre-empt, any potential for improper disclosure of their confidential proceedings. After all, besides the company secretary in his or her role as secretary to the committee, there will be other invitees to the committee sessions, for example, the head of the finance function, chief of internal audit, and so on. While the integrity and objectivity of these participants is not doubted, the committee chair may be well advised to enjoin on all the participants the imperatives of ensuring confidentiality of the proceedings to protect the interests of concerned employees and others, encouraging transparent discussions, and thus enhancing the effectiveness potential of the committee itself. Such traits of professional independence, discretion and confidentiality may well develop over a period, but till then committee chairs and members may have to be consciously sensitive to the potential for erosion of their credibility and effectiveness.

A THREE-PRONGED APPROACH TOWARDS AUDIT COMMITTEE EFFECTIVENESS

Granting that an audit committee has the necessary independence, objectivity and competencies in good measure, its effectiveness can still be seriously threatened if the necessary infrastructural support is not in place. Three such areas can be identified: an independent finance and assurance functions, an independent compliance function, and independent secretarial function, the latter two often combined in the position of a company secretary. Traditionally, all these functions have been treated as part of the overall general management support structure reporting to the chief executive or, depending upon hierarchical positioning, to the chief financial officer. While administrative convenience will still support such an arrangement, active involvement of the board and especially its audit committee in their incumbents' choice and their independent functioning is absolutely essential, given their unique support role to them in the discharge of their fiduciary obligations to the company and its shareholders. The Companies Act 2013 does well to mandate that *key management personnel*[10] are to be appointed by the board and as such become part of the fiduciaries of the company with ultimate accountability to the shareholders.

A Concept of Flow-through Fiduciary Obligation

Supporting this proposed board and audit committee involvement in these functions is a hitherto hardly explored concept of *Flow-through Fiduciary Obligations*. The fiduciary responsibility of the directors has already been noted; the flow-through concept is an extension of these obligations to people who support the directors in the discharge of their obligations. Because the officers heading these functions (unlike the directors) are not directly appointed by the shareholders in general meeting, and yet are an integral part of the governance system of a company enabling the directors to discharge their obligations, this concept introduces a flow-through mechanism by which they constructively inherit these obligations to the extent they are delegated these functional responsibilities. What this would mean in practice is that although these functionaries may be organizationally and hierarchically subordinate to the chief executive, they also have an overriding responsibility for acting in the best interests of the company and all its shareholders as determined by the board and its committees even if that led to conflict situations within the executive ranks. A commonplace example would be the CFO rejecting an executive attempt to account as sales revenue at month-or-year-ends transactions that fail the revenue recognition tests; although this action may be seen as a routine mechanical application of a 'rule' the underlying fact is that the CFO is in fact discharging (perhaps more intuitively than deliberately) his accounting and reporting obligation to the shareholders to reflect a true and fair version of the activities of the company according to accepted standards of accounting principles. Failing to do so would be a breach of what may be called the flow-through fiduciary obligation the CFO is subject to as part of his or her duty to enable the board to discharge their fiduciary responsibility to the shareholders.

It is apparent that this conceptual construct is also underlying certain legislative and regulatory mandates such as for example seeking signing and certification of financials by the CFO along with the CEO.

Independence of the Fiduciary Functionaries

Given this position, what should audit committees do to reassure themselves that these functionaries perform such that they not only meet their own flow-through fiduciary obligations but also in the process assist the committees (and the board) in satisfactorily discharging their own obligations? Clearly the independence of these functionaries from their hierarchically superior executive management needs to be preserved and assured. This could be ensured by the audit committee actively participating in all the processes relating to their appointment, performance evaluation, career progression, job security, and so on, so that the professionals can pursue their tasks with independence and integrity, solely for the benefit of the corporation and its shareholders.

Finance and Assurance Functions

Professionals in the finance and internal audit or assurance functions *employed* by the company have reporting relationships within the company hierarchy, and their own personal progression is determined by the evaluations of their performance by seniors within the organization. Often, effectiveness of the control and surveillance functions in the company are impaired or inhibited by such equations, leading astray all but the most committed and independent among the functionaries. A conscientious CFO may be accused of lacking in 'business orientation' or 'risk-taking' when performing his or her legitimate function diligently. An 'inconvenient' internal auditor could be transferred out on 'promotion' to another position in the interests of career progression or 'broadening' of the incumbent's business exposure. While generally these initiatives may be well intended and fully justified, the task of the audit committee is to guard against moves that deprive it of reliable and professional support, and even more importantly, discourage independent professional inputs of value in the discharge of its own responsibilities.

There is thus a strong case for the appointees to positions of chief financial officer or the chief internal auditor to be vetted by the audit committee and cleared by the board, with any changes in these two incumbencies also being routed through the same process.[11] Such a routine ensures that the incumbents have the confidence and support of the board and the audit committee, key ingredients for their independent professional performance. The key to successful management of hierarchical equations lies in achieving a measure of cordiality in operating relationship concurrently with zealous professional turf-protection that would ensure and encourage integrity in the discharge of respective functional responsibilities. To mitigate any dilution of executive authority, the audit committee could perhaps decide to exercise 'oversight' authority on performance appraisal systems in general, and especially as they apply to the CFO and chief of internal audit and assurance. As with other matters, the committee could adopt a probing approach to satisfy itself that the actions (and inactions) concerning such professionals in terms of their progression and development are well founded. In this manner, the committee may be able to protect the administrative suzerainty of the executive while ensuring that the professional independence and credibility of its own support systems are not compromised.

A related question that has received critical attention in recent years is the efficacy of a company's in-house internal audit function reporting to its chief financial officer, as seems to be the common practice in many organizations. An emerging trend is for the internal audit function to split its reporting relationships between the audit committee (for strategy and functionality) and, the CEO and not the CFO (for administration). Of course, while being superior to the prior dispensation, this arrangement leaves the function with two masters—organizationally not the best of structures—especially when one of these, the audit committee interfaces only at two or three-monthly intervals scheduled around committee meetings. Nevertheless, this arrangement appears to be the preferred option, especially with the audit committee chair being available to the chief internal auditor in-between committee meetings on a need-to-interact basis.

Similar considerations apply to external firms of accountants and others to whom part or the whole of the internal audit and assurance responsibilities are outsourced. Such firms do not obviously have the direct reporting obligations to the shareholders as the external statutory auditors do but the concept of flow-through fiduciary obligations ought to apply to them as they do to the in-house internal auditors. The audit committee should ensure that their appointment, scope, remuneration and other terms are duly approved by them (in consultation with the chosen firms) and the contract specifically highlights their reporting relationship to the audit committee and through them to the board. Removal of outside firms and their replacement should follow some consistent norms of rotation; any mid-term separations should be justified to the audit committee's satisfaction.

Compliance and Secretarial Functions

These are the other two key fiduciary support functions. The company secretary is a key official in the governance regime of corporations. More than two decades ago, the Cadbury Committee in the UK highlighted the critical contributory role of the company secretary.

Indian law requires every company including a listed company above a specified size to have a fulltime company secretary, the position being listed as among *key managerial personnel* whose appointments and removal are matters for board consideration and decision. The company secretary is to 'report to the board about compliance with the provisions of this Act, the rules made thereunder and other laws applicable to the company'.[12] Given the importance and trust of this position (which will by definition be privy to the most confidential of all discussions at board and committee meetings and have to act as the conscience keeper of the company in terms of ensuring compliance with all legal requirements) it is critical that the incumbent is able to operate in an ambience of unhindered independence from the executive management (notwithstanding hierarchical reporting relationships for administrative convenience) and to serve the company, its board and committees as the in-house adviser and intermediary between the executive and the board and its committees. Much of the compliance management and reporting will be to the audit committee in the first instance and it is essential that there is developed a close working relationship between the company secretary and the audit committee chair and members, not unlike the relationships the CFO and the chief of internal audit and assurance need to have with the audit committee chair and members.

STAYING UPDATED

The oversight arena of audit committees is indeed quite vast and subject to dynamic changes and improvements in their technical content. Accounting, auditing and reporting standards around the world are constantly under professional review to ensure that they keep pace with the changing business and regulatory requirements. While a member with specialist expertise in these areas can undoubtedly brief his or her colleagues on the committee of any significant developments, it is a good practice for the audit committee to request expert independent briefings on such changes as and when they occur, and especially in relation to the company's business and operations.

Companies with international operations or presence have a further dimension of compliance to contend with. The committee should ask for a detailed compliance checklist of requirements in relevant jurisdictions using for the purpose local experts to supplement in-house expertise. Such listings should be reviewed by the committee at least annually and updated periodically when major changes are proposed or mandated. Countries where regulations are available only or mostly in local languages (like in Japan for instance), companies will face a unique problem of overseeing compliance; it will be useful in such cases to obtain official translations if available or get local experts to translate so that informed compliance actions may be initiated and monitored.

AUDIT COMMITTEES IN INDIA

In India, audit committee practices and procedures have been evolving over time in tandem with the improvements in the overall corporate governance ambience, partly mandated and partly dictated by market forces. To the extent that minimum audit committee duties are enumerated by legislation and regulation,[13] a basic framework is available to such companies which over a period of time, they can improve upon. The key is to establish a proper business case for such audit committee surveillance and contribution. Those companies who demonstrably adopt and stand by true audit committee independence and oversight would most likely succeed in reducing the perceived governance risk and benefit from consequent improvements in their valuations.

FALLIBILITY OF AUDIT COMMITTEES

While undoubtedly the potential of audit committees is indeed quite significant, expectations must necessarily be tempered by the limitations under which they have to operate. Their members are largely and in several jurisdictions wholly non-executive and thus can devote only part of their working time; despite their probing skills and domain expertise, they normally lack the inside view of their companies' business activities and largely depend upon the information provided by the executive and the effectiveness of internal assurance systems. Depending upon individual competencies and collective synergies of audit committees, the gap between the theoretical and the realized potential can vary widely among different audit committees. This arguably explains why some outstanding audit committees in terms of membership competencies were still unable to preempt major corporate frauds and deviant behaviour in their companies.[14]

There are also some dissonant voices on the usefulness or effectiveness of audit committees, especially in a non-US context. Using the Actor Network Theory (ANT), Spira[15] describes two networks in the context of audit committees:

'[S]upport for audit committees is based on the assumption that the quality of financial reporting is closely related to the independence of external auditors. ...[T]his "quality" is threatened by attempts by the executive directors to enroll the auditors in employing accounting policies which, while strictly legitimate within current generally accepted accounting practice, fall into "grey" areas and might be viewed as "creative". ...[The] solution is to interpose the audit committee, composed of non-executive directors, between the auditors and the executive directors. ...in theory providing an obligatory passage point through which the auditors are enrolled into their "independent" network, preventing direct influence by executive management.'

Spira points out that this intermediary passage point tends to break down (and hence becomes dysfunctional) in practice because of the close working relationships with the executive management especially the finance director, a situation that could be mitigated or even negated if the audit committee chair has a finance background. The competition for enrolment of auditors by the finance director on the one hand, and the audit committee on the other, is an unstated but constantly enacted play in most companies; audit committee effectiveness is therefore limited and inconclusive. Although this is contrary to the mainstream thesis, it is easy to relate to this view especially since:

- External auditors work closely with executive management,
- Their positive networking could lead them to more audit and non-audit work in group entities
- Their fees are often left by the shareholders to be decided by the board which effectively translates in to executive management who make the recommendations, and
- Their contractual obligations to the shareholders are often blurred because of the distance between them (they 'see' only some of the absentee shareholders who attend members' meetings) and hardly are able to relate to an amorphous and constantly changing body of shareholders as opposed to the proximity of executive management

Two countervailing forces could possibly salvage this situation:

- First, a powerful professional discipline enforced by the institutions that grant auditors their license as 'reputational agents' whose conduct and considered opinion could be trusted by those who engage them and those who rely on them for their investment and other decisions
- Second, a much closer association with the board and the audit committee through regular briefings and executive sessions (without executive management being present) that builds a rapport between auditors and the audit committee and reaffirms the auditors' allegiance and accountability to the shareholders represented by the board and the audit committee

Audit committees could indeed fulfil their assigned and desired goals if, with regard to the enrolment of external auditors on their side, they could tilt the balance in their favour, and every attempt in that direction is worthwhile. A major contributory would be financial literacy and accounting affinity that would clearly establish better commonality of interest and objectives between the committee and the auditors than that between the auditors and the financial executive. The other is to ensure that external auditors are compensated adequately and appropriately for their contribution.

III

Compensation and Nomination Committee

Next in importance is the compensation or remuneration committee. Indian law combines it with the nomination committee discussed later in this chapter. Even otherwise, the true scope of the compensation committee does include not only executive management remuneration but also setting the tone at the top for general employment policies and practices to be followed in the corporation.

THE RISE OF THE COMPENSATION COMMITTEE

Unlike the audit committees, compensation committees are of relatively recent origin. In the UK, they were recommended by the Cadbury Committee in 1992, while the Canadian guidelines suggested their adoption in 1994. In the US, the New York Stock Exchange rules required listing companies to have a compensation committee consisting of independent directors, while NASDAQ listed corporations had the option of a similarly constituted compensation committee or the independent directors on the board fulfilling these requirements. In India, compensation committees are mandatory for listed companies.[16]

Objectives

There is more to the compensation committee than just executive pay, important undoubtedly as it is. At an organizational level, the committee could set the policy level tone on fair and reasonable employment and working conditions, objective and transparent performance appraisal processes, adequate internal communication and grievance redressal mechanisms, and so on, besides mandating on matters such as child labour, workplace gender and class based harassment, employment of the disadvantaged, and other issues such as inclusive development and environmental protection as they concern human resources deployment and development. At the top management level, the committee would be engaged in compensation plans and ownership alignment through stock ownership schemes, succession planning, and executive development and career progression. At the top of its agenda, of course, will be the CEO and executive director compensation terms and periodical performance evaluation, and variable pay determination.

Membership and Independence

International best practice is unanimous in suggesting independence and objectivity as the prime requisites for compensation committee membership since the committee is to determine compensation levels including performance-based variable components of executive directors including the managing directors.

In the US and the UK, compensation committees are to have only independent directors. The Indian requirement does not go far enough in this regard. The Companies Act 2013[17] mandates a minimum of only half the membership of the committee to be independent.

The possible explanation for not asking for a full complement of independent directors on the committee could be the nature of concentrated ownership structures in the Indian corporate sector. Excluding the controlling shareholders from the compensation determination process involving not only executive management but also of other employees was perhaps considered potentially dysfunctional in practice. The fact that only one half of the committee needs to be independent also opens up the possibility of the committees' decisions being taken validly in the absence of any independent director since (unlike in the case of the audit committees) the listing agreement does not mandate the presence of at least two independent directors to form an acceptable quorum for the meeting. As a step in the right direction in what hopefully will only be a transitory phase, the legislative and regulatory initiatives are welcome but certainly not strong enough in terms of best practice requirements.

An objective, unbiased membership is the key to the successful performance of the compensation committee. As in many other cases, such a trait is not only required to be in place but also be seen to be so. Interlocking directorates with directors reciprocally sitting on each other's boards are one such red herring factor that could vitiate committee objectivity. Some countries have prohibited such reciprocal arrangements where an executive director of Company A sitting on the compensation committee of Company B whose executive director sits on Company A's compensation committee deciding his compensation. Clearly Indian requirements do not go that far as yet in ensuring objectivity in compensation decision making processes.

EXECUTIVE COMPENSATION

Qualitatively, the principal purpose of the compensation committee is to bring about a measure of objectivity and discipline in matters relating to executive remuneration, especially of the chief executive and his top management team. Given that primary role, how should, and do boards tackle this onerous and sensitive issue?

APPROACHES TO EXECUTIVE COMPENSATION[18]

Broadly, there could be three approaches to determine executive pay in corporations generally and in publicly traded companies in particular: optimal contracting, managerial power, and public policy approaches, as briefly described below.

Optimal Contracting Approach

Based on the agency theory of corporate governance, executive pay is negotiated at levels that would dissuade them from pursuing their own material interests through expropriation of what rightfully ought to belong to the shareholders. Managerial remuneration will tend to be pegged at levels where the executive will be discouraged from 'plundering' the wealth belonging to the principals, the shareholders. An extension of this proposition would concomitantly seek to 'align' executive interests to shareholder interests by converting them in to shareholders themselves by offering them stocks and options besides attractive cash compensation both to motivate them to perform better and to retain them from going out looking for greener pastures, holding them back with 'golden shackles'. 'The optimal contract is therefore the one that minimizes agency costs (that is, the sum of contracting costs, monitoring costs, other costs incurred in achieving a certain level of compliance with the principal's interest) and the costs of the residual divergence.'[19] Although this approach is widely adopted in theory and in practice, the probability of serious error in this estimation must be quite high judging from the extent of overt and covert usurpation by the executive of corporate resources that surface in various cases of corporate distress and misdemeanor from time to time.[20]

Managerial Power Approach

While the optimal contracting approach with all its inherent uncertainties is intuitively very appealing, the bargaining equations between the employers and the employed can and do vitiate this process in practice. Outstanding talent at the top management levels is scarce[21] and hence commands a premium in a competitive market for such talent. Specific requirements of individual corporations (depending upon their business circumstances and business needs) may further exacerbate the situation and tilt the power balance farther towards the executive than the boards may have bargained for. Especially in economies with a predominance of dispersed corporate ownership (such as the US), this can turn out to be a critical factor in determining executive compensation. The process is further compounded by the fact that the market for CEOs, limited in size as normally it is, tends to feed upon itself in terms of peer pricing, with compensation consultants (whose earnings largely depend upon absolute compensation numbers eventually contracted) fuelling escalation of executive pay.[22] Board compensation committees comprise generally of incumbent or former CEOs of other corporations and are usually quite supportive of high compensation levels to this elite group.

Immediate cash payouts to retiring CEOs in India do not normally reach such sky-high numbers but that is not to say preferred CEOs do not command handsome benefits post retirement. Sale of upmarket residences at throwaway prices based on archaic valuation rules, attractive retainers and consultancies (state owned Air India has been in the news for engaging a retired CMD to recruit foreign pilots for the carrier), preferred engagement on out sourced contracts for services or manufacture, and so on are some of the often undisclosed and unreported golden parachutes that companies resort to.

In the result, managerial power tends to be strong enough to successfully demand excess rent in terms of its pay and perquisites for itself, stemming from the demand-supply gap of suitable talent, peer pressures and motivated consultants.

Public Policy Approach

This model is based on the principle that executive pay even in the private sector needs to be aligned to the general levels of compensation for jobs of similar responsibility elsewhere in the economy, often including the pay levels of comparable positions in the bureaucracy. This approach is usually justified on the basis of public policy requirements that call for reduction of inequalities in society. In this approach, executive pay as disclosed is a function of the limits and constraints imposed by state. Post-independence, India had embarked upon a supposedly egalitarian drive to contain executive salaries in the private sector at abysmally low levels. An undesirable fallout of such restrictive policies is that such compensatory mechanisms to make up for the shortfall in approved pay may continue partly or wholly even when, as is the case in post-economic-liberalization India, such regulatory constraints are relaxed or removed.

FEASIBILITY OF BOARD ASSERTIVENESS

In both the optimal contracting and managerial power approaches, company boards have tough and difficult choices to make. On the one hand, they have to do the best by their shareholders getting the most suitable CEO who can deliver expected results on a sustainable basis at the optimal cost to the company, neither more nor less. On the other, they need to be 'nice' to the CEO since in a sense the non-executive directors (who have to formally decide the pay package for shareholder approval) likely feel obligated to the CEO: 'rather than acting solely in the shareholders' interests, [they] become[s] "captured" by the CEO'.[23] The reasons are many:

- Getting to be a director (first executive, and later non-executive as well) is the ambition of most professionals; once having been there, no one generally would want to risk losing the distinction
- One does not wish to be branded as a 'difficult' director; such a reputation can be injurious to further progression in the close-knit circles of boards and directors
- Board memberships offer good monetary rewards (especially in a post-retiral scenario) besides other status-related perquisites of high flying life styles; few people would do anything to jeopardize such hard-earned benefits in later life

The fall out of such considerations is that the so-called independent elements in board membership (barring a few honourable exceptions) can rarely be expected to 'bite the hand that feeds.' Greater disclosure on how compensation packages were arrived at, as is now required, together with the thought interested shareholders will not be able to vote on their compensation packages at shareholders' meetings, would probably bring in a measure of greater circumspection in executive pay escalations.

Executive Levels of Coverage

While there is no ambiguity on the compensation committee's role with regard to executive and whole time directors including managing directors, there is room for some ambivalence in many jurisdictions on the committee's role with respect to other executives in the senior and top management categories who are not members of the board. In the US, for example, regulations rightly include within the ambit of the compensation committee responsibilities all remuneration including incentive compensation and equity based plans of senior management personnel (generally referred to as Section 16 officers) who are not on the board. Section 16 officers (other than the CEO) are the president, secretary, treasurer or principal financial officer, controller or principal accounting officer, any vice president in charge of a principal business unit, division, or function (such as sales, administration, finance), and any other person who performs similar policy-making functions.[24] Indian law extends the committee coverage to all executives on the board and also all key management personnel even if they are not on the board.

NOMINATIONS AND GOVERNANCE

The concept of nomination flows directly from the perceived need to achieve the elusive 'ideal' board composition in companies. Given the overwhelming support worldwide to the imperatives of board independence through the presence of independent or non-aligned directors, the entry and continuance of board members had to be routed through a screening and filtering mechanism exclusively by all, or a sub-set of incumbent independent directors. This was the rationale for a committee of directors addressing nomination issues. Since the director selection process itself was an inherent constituent of the overall governance structures in a corporation, many corporations have found it convenient combine with this function a review and recommendation role in respect of their corporate governance processes and practices.

OBJECTIVES

A major instrument of continuing board capacity and competence in the interest of the company's shareholders is its ability to renew and regenerate itself from time to time. This helps to avoid exposure of its members to potential complacency, fatigue or other impairment of their ability to perform optimally. It is with this objective in mind that regulation in most countries require a proportion of the directors (a third of the number in India) to retire each year so that in theory the entire board (with the exception of a few executive and other prescribed directors) can be wholly replaced every three years.[25] However this commendable objective of board renewal is generally frustrated in practice since most often the same directors offer themselves for re-election and get back on the board for another innings of three years! Still, vacancies in director positions may arise when the company decides not to field a retiring director for reelection for whatever reason, or to expand the board to strengthen competencies, or even to accommodate a family member in case of promoter controlled companies.

The primary objective of this function is to be ready with suitable candidates when such situations arise. This would involve regularly scanning for and short listing potential candidates. This would be particularly relevant in the choice of independent directors and re-nomination of retiring directors. To ensure the nomination processes and recommendations are entirely objective and without any pressures from the controlling promoters or executive management, many country regulations seek a wholly independent committee. This desirable objective is often tempered in countries where corporate ownership and control are in the hands of dominant promoter shareholders. Thus, the Indian requirement is not for a wholly independent nominating committee but one comprising entirely of non-executive directors with at least half of them also qualifying as independent. The views of the controlling shareholders and executive management where necessary may be obtained by inviting the promoters to relevant parts of the deliberations.

An important process related recommendation relates to the consultation to be engaged in before recommending new nominees for board consideration. These include competencies and skills of the board as required and as existing, any gaps to be filled and the time availability and application potential of the proposed nominee such that the perceived gaps in board competencies are addressed effectively.

It is in this context that the various theoretical foundations discussed earlier become important guideposts for facilitating the work of nomination committees. For example, if the focus is on agency-theory-based control aspects of governance, one should be looking for candidates with a probing investigative mindset, with financial, accounting, legal and even forensic backgrounds, or appropriate business and domain exposure. A resource dependence approach may dictate search for candidates with necessary business or other networking connections that would open doors of opportunity to the company or help in improving business or stakeholder interaction. A diversity theory approach may be necessary in case of boards that are short on the diversity dimension in terms of multiple nationalities (especially in companies with global footprints), ethnic, regional and gender representation, and so on. Care should however be exercised to ensure that nominations on these grounds do not lead to undesirable interlocks or reciprocal directorships which may be perceived as bringing more challenges than opportunities, more problems than benefits.

IV

Other Committees

STAKEHOLDERS RELATIONSHIP COMMITTEE

We have already discussed some of the theoretical imperatives of managing stakeholder issues even while operating the company for the benefit of shareholders. While there is growing recognition around the world of the role and rights of relevant stakeholders in corporations and related corporate responsibilities, India is probably the first major country that has legislated on this matter.

Reflecting this shifting emphasis in required board accountability, the Companies Act 2013[26] mandates companies that have more than a thousand shareholders, debenture-holders, deposit-holders and any other security holders at any time during year to constitute a stakeholders relationship committee headed by a non-executive director. This committee is tasked with the responsibility to consider and resolve stakeholder grievances. Stakeholders for this purpose include shareholders as well and will need addressing by this committee.

CORPORATE SOCIAL RESPONSIBILITY COMMITTEE

Similarly, while corporate social responsibility has been attracting increasing recognition around the world in recent decades, India has legislated for board level attention of such issues and has even prescribed mandatory minimum spending norms on such issues that corporations should comply with. Large companies with substantial profits[27] are required to constitute a board level corporate social responsibility committee with at least one of its members qualifying as independent. Among the responsibilities of this committee are to:

- Formulate and recommend to the Board, a corporate social responsibility policy indicating the activities to be undertaken by the company[28]
- Recommend the amount of expenditure to be incurred on the activities; and,
- Monitor the corporate social responsibility policy of the company from time to time

Based on the policy recommendations of the committee, the board is required to approve the company's CSR policy and disseminate it to shareholders and to other constituents. It should also ensure that the company's spend on approved CSR activities each year is not less than two percent of its average net profits of the three preceding years. The mandate also requires the spend to be focussed preferably in and around its area of operations; and in case the actual expenditure falls below the prescribed amount, the board is required to explain the reasons in its annual report to shareholders.

Whether corporate social responsibility issues are to be legislated at all or left to the wisdom of company boards and their shareholders is a larger debate. So also is the question whether CSR expenditure should be treated as add-on only when making profits or considered as a responsibility and cost of doing business irrespective of a company's profitability. For now, the law makers have decided to impose this obligation by statute and one will have to fall in line and perhaps review the impact a few years hence.

CHAPTER 5

BOARD EFFECTIVENESS
Managing the Dynamics

We have wept long enough. No more weeping, but stand
on your feet and be men.

—SWAMI VIVEKANANDA[1]

I

Processes

There is a commonly held erroneous view that processes and procedures are avoidable impediments in the way of more pressing business discussions. Adherence to required processes is fundamental to the effective performance of the board in corporations. In recognition of the their importance to good governance, this chapter begins first with a discussion on board processes.

MEETINGS AND THE BOARD CHAIR

Getting the best out of the board in the interest of the company and its shareholders is the principal job of the board chair. This responsibility covers the following.

- Setting the agenda for board meetings
- Ensuring that all that needs to be brought up to the board is in fact so brought up
- All necessary papers and relevant background information are made available to the directors sufficiently in time to enable their meaningful participation and contribution
- Allowing adequate time and drawing out those reluctant to articulate their view
- Taking a balanced and objective view on the sense of the discussions, and ensuring that the decisions taken are faithfully and accurately reflected in the minutes of the meeting and effectively followed up

It is often said that a successful chair must possess extraordinary skills of persuasion, patience, perseverance, perspicacity, and perspective to be able to guide the deliberations towards a balanced collective decision. Constructive dissent must be encouraged and welcomed; strong disagreements maybe recorded if so desired. Main board processes can be grouped under three categories—those to be observed before, during, and after the meetings; some of the key tasks and activities in this context are set out in Exhibit 5.1.

Exhibit 5.1: Enhancing Board Effectiveness: Process Best Practices

Phase	Task	Activities
Before Meetings	Setting the Calendar	• At beginning of each year, set up agreed dates, timings and venues for meetings of the board and committees • Adhere to these dates barring exceptional circumstances • Helps the executive to schedule their board-related work; directors can block these dates, improving attendance
	Setting the Annual Agenda	• Enumerate under three categories (routine and statutory, performance-related, and future-related) the board tasks to be completed each year • Category I tasks include compliance, routine resolutions for bank operations, powers of attorney, delegated authority, minutes approval, etc. • Category II tasks include performance review, internal audit reports, quarterly financials, interaction with statutory auditors, etc.

		• Category III tasks include visioning exercises, annual plans, strategic issues like inorganic growth through mergers and acquisitions, top management succession, etc. • While Category I and II items would recur in every meeting, Category III items may be staggered such that over the full year they are addressed comprehensively
	Setting the Meeting Agenda	• In consultation with the CEO and the concurrence of the chairman, formulate the agenda for each meeting • Include Category III items pre-scheduled in the annual agenda for a particular meeting and get concerned functions to commence preparations well in advance • The company secretary to liaise with concerned functions to similarly get the papers for the recurring Category I and II items on time • Circulate the agenda with relevant papers well in advance of the meeting date
	Board Papers	• Aim to achieve the golden mean in terms of board papers quantum—neither too detailed nor too sketchy • Wherever possible, preface each item paper with a pre-formatted summary of the issue, alternatives, decision requirements and timing, financial and other governance

		impact. This helps directors to focus on the issues at hand on an informed basis • More detailed information may be provided as appendices for in-depth study as desired
	Offline Meetings/ Circular Resolutions	• Hold offline audio-video meetings of the board or the committees in case of emergent matters that require attention before the next scheduled physical meetings • In case of unexpected developments requiring board concurrence, obtain approvals by circular resolutions (if necessary preceded by an offline meeting) with full details in support
	Pre-meeting Briefings	• In case of complex or sensitive issues, pre-briefing of some or all the directors by the CEO or other senior executive may be desirable to save collective board time. This may be particularly relevant in case of technical, financial or legal issues where some directors with domain expertise may require such prior briefings • This is also used to enlist support of directors who, without such full briefings, may be inimical to proposal
		• It is important to get independent directors to attend meetings to fully benefit from their participation

During Meetings	Quorum	• Good practice to ensure that internal requirements for quorum include obligatory presence of majority of independent directors
	Time Frame	• Allocate pre-fixed time for each agenda item so that board and committee time is equally distributed in terms of importance of the topics • Allow spill-over time between meetings of committees and the board to provide for any time overrun
	Actions Taken	• Key to effective monitoring is a review of actions due and taken • No item should be taken off the 'actions due' list unless it is fully addressed and the board/committee signs off
	Presentations	• Welcome in terms of focus and ease of understanding, but should not pre-empt discussion by directors • Should be read in to the minutes of the meeting
	Table Items	• Eliminate or largely minimize items presented at the meeting but not included in the agenda, unless on grounds of sensitivity or urgency • Prior oral briefing of directors preferable in case of sensitive table items
	Executive Sessions	• Limit attendance and participation to need-based invitees and even then only for the duration of discussion on concerned topics

		• Maintain confidentiality of privileged communications by invitees both to encourage them to be candid and to avoid any victimization by the executive later on
	Minutes	• Draft minutes to be ready for circulation after clearance by the board/committee chairmen within a maximum of one week • Should be concise and yet comprehensive enough to record the sense of the discussion and major views expressed • Any serious dissonance must be recorded faithfully with attribution to the director(s) and any dissent, if required by the director, must be recorded with attribution
After Meetings	Actions Arising	• Board decisions requiring follow up actions and feedback must be entered in an 'actions due' list that should provide brief account of the decision and action to be taken, the person/function responsible for auctioning, and the due date by which such action should be completed • At each meeting of the board/committee, status of action taken on all items on the 'actions due' list (and not only the items from the immediately preceding meeting). No item should be taken off from the list without board/committee approval, until the action is completed and the board/committee apprised

II

Coping with Conflicts of Interest

One of the most challenging aspects of corporate governance relates to conflicts of interest in stewarding the operations of the company's business. In a corporate context, conflicts of interest arise when a transaction between the company and an executive, an office holder, a director, or an organization in which any of them or their close relatives have a controlling interest, has the potential to extract private benefits to the detriment of the company's and its shareholders' interests. Transactions involving corporate directors and the company are indeed the most vulnerable on this count because of the fiduciary obligations which prohibit directors seeking any personal gains for themselves while dealing with the affairs of the company. The important point is that not only do such conflicts arise in day to day business but that one needs to be conscious of that potential and evolve processes to pre-emptively avoid them or at least proactively mitigate their ill effects on the company and its shareholder population. A major responsibility of corporate boards is to develop mechanisms to identify and appropriately steer clear of potential or actual situations of conflicts of interest in the course of the company's business operations, or where appropriate, ensure utmost transparency and disclosure to the board and the shareholders for an informed appreciation of the facts and circumstances before their approval is granted.

THE NATURE OF DIRECTORIAL ACCOUNTABILITY

Virtually every business transaction offers scope for conflicts of interest between and among the players. A simple buy-sell transaction involves an inherent divergence of interest between the parties, in that the buyer seeks to get value for money while the seller targets money for value provided. So long as the contracting parties are aware of the details of the product or service being bought or sold, without recourse to misrepresentation or subterfuge, and the transaction content is not illegal or against public interest, the parties are left to judge for themselves the fairness or attractiveness of the transaction from their own view point with no perceived conflicts of interest. It is only when a party to the transaction is charged with the extra fiduciary duty towards another to ensure the latter's interests are protected and furthered, that a potential for conflict of interest between them arises. Fiduciary duties are derived both from common law as laid down by judicial pronouncements over time, and legislative or regulatory requirements that mandate certain dos and don'ts including a minimum required level of disclosure of information. Listing agreement provisions applicable to publicly traded companies and statutes such as in the Companies Act are examples of such interventions.

There is, of course, a further, possibly even more important ethical dimension to corporate conflicts and their pre-emption. While law and regulation can prescribe, and the judiciary can interpret such conflict situations and their fallouts, there is a more demanding criterion of establishing what is fair and equitable. What is right, and what is wrong? What is good, and what is evil? To fail in adequately discharging the 'trust' reposed in one will certainly, in most regimes, be considered wrong and evil.

'FAIR DEALING' BY DIRECTORS

Directors owe an obligation of fair dealing to their company and its shareholders. This calls for appropriate and comprehensive disclosure of the interests involved, leaving it to the other *non-interested* directors (and non-interested shareholders) to approve the transaction because of its possible overall benefit to the corporation. Two dimensions need to be considered—one, relating to the conflict of interest per se, and the other, to the material facts of the transaction. Fairness itself is often a range rather than a fixed point. The company can consummate the transaction at the lower instead of the higher end of the range, or even perhaps decline to go through with the transaction on grounds of probity or propriety.[2]

Another critical principle in the field of conflict of interest situations is that directors may not advance their pecuniary interests by engaging in competition with the corporation, without the disinterested directors on the board authorising (or ratifying) such action in the larger interest of the company, or approved by disinterested shareholders, if they are convinced the company's interests are not prejudicially impacted. Regrettably, Indian regulation and conventions still do not look down upon such common directorships in competing businesses, with even the banking sector not being wholly free from this malaise.

CORPORATE OPPORTUNITY

The related issue of *corporate opportunity* seeks to prohibit (or after the event, penalize) the directors and officers in their fiduciary capacity from expropriating to themselves (or their affiliates, associates or other related entities) a maturing economic opportunity which their company is actually, or potentially, capable of pursuing for its own benefit and that of its shareholders. Corporate opportunities clearly relate to the possible benefit accruing to the company had it not been usurped by a director or officer of the company and hence more difficult to address.

COPING WITH CONFLICTS OF INTEREST

How should boards and regulators address such conflict situations in the best interest of the company and its shareholders? Some of the possible measures are.

Totally prohibit the fiduciary from acting in a conflicted situation, like for example, lawyers being traditionally barred from representing different clients with conflicting interests, or, financial intermediaries acting for parties with potentially conflicting interests (such as advising a company on sale of securities as well as acting as brokers buying the same securities for their pension funds). An 'efficient' market for corporate control may act as a deterrent to conflicted managements with the ever-present threat of competing managers offering to take over the company and deliver better shareholder returns. Many hostile takeover situations actually bank upon the possibility of minimizing leakages in the system besides of course, genuine cost reductions and revenue growth optimization.

Building 'Chinese walls' in financial conglomerates is quite common, with measures like separation between back-office and front-office, between client trading desks and proprietary trading desks, inducting independent directors on company boards, independent compensation and audit committees, and so on. The efficacy of these initiatives, especially those relating to corporate boards, will depend upon the organizational buy-in and adoption of such measures in spirit rather than only in letter.

Disclosure is another measure that has found increasing favour with regulators around the world. The primary objective of this is to overcome information asymmetry between the parties.[3] To be effective though, disclosure needs to be transparent and complete—a pre-condition that is often observed more in breach than in compliance.

RELATED PARTY TRANSACTIONS

Virtually all conflicted dealings in corporations tend to be related party transactions (RPTs) where the corporation entering into contracts with the other party is a person or other legal entity related in some way to the corporation, or its directors or officers, or their relatives and close associates.[4] The basic presumption in case of related party transactions is that they are not in the best interests of the corporation unless proved otherwise.

Not all RPTs need to be illegal or bad for the companies. In many cases, these transactions may well contribute to the wealth maximization efforts of the company. For example, companies may set up subsidiaries in overseas territories, either due to local regulatory regimes or for better organizational structuring and transactions between the parent and the subsidiaries may have none of the undesirable overtones normally associated with conflicted transactions. But even in such cases, the board and the directors especially of the subsidiary (because of its relative position of vulnerability) have to ensure that the interests of the other non-controlling shareholders are not prejudicially affected by such RPTs. Even in case of 100 percent subsidiaries, because of their different sets of stakeholders, their directors may have to exercise due vigilance in ensuring that the interests of the subsidiary are not impaired because of such RPTs with the parent or dominant controlling shareholder.

CONFLICTS IN PRACTICE

Corporate business formats are inherently conflict-prone because of the interplay of the divergent interests involved: the goal non-congruence between and among shareholders (both dominant and absentee), other stakeholders, the company and its board, individual directors, executives, and the state. It is important to note that the transactions described here are not necessarily unlawful or illegal. In fact, some of these instances have even stood the test of judicial scrutiny. They are narrated here only to highlight the constant struggle between what is just and equitable on the one hand, and what is just legal, on the other.

ON BUSINESS STRATEGY

Providing strategic direction and guidance is a key component of the board's stewardship function. This is also an area of potential conflict of interest between and among directors representing different shareholder constituencies, especially in companies with dominant shareholders. For example:

- Group interests and policies tend to take precedence over what might be in the best interests of the company itself and its other shareholders. Illustratively, Britannia Industries, the breads, biscuits and dairy major had to exit its Soya business in the early nineties just because its US based parent, R.J.R. Nabisco did not find that business an appropriate fit in their global business scenario. Much will depend upon the strength of conviction of the other directors on the board and their ability to stand their ground in the interest of absentee shareholders. A common feature of transnational companies operating in host countries (with or without local partners) is the restraints on technology development, overseas markets, captive input sourcing, and so on. While these are justifiable from the perspective of the parent, the host country directors will have to balance these costs with the benefits of foreign collaboration and look after the interests of their absentee shareholder population

- Dominant ownership and the personal ambitions and aspirations of controlling shareholders are also a potential cause for conflicts in boards which often may not openly surface, eventually to the detriment of absentee shareholders. Unrelated investments and diversifications have been the root cause of many a corporate distress and even failure. A case in point is the UB Group and Kingfisher Airlines, with the latter being driven by the dominant promoter and in the event, failing. Undoubtedly, in the aggressive pursuit of such adventures where the bandwidth required to operate them professionally and successfully is absent, the role of the domineering promoters with a penchant for glamorous and high profile diversifications can clearly be seen. The extent to which directors of the promoting companies are able to moderate or restrain such investments and the directors of the investee company are able to insist on installing executive management with the required expertise are entirely dependent upon the profile of the respective boards and their ability to prevail over the dominant shareholders

ON GAINING CONTROL

- Who will be in charge of a corporation is a theme that never fails to generate conflicts not only among the warring shareholders and executives but also between and among the directors of a company. Especially in a country like India where family ownership is predominant, succession issues within the family often spill over to the company's board and its directors, often causing wealth erosion to the other absentee shareholders. A case in point was the family feud between the Ambani brothers in Reliance Industries, among the top Indian corporations. Somewhat similar situations can arise in case of multinational subsidiaries and affiliates as well, where a parent with a significant minority stake desiring to acquire management control over its affiliate is opposed by the rest of the directors on the board as happened in ITC in the late nineteen

- Such conflicts also arise when control is sought to be wrested from a seemingly inefficient promoter-management through a hostile takeover bid. In such situations, a very low promoter holding can be a great disadvantage to the incumbent management who need to bolster their entrenchment through other means such as political or institutional support [**Case summary 5.1, DCM and Swraj Paul**]. The conflict in such instances is between the entrenched promoter directors and the absentee shareholders who are denied an opportunity for more efficient wealth creation performance

ON MERGERS AND DIVESTITURES

- Conflicts can arise when companies or businesses with common parentage are merged or hived off. It is always a challenge for the board of a company to ensure that the transaction is in the best interest of its shareholders and they are not short changed by interested parties. As RPT, such initiatives are presumed to be injurious to the subject company unless the directors in their wisdom are satisfied to the contrary. Such mergers, though, need not inherently be disadvantageous to the company but the directors will have to ensure that the proposal is beneficial to their absentee shareholders [**Case summary 5.2, iGate Global Solutions**]

- Similar considerations apply in case of divestitures as well. Often, speculative investments are made by companies and later when they apparently do not turn out to be successful, the dominant shareholders 'offer' to buy them out to help the company and its absentee shareholders.

Independent directors in such cases may have to satisfy themselves that the divestments are in the interests of the company and its absentee shareholders and they do not amount to usurpation by conflicted promoters or the executive of a valuable business opportunity from the company

Some of the key issues to be addressed in such conflict situations are

- Why is a business or subsidiary being merged with, or moved out of the company? Irrespective of the parent's perspective, does the company stand to benefit by such a transfer?
- Is there a corporate opportunity that is being usurped by the transaction? Is the company being burdened with any unacceptable risky business addition?
- Is the valuation fair and reasonable to the company? One should also be on guard especially if the valuations look too good to be true as happened in the Satyam case where the promoter affiliates were reportedly willing to transfer their businesses at 'attractive' valuations
- Many leveraged buyouts by the executive also fall in to this category of conflicts[Case summary 5.3, RJR Nabisco]. When executive management (especially in a widely dispersed share ownership structure) proposes to acquire their company for whose performance they were responsible, there is a presumptive conflict of interest between them and the company and its shareholders. Boards in such instances have the responsibility of critically examining and pre-empting, in shareholders' interest, executive actions (and inactions) in the immediate past and during the negotiations phase to ensure risks of

deliberate asset stripping or value destruction aimed at minimizing their acquisition cost. Although not always done, boards may find it helpful to curtail executive authority for major decisions impacting firm valuations once the buyout proposal had been announced. This can be justified on the ground that with the buyout intentions being made public, the concerned executives are to be seen as potential buyers of the company whose continuing access to insider information and executive authority would lead to and further accentuate asymmetry of information between them and the board, and as such be detrimental to shareholder interests.

ON INSIDER INFORMATION

- Major conflicts of interest arise when directors, both executive and non-executive, indulge in using for their personal benefit or that of their immediate family and friends, proprietary or privileged information they receive as directors for board deliberations and decisions. Such breach of trust sets the concerned director squarely in conflict with the company and its shareholders [**Case summary 5.4, Rajat Gupta**]. When such abusive practices are resorted to by directors in executive management, the crime becomes even more unpardonable. Insider information abuse is not easy to detect (especially when indulged in by celebrity directors and trusted executive directors) or establish and hence a large number of such abusive transactions go unpunished; there are also instances which, because of difficulties in prosecuting or in the interests of speedy dispensation of justice, tend to get settled with the regulators or prosecutors without admission of guilt

III

Reporting and Communication

Corporate communication covers a wide variety of dissemination processes that are aimed at keeping different stakeholders and constituencies well and truly informed. A great deal of communication needs to, and does indeed, take place on various matters pertaining to the corporation, for example, on financial results, products and services, and personnel policies, and so on. Our focus here is however, limited to the policy dimensions of board communications and ways to enhance their usefulness and credibility to the intended audience.

As companies grew and trading in their securities increased, it became necessary for the market players (besides shareholders) to be informed of key performance details frequently, leading to regulatory mandates requiring publication of quarterly financials. Meetings of shareholders, analysts' calls, chairman's speeches and so on are further measures of both oral and written communication to shareholders and other investors; in modern times, the speed of communication has been vastly enhanced with the advent of electronic media such as company web sites and various other wire services which facilitate almost instantaneous transmission of messages and reports companies wish to disseminate. But speed is only one measure of the effectiveness of corporate communications; the other important dimension relates to their completeness, clarity, and credibility, all of which when fully met, add to the reputation of the company with its attendant benefits.

There is another dimension to good communication—it acts as a countervailing check on company managements since they would be operating under the informed eyes of others in the know. Jeremy Bentham, the eighteenth century English philosopher and the founder of the Utilitarian approach to ethics, applied to corporate management and its reporting responsibilities, what he labelled the *panoptican* principle,[5] literally implying an instrument by which all is seen, in the firm belief that 'the more strictly we are watched, the better we behave.'[6] To Bentham, publicity or disclosure and communication in modern parlance, was key to accountability. He wrote, '[A]ccounts must be… published…regularly—and will be scrutinized by many a benevolent…suspicious…envious …eye; accounts…giving the most perfect transparency…the eye of the public is drawn upon the subject, and operates as a check [upon] personal interest and favouritism.'[7]

DISCLOSURE: THE ROAD LESS TRAVELLED

Corporate information disclosure has had an unedifying history. In 1932, Berle and Means summarized the state of corporate disclosure practices and the broad legal requirements then prevalent in the US, noting that 'no state requires disclosure of the facts considered usual in the normal open market situation. … It will be noticed that in dealing with corporate information the underlying assumption is that such information must be considered as a private matter, of interest only to its shareholders; and even in that regard limit in the extreme the information which the corporate management must make available, even to its own shareholders.'[8]

Such an approach to disclosure could possibly be traced to the evolution of the corporate ownership of the organization itself that generally evolved from partnerships, into incorporated entities. Initially, most of the shareholders were also co-partners and were engaged actively in managing the operations of the company, and were consequently in the know of facts pertaining to the business, with no special 'disclosure' being necessary. The issue of disclosure became important only with the proliferation of 'absentee' shareholders with no involvement in the management of their corporations' businesses, and thus had no clue as to what was happening inside unless they were made aware of it. Even purchases of stock in companies were often on the basis of very little information about the company or its business, or its directors and managers. In England, for example, it was only in 1844 (when the Companies Act was legislated) that the principle of compulsory disclosure relating to promoters, prospectuses for soliciting share subscriptions, and publication of annual reports and audited true and fair balance sheets were mandated.

Indian experience has not been dissimilar, as Indian corporate legislation has closely followed related developments in England. As already noted, the Indian business scene was dominated by British managing agencies in the nineteenth and early-twentieth century. Lack of appropriate disclosures and transparency in operations were among the various corporate abuses common to that period. With the abolition of managing agencies in the second half of the twentieth century and the enactment of a monumental Companies Act in 1956, disclosure requirements both at the time of public offer of securities and annually thereafter were strengthened. The extent and patterns of corporate abuses in the earlier era, further compounded by the socialistic political agenda of the post-independent regime, led to an overly distrustful approach to restraining corporate behaviour and escalating disclosure requirements. Of course, in tune with changing times and India's increasing integration with global business, there have since been several relaxations in recent years and the trend is set to continue. Listed companies are additionally subject to the requirements of the capital market regulator and the stock exchanges, while the Reserve Bank of India has mandated and recommended its own set of disclosures for the banking and the non-banking financial services sectors.

Communication and disclosure, though, would be of a superior quality only when corporations look at them as value-adding initiatives, not merely as avoidable cost and effort intensive compliance exercises.

BOARD ROLE IN COMMUNICATION POLICY OVERSIGHT

Among the earliest governance guidelines that specifically refer to communication policy as part of board stewardship responsibilities was the 1994 Canadian document published by the (then) Toronto Stock Exchange. It stipulated that[9]

'The [fourth] principal responsibility of the board is to ensure the corporation has in place a policy to enable the corporation to communicate effectively with its shareholders, other stakeholders and the public generally. This policy must effectively interpret the operations of the corporation to shareholders and must accommodate feedback from shareholders, which should be factored into the corporation's business decisions. We also note the critical role of the media in publishing and interpreting corporate information.'

In India, the Kumar Mangalam Birla Committee Report also highlighted the imperatives of communication and disclosure, stating that

'The shareholders' role in corporate governance is...by requiring the board to provide them periodically with the requisite information, in a transparent fashion, of the activities and progress of the company. ...Adequate financial reporting and disclosure are the cornerstones of good corporate governance.'[10]

In a corporate context, the company and its board are obliged morally and legally to keep their shareholders and other stakeholders fully and transparently informed about the state of affairs of the company whose governance has been entrusted to them.

AN INFORMATION DISCLOSURE AND ENHANCEMENT MODEL

Information asymmetry between contracting or negotiating parties is a major contributor to arbitraging potential since the party in possession of superior information will be at an advantage over his counterpart. Public policy and societal preferences for a reasonably well ordered contracting environment lead to the prescription of minimum levels of information disclosure. In some contracts like those relating to life, fire and marine insurance, the principle of *uberrimae fide*, or utmost good faith, is required by law whereby the assured party is obliged to make full disclosure of all material facts which would influence the insurer's decision to offer a contract of insurance and its terms including the price.

And yet, fundamentally the world of business and commerce thrives on information asymmetry. The general mercantile principle of *caveat emptor* (let the buyer beware) still applies to a vast majority of such transactions, except where law otherwise mandates disclosure. While there is plenty of vocal support and commitment to the concept of level playing fields, when it relates to information sharing and disclosure, the biblical golden rule of 'do unto others as you would have them do unto you'[11] is often observed in breach than in compliance. Corporate (and individual) reputations are inversely proportional to the levels of information asymmetry in their dealings with others.

Given this overall proclivity towards poor and inadequate communication, the effort is always to look for ways in which the disadvantaged party could reduce the information asymmetry and its consequent impact. This often leads to intermediation between information owners and information seekers. In the context of societal resource allocation to individual business units in a capital market economy, household savings could flow directly to firms as in the case of direct equity investment, or go through financial intermediaries such as banks, mutual funds, pension funds and insurance companies. Again, firms could communicate directly with investors through the media and their own information channels or go through information intermediaries such as financial analysts. The information intermediation could be regulatory (as in the case of independent auditors) or discretionary (as in the case of financial analysts). In either case, the effort is to review and evaluate the information provided by the firms, and pass it on to the information seekers with their professional assurance (in case of auditors) or value addition (in case of financial analysts).

Exhibit 5.2 offers a stylised model of the dynamics of the information dissemination process from information owners to information seekers. In summary

- First, the firm may only have part, and not all of the information relevant to information seekers. This may be due to executive indifference or inefficiency in scanning the environment for relevant data, its collection, processing or interpretation, often on grounds of resource scarcity or related costs
- Next, executive management (directed by board policy) would decide on the extent and tenor of communication. Disclosure can be in response to statutory and regulatory

mandates or discretionary. Within the former, the choice ranges from what is referred to as check-box compliance where disclosure is the barest minimum that the firm can get away with without being held for non-compliance, to full and fair disclosure where it meets criteria like 'substance over form' and 'spirit over letter' of the mandatory requirements. In the model, the former is referred to as partial and the latter as complete

- Similar decisions would apply to discretionary or voluntary disclosures of information. Here again, there can be partial or even no disclosures at the option of the company. Alternatively, there can be complete disclosure based on the conviction that it is in the interests of the company and its reputation with its consequential bottom line benefits. Research suggests that such additional information availability, leading as it does to a reduction in the information asymmetry between information owners and information seekers, minimizes the uncertainty component, contributing to a lowering of the cost of capital of the firm

- The next step in the process is evaluation and validation of disclosed information by external agencies. The model reflects four categories of information intermediaries between the firms and the investors in a mandatory or discretionary format: regulators (corporate law policy makers and administrators in case of all companies, and stock exchanges and capital market regulators in case of publicly traded companies), independent auditors (and accounting standards setters), financial intermediaries (analysts, credit rating agencies, proxy advisors and equity researchers), and investigative financial and business journalists from the print and audio-visual media.

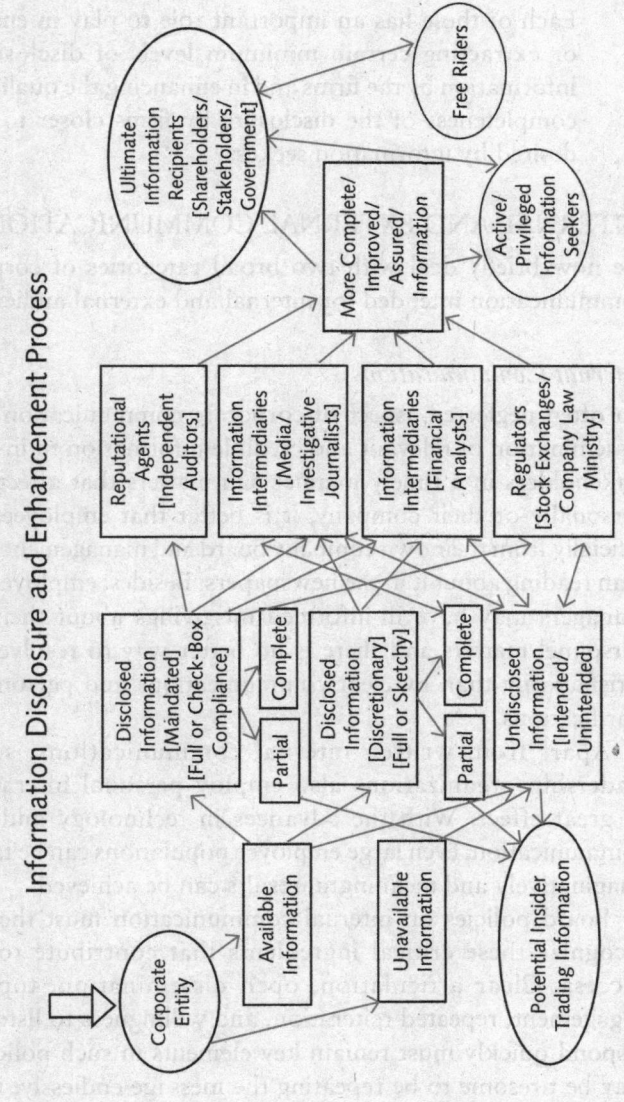

Exhibit 5.2: Information Disclosure and Enhancement Process

Information Disclosure and Enhancement Process

Each of these has an important role to play in ensuring or extracting certain minimum levels of disclosure of information by the firms and in enhancing the quality and completeness of the disclosure by firms closer to levels desired by information seekers

INTERNAL AND EXTERNAL COMMUNICATIONS

We now briefly deal with two broad categories of corporate communication intended for internal and external audience.

Internal Communications

An often neglected aspect of corporate communication is the dissemination of relevant and credible information to in-house stakeholders in a timely manner. On matters that affect them personally or their company, it is better that employees hear officially from their own company board and management rather than reading about it in the newspapers. Besides, employees and managers may have ill-informed misgivings about their own personnel matters and there is no better way to resolve them satisfactorily than by clear communications and personalized clarifications.

Apart from written internal communications, several leadership organizations also employ personal interactions to great effect. With the advances in technology and good communication, even large employee populations can be tackled imaginatively and meaningful results can be achieved.

Board policies on internal communication must therefore recognize these critical ingredients that contribute to their success. Clear articulation, open dissemination, top-level engagement, repeated reiteration, and willingness to listen and respond quickly must remain key elements in such policies. It may be tiresome to be repeating the message endlessly; it may be tempting to share the communication with the inner circle of colleagues and associates and let them carry on the good work downstream. The results would not be the same.

External Communications

While external communications cover a wide variety of recipients, our focus here is limited to the investor community in general and the company's shareholder population in particular. By virtue of being trustees for the shareholders the directors are obliged to report back periodically on the state of affairs of the company and the results of its operations. This is usually done through the medium of an annual report to the shareholders who are on the register of the company at a given date. This requirement is of such paramount importance that the minimum required contents of such a communication have been mandated by law and regulation. In case of listed companies, quarterly summary financials are to be sent to the respective stock exchanges within fifteen minutes of the board approving them and, thereafter, published in the print media mandatorily. Such is the importance of the responsibility of the board of directors with regard to communication to the shareholders.

Besides these requirements, there are several other shareholder related communications that companies make in practice. Thus,

- Listed companies hold analyst's briefings to respond to any queries, participate in audio-visual media interviews and of course, have their chairmen deliver speeches at the annual meetings of shareholders. Companies often utilize these opportunities as useful media of communication

- Decades ago, P.L. Tandon, then chairman of Hindustan Lever (now Hindustan Unilever) pioneered the practice of converting these speeches into economic and strategic discourses on various issues of national interest and company impact; it is now virtually standard practice for company chairmen of large listed corporations to follow suit, showcasing how their companies were dealing with and responding to the needs of changing times. Some company chairmen have adopted the practice of writing personalised letters as part of the company's annual reports to shareholders. Clearly such letters are not the responsibility of the board and hence may be used to convey information without, perhaps, the attendant legal responsibilities

- Company websites provide a good and effective medium for online corporate communication though admittedly their reach is limited to the computer-savvy

- Communications going out in the name of the board, for example, the annual directors' report to shareholders and the financials of the company should adhere strictly to the cannons of good communication—clarity, credibility, correctness and completeness—for the recipients to make informed judgements. Although such communications may have been drafted by the executive management, investor relations agencies, or the independent auditors (in case of notes to accounts), it is up to the board to satisfy itself that the final version of the communication complies with the required standards. This will enhance the reputation of the board and the corporation and consequently its perceived value in the mind of the recipients. Generally, linguistic gymnastics and obfuscation in the drafting of such communications do not, contrary to popular belief, achieve their intended purpose of shielding the company from probing minds of discerning investors and analysts. On the contrary, they often unwittingly create embarrassing situations for the company (Exhibit 5.3). Boards owe it to their investors and other stakeholders to render a truthful and complete account in their communications couched in simple and easy-to-follow language.

As in many other aspects of good corporate governance, companies and their boards need to judge for themselves what level of disclosure is appropriate and transparently beneficial to the proper assessment of their companies by their co-investors who are not in operational control. Regulatory mandates are just one, and a minimum one, of the benchmarks. Failure to recognise this market expectation is likely to be injurious to the corporations themselves in the long run, both in terms of their valuations and as triggers for further mandatory and legislative interventions.

Exhibit 5.3: An Embarrassing Example from a Published Directors' Report

'While operating profit is marginally lower than in the previous year, it is noteworthy that no benefit was sought to be derived from an increase in inventories of finished goods as happened in [the previous year]'

—A leading consumer goods company belonging to a reputed group

---

IV

Board Evaluation

Corporate boards and directors have a job to do and although being at the top it is difficult to accept, it is fair that they should have their performance evaluated just as every other player in the corporation. In India, the Companies Act requires the company's Nomination and Remuneration Committee to carry out an evaluation of every director's performance.[12] Methodologies of such evaluations can differ, parameters can vary, and country and cultural bias could vitiate comparisons, but the fact remains that corporate boards and directors in well developed markets are being increasingly judged by their societal peers and investing publics. In India, with its predominance of promoter and other dominant ownership structures, one can only speculate how effective and functional such evaluations would be, especially in case of the promoter sponsored CEOs and other directors; it may however be worthwhile to begin the process so that it may settle down and mature concurrently with improvements in acceptance of general standards of good governance as well as the development of capital markets, investor expectations, and contests for corporate control.

There are two aspects to board evaluations—the performance of individual directors and the effectiveness of the board as a collective body.

EVALUATING INDIVIDUAL DIRECTORS

One reasonably sound is option is evaluation by peers where each director on the board evaluates every colleague on several parameters such as attendance, contribution, participation, preparedness, commitment, connections, functional skills, business acumen, and so on. In order that the feedback is free and uninhibited, it may be worthwhile for an external consultant to design and process the appraisal forms and responses, and leave it to the non-executive chairman (or the independent lead director) to share the collective perceptions of the board with each director individually. Another option is for the external consultant to individually discuss with each director his appraisal by peers and offer counsel and guidance for improvement; this should be followed by a briefing of the entire board on the aggregate results and action issues emerging from the evaluation and mentoring exercise. If remuneration is dependent upon such performance appraisals, this would also serve as an objective and impartial format for deciding the quantum of reward. As an incidental bonus, directorial independence would also largely be protected in this system, since the rewards would not be seen as some largesse personally handed down by the promoters or the CEO but earned on the basis of peer evaluations.

EVALUATION PROCESSES

That the board is a collection of individuals with mutually complementing skill sets working together in the interests of the corporation and all its shareholders has been noted already. To expect each director to perform equally on the three roles of contributing, counselling and controlling is unrealistic. Some parameters of measurement (such as attendance, participation, commitment, preparation, etc.) may be common to all while certain others (such as business or functional domain expertise, experiential wisdom, or probing and forensic skills) will vary with each individual. In designing evaluation formats and interpreting evaluation scores these factor would need to be adequately addressed. It would also be useful to agree these metrics with individual directors in advance so that the eventual evaluation feedbacks would be reasonably well received. The evaluation format should also provide for performance as a board or committee chair, as a lead director, and as committee members, as applicable.

Each director may be required first to self-evaluate his or her own performance against such agreed benchmarks of performance, and then evaluate every other director including the board chair, the lead director, the managing director and the executive directors (the latter two on their role as directors and not as executives). Performance may be graded on a scale of say one to five with the mid-point representing meeting expectations.

Following are some suggested criteria for all directors, executive and non-executive. Questions for eliciting responses would of course have to be suitably framed.

As Directors

- Attendance at board and committee meetings
- Preparedness levels, both in terms of interest and contribution
- Relevant and value-adding participation
- Communication skills
- Involvement in company affairs, offline as well as at formal meetings of the board and committees, in terms of time commitment, familiarity with environmental developments bearing upon the company, and so on
- Role as company's ambassador and public relations representative, and their contributions in presenting a positive (but obviously not untruthful) image of the company in their interactions within and outside the company
- Professional and/ or specialist skills in areas of value to the company, their reputation as opinion makers, and their own personal achievements

As Board and Committee Chairs, Lead Director

- Leadership qualities as evidenced in the efficient conduct of meetings and ability to obtain optimal contributions from colleagues

- Time commitment in preparing meeting agenda and ensuring adequate and timely dissemination of information to members
- Handling of shareholder meetings, analysts presentations, and in general providing a positive (not untruthful) image of the company
- Ability to counsel and control, where appropriate, executive management and to ensure that board policies and decisions are faithfully, effectively and promptly implemented

EVALUATING THE BOARD AND COMMITTEES

In theory, the potential of the board (and the committees,) like any other groups, ought to be more than the sum of its parts. Whether this translates in to realization in practice is the question that collective evaluations seek to address. Among the parameters that could be used for the collective evaluations are the following.

In Terms of Board Work

- Was the board (or the committee) able to complete the annual work schedule it had set out for itself for the year?
- Were the board papers, presentations, minutes, and so on satisfactory in terms of content, delivery and promptness?
- Were the time allocations for meetings and items under discussion adequate?
- Was participation by directors satisfactory?
- Were the executive sessions satisfactory?

In Terms of Results

- Were the value creation objectives achieved? (Metrics could be EVA, market cap, and so on)

- Have non-financial objectives been achieved? (Rankings in terms of size, peer performance, admired companies, preferred employers, preferred vendors, and so on)
- Have board regeneration and composition objectives been achieved?

Required background data will have to be prepared and provided to directors so that they can evaluate performance on an informed basis. These parameters are illustrative and companies will have to develop their own metrics for evaluation purposes depending upon their circumstances and priorities.

PROCESSING AND DISSEMINATION OF EVALUATION RESULTS

The next step concerns the manner in which the completed appraisals are to be processed and used. Three alternatives are available.

- Individual directors retain their self-appraisal for their own information and use it for self-correction and self-improvement. The purpose of the evaluation process is to provide directors the opportunity to step back and objectively assess their contribution and make course corrections, if any. If any director so desires, he may seek counsel from the external counselor, the board chair or the lead director or the chair of the governance or nomination committee (or even just a senior and more experienced colleague director) to chalk out a suitable personal programme of self-improvement.

  As an extension, peer appraisals are done in addition to self-appraisals. These are anonymously collected and summary scores and comments are passed on to individual directors to whom they relate. In this option, directors have the benefit of not only looking at themselves but also of gaining some perspective as to how their colleagues perceive their contribution

- In the second option, all appraisals, both self and peer, are pooled together anonymously, and summarized for discussion at a full meeting. (In some cases, this may be routed through a board committee, usually comprising board and committee chairs and the chief executive.) The important point to bear in mind is that only summaries and aggregates are discussed in the full board, without mention of specific names of either the assessors or the assesses, except in the case of the chairs. To facilitate open discussion, the chairs may opt out of the meeting during this part of the discussion, and re-join later to hear the summary observations regarding their performance

- The third option takes this process even further. After the individual appraisals are compiled, an external consultant, the board chair or an *adhoc* committee of senior directors discusses it with each director individually, and chalks out any orientation or other training programmes that may be mutually considered useful for the concerned director. Much of the mentoring and experience sharing involved in such an exercise is generally of immense value to the individual directors and to the board collectively in improving overall effectiveness. Clearly, this calls for a great deal of maturity on the part of everyone involved both in providing and in taking the feedback in the right spirit and for constructive enhancement of individual and collective board performance

APPLICATIONS FOR EVALUATION FINDINGS

Most of the benefits accruing from the performance evaluation of managers and employees also apply to evaluations of the board and directors. Additionally, in the context of corporate governance, some of the applications to which these evaluations can be administered are

- Toning up the board, in terms of its constituents and optimally benefitting from the skills and expertise available to the company. These evaluations may indicate gaps in the availability of specific skills or knowledge which the board may then begin to remedy through further additions or by more focused application by its members

- Deciding upon training inputs and other initiatives where the board and the individual directors concur. This will help in improving the capability of the board

- Deciding upon the remuneration of non-executive directors. (In case of executive members of the board, these appraisals may be used as additional inputs while appraising their performance as executives). While many company boards follow the easy route of rewarding all directors equally, such a practice may not be conducive to appropriate motivation of the members whose contribution and commitment may be of a higher order. Performance appraisals by peers could well be the most acceptable way to determine differential remuneration to directors

- Facilitating the process of recommendation for reappoint-ment of directors at the end of their term. Those with consistently poor performance during their tenure may be identified and eased out without much embarrassment.

- Contributing directors would be motivated to continue and better their personal performance when they realize their work is receiving peer recognition. Often, this could be a stronger motivator than mere monetary rewards

Case summary 5.1: DCM, Escorts and Swraj Paul

In February of 1982, Finance Minister, Pranab Mukherjee announced a 'Portfolio Investment Scheme' (PIS) to encourage non-residents of Indian origin to invest in Indian companies, thus improving the inflow of foreign exchange that was desperately needed to cope with the country's adverse balance of payments situation. In case the overseas investors were companies, at least 60 percent of their ownership should be held by people of Indian origin to qualify for this investment route. There were also provisions restricting individual holdings to 1 percent and collectively to 5 percent (introduced on 2 May, 1983) of the investee company's equity. Reserve Bank of India had prescribed procedural rules that had to be complied with.

Caparo Group (Caparo) was a company incorporated in the UK and 61.6 percent of its equity was owned by Swraj Paul Family Trust, whose exclusive beneficiaries were Swraj Paul, his wife and several other members of his immediate family. The investments in DCM shares had been made through 13 Caparo subsidiaries (one 98 percent owned and the rest wholly owned) and thus qualified to buy into DCM's equity under the PIS. There was one catch though which Paul took advantage of: the 5 percent upper limit in the aggregate did not apply to any shares bought prior to 2 May, 1983, the date of the policy announcement prescribing the 5 percent aggregate ceiling. The net result of these purchases added up to some 13 percent of DCM's voting equity; in contrast, the DCM promoter family held only 9 percent. The Indian financial Institutions led by government owned Life Insurance Corporation of India (LIC) owned some 52 percent of DCM's equity.

Sensing a potential takeover threat, the DCM board rejected the share transfer applications of the Caparo companies. Concurrently, Escorts (another major group in northern India) was also facing a similar situation with Caparo seeking to buy into their equity using the same processes; its board also rejected the share transfers on the ground that some of the investing companies were under investigation by government agencies. Given the commonality of facts and circumstances, Escorts took the legal route for judicial remedies with DCM playing an interested observer's role.

Escorts challenged, using numerous technical objections and even claiming bias and non-application of mind, the government's decision and Reserve Bank's concurrence that shares bought before 2 May, 1983 were not subject to the 5 percent ceiling; it was argued that, among others, such purchases by Caparo could not be regularized by a subsequent notification and that 'prior' permission was a must for them to be legitimate. At the High Court level, Escorts (and by analogy, DCM) won their point but their happiness was short lived since, on appeal by LIC, the Supreme Court overturned that decision in December 1985 and held such 'prior' permission was not specifically prescribed by, and could not be read into the legislation.

Thus cornered, DCM and Escorts were left with no alternative but to fall back upon their political connections. Vivek Bharat Ram sought the help of Rajiv Gandhi, who had taken over as Prime Minister following the assassination of his mother, Indira Gandhi. Reportedly, Rajiv Gandhi called Swraj Paul and *told* him to settle the matter out of court. Details of the settlement are not in public domain but the fact is Paul backed off and DCM (and Escorts) continued as before. Paul, who was close to Indira Gandhi and had often met Rajiv in this connection to salvage his infructuous investments, recalled the unstated change in the implementation of government policy and concluding 'there was no purpose in fighting the Prime Minister of India', decided to agree to a proposal to sell off with the assurance of no financial loss, which in the event never worked out; repatriation of his sale proceeds apparently took some ten years without any recompense for loss of interest or currency erosion.

This episode also offered much learning to corporate India, till then protected from contests for control, and treating corporations as personal fiefdoms that could be run with minimal promoter holdings. Many of them hurried to find ways of increasing their equity; on the flip side, the much propagated PIS failed to enthuse non-resident Indian investments in Indian corporations.

Source: Supreme Court, Bharat-Ram, Paul

Case summary 5.2: iGate Global Solutions
Merging Group Subsidiaries

iGate Global Solutions (IGS) went public in India in 2000 as Mascot Systems, a mid-tier software services company; like most others in the industry, Mascot sourced a predominant proportion of its business from the US. As part of the going-public process, its seven-member board had been broad based and strengthened by the induction of three prominent independent directors: an eminent banker who had retired as the chairman of India's largest commercial bank, a corporate lawyer with an international practice and reputation to match, and a corporate governance academic with significant industry experience at board levels. *Post* the public issue, the original promoters, Nasdaq-listed iGate Corporation (iGate) in the US, owned some 85 percent of its equity; the founding iGate chairman was also the chair of the Mascot board, which in addition had on it iGate's co-founder. Such high level participation in a subsidiary reflected the importance of Mascot's significant contribution to the Group's revenues and profits as much as its perceived potential in the context of Indian IT industry's exponential growth as a preferred outsourcing destination.

In 2002, iGate proposed, as part of its group businesses restructuring, merger of two of its wholly owned subsidiaries, eJiva and Aquaregia Technologies (Aquaregia) with IGS. This was followed by another similar proposal in 2004, seeking merger with IGS, another group subsidiary, Pittsburg-based Symphoni Interactive (Symphoni), a company offering Strategic Consulting Services, Technology Solutions, and Implementation Services which alone, accounted for almost 74 percent of revenue. IGS promoters felt there was a good strategic fit between the businesses of IGS and these three companies (except for a small segment of Symphoni which was eventually excluded) that offered synergies.

The key problem however was that the entire proposals were in the nature related party transactions since the three US subsidiaries were wholly owned by the controlling owners of IGS, which as an Indian listed company had several thousands of other absentee shareholders whose interests the IGS board had to protect. So, when the eJiva and Aquaregia proposals were brought up to the board for approval, the three independent directors desired to have the proposals objectively evaluated. Accordingly the board constituted a committee comprising the three independent directors who in turn appointed SBI Capital Markets (SBICM), a Category I merchant bank to do an independent valuation. SBICM's valuation report was duly presented to the committee who met in executive session without any other non-independent or interested directors or executives being present, and being satisfied recommended to the full board its acceptance. This healthy practice was repeated in 2004 when the Symphoni proposal was brought up to the board. By then the board and the promoter directors were accustomed to such independent evaluation as a good governance practice, and any unstated reservations that may have been felt in 2002 were no longer a problem. A similar committee of independent directors appointed SBICM again to evaluate the Symphoni proposal which was duly considered by the committee in executive session before being presented to the board for acceptance.

There were important takeaways for the company, the promoters and the independent directors. Not all related party transactions are biased against the non-controlling shareholders but such objective evaluations by the independent directors on the board assure shareholders that their interests are not only protected but are also demonstrably seen as being protected. It also meant that when independent directors insist on certain good practices as a measure of good governance with the consequent impact on the reputation of the company, the promoter directors generally tend to fall in line and get used to such scrutiny even though they may initially experience a measure of discomfort. After all, no promoter can be averse to the beneficial effect of such good practices on company reputation that eventually gets reflected in market valuations.

Source: Courtesy, Company Proprietary Documents

Case summary 5.3: RJR Nabisco and Ross Johnson

The year was 1988. On October 19, the day before a scheduled board meeting, Frederic Ross Johnson, R.J.R. Nabisco's President and CEO was hosting a dinner for his company's outside directors. It was here that Johnson informed his stunned board colleagues that he together with a few other senior executives was proposing a leveraged buyout of the $13 billion company, at the time trading at $55 a share. The formal proposal that followed a few days later indicated a purchase price of $75 per share. As in virtually all such management buyouts, Johnson was sanguine that it was his play and the board would accept it as a matter of course without too much of debate or disagreement. After all, he had ensured excellent personal relationships with the board members who had been pampered with pay and perquisites that were the envy of corporate America. And the offer price at a 36+ percent premium over market would be enthusiastically be welcomed by shareholders, a factor that should facilitate smooth board clearance. But he couldn't have been more wrong.

From the moment Johnson announced his intention of buying out the company, to Charles Hugel, the board chair (himself the CEO of a $3.5 billion company, Combustion Engineering) and his co-directors, Johnson ceased to be 'one of us' and became a greedy buyer with whom they had to negotiate in the best interests of the shareholders. This was evident at the dinner itself when Johnson and the directors who were potential buyers were asked to leave the rest of the board to discuss the matter; this positioning continued throughout the negotiations later on. The management contract Johnson had drafted and agreed with his reluctant investment bankers, Shearson Lehman did not help matters either: with an original management investment of a mere $20 million for 8.5 percent of the company, its members were to make $100 million over five years and come away with 18.5 percent of the equity, potentially worth billions if they could meet an ambitious set of operating targets. The management group comprised only six names besides Johnson's: Horrigan Jr, the head of R.J. Reynolds Tobacco; Welch Jr, chairman of Nabisco Brands; Robinson, the parent company's CFO; Henderson, chief counsel; Martin, an executive VP; and Sage II, an outside director. To the non-interested members of the board this was nothing short of too much for the too few and greed of the highest order. Also, given earlier estimates that placed the valuation at around $100 per share, Johnson's $75 offer betrayed an effort 'grabbing the company cheap' especially by a CEO who had failed in his two years of tenure to get the market valuations up anywhere near the best the company had ever had of some $72 per share.

Immediately after the fateful dinner, the board announced it was considering an offer of $75 per share from the management; this evoked interest from other potential buyers including Kohlberg, Kravis and Roberts (K.K.R.), who eventually won the battle with an offer of $109 comprising cash and payments in kind. This was slightly lower than the final management offer of $112. Because of the composition of the offers (cash, securities etc), the board's advisors came to the conclusion that both offers were 'substantially equivalent' and asked the board to take a call; board's choice was K.K.R.. Several possible reasons have been speculated upon for this board decision: the directors may have played safe to avoid any 'insider dealing' allegations of colluding with incumbent management; despite the cordial relationships between the CEO and the directors, they did not forgive him for the surprise he sprang on them on this deal; K.K.R. were much more flexible during negotiations than Johnson and his advisers; K.K.R.'s package gave shareholders a better opportunity for returns on the convertible securities because of the longer four-year time frame; K.K.R.'s plans were more employee friendly than Johnson's, who anyway had antagonized many old hands earlier by transferring headquarters to Atlanta from the tradition bound Winston-Salem where R.J.R continued to be the largest employer; the attempts of incumbent management to deny, delay and even distort information when asked for by K.K.R. and other bidders during the due diligence process; and finally, the directors could not forget Johnson's initial plans of buying the company cheap and the greed that shaped his management contract with Shearson Lehman even though it had been diluted significantly as the negotiations wore on.

Johnson not only lost the bid but also his job as the high profile, jet setting CEO of R.J.R. Nabisco since K.K.R. would not have him and his team in the post-acquisition scenario. The Winnipeg-born Canadian with his accounting background and business acumen that propelled his rise over the years had ultimately found his match in Hugel and his board colleagues who correctly chose to side with the shareholders than with executive management which attempted to expropriate to itself value that rightfully belonged to shareholders.

Case summary 5.4: Rajat Gupta, Raj Rajaratnam and Goldman Sachs

It was Friday, June 15, 2012. The Federal Court of the Southern District of New York, with Judge Jed Rakoff presiding, was in session with the packed court room waiting in hushed anticipation. The Jury of twelve, four men and eight women, had reached their verdict and the foreman reeled of a series of 'guilty' pronouncements on the different counts the accused was charged on. The unruffled defendant who in all his composed dignity intently listened to the verdict was Rajat Gupta, three-term head of the international consultancy McKinsey & Co., much sought after company director, philanthropist, and arguably the most successful Indian American. The charges related to alleged insider trading on non-public, price-sensitive information he was privy to as a director on the board of Goldman Sachs, among the biggest players in financial markets.

Raj Rajaratnam, a Sri Lankan American, was at that time the Managing General Partner of Galleon, among the largest hedge fund advisers and managers, and was counted among the richest in the US. As happens in securities trading, much of his success was due to his uncanny reading of markets and companies but more often based on privileged information not in public domain that he ferretted out from his wide network of friends and business associates. He was connected to Rajat through a common contact, Anil Kumar who was also from McKinsey. Rajat and Raj developed a business relationship that would eventually lead to Rajat investing heavily in hedge funds himself under Galleon management. That Raj was often less than faithful to Raja's interests was a matter of concern but not serious enough to break their friendship.

Among the several positions that Rajat held in the corporate world was his membership on the board of Goldman Sachs. In the wake of the global financial crisis that impacted virtually every financial institution, Goldman Sachs was facing difficult times with the prospect looming large of the company making a loss of $2 per share (the first loss in its history) during the quarter ended 28 November, 2008. As was his normal practice, Lloyd Blankfein, the CEO felt it necessary to keep his board informed and called for a meeting on 23 October, 2008, which Rajat joined by phone. 23 seconds after the meeting ended, Rajat called Raj and spoke for about 13 minutes. Galleon avoided potential losses of $3.80 million by exiting their positions in Goldman Sachs by the time the company announced the loss numbers on December 16.

Even more critical was the privileged information that the Goldman board was provided for their approval on 23 September, 2008 of the proposed investment of $5 billion by Warren Buffett's Berkshire Hathaway. Rajat was again participating by phone; he phoned Raj 16 seconds after the meeting call ended. In the five or six minutes left before closing time at New York Stock exchange that evening, Raj managed to buy over two lakh shares of Goldman and with stock prices shooting up after the public announcement after 4 pm, when the NYSE trading closed for the day, Raj made a profit of some $1.23 million. Taken together, these tip-based trades resulted in illegal gains to Galleon of over $5 million.

There was no evidence that Rajat personally made any profit on these transactions but the fact was that he had breached his fiduciary duty to the company and its shareholders. There were no recorded tapes of the conversations between Rajat and Raj directly proving inside information as described was indeed passed on but circumstantial evidence of the sequence of board meetings, Rajat's calls and Raj's trading actions was compelling. Judge Rakoff had no doubt that, 'Gupta, though not immediately profiting from tipping Rajaratnam, viewed it as an avenue to future benefits, opportunities and even excitement.' Rajat was sentenced to two years imprisonment and a fine of $5 million. The matter is under appeal and pending a decision, Rajat's jail sentence was kept in abeyance. Irrespective of what the final outcome of this litigation (and SEC's separate civil action), one fact stood out towering over everything else: his reputation as an inspiration to several hundred thousands of people he touched—with his competence, compassion, and compelling character—had taken a beating beyond repair. Whether he succeeds in appeal or has to serve his jail sentence, life for Rajat can never be the same again.

Source: Indictment and Sentencing Documents (2012), Raghavan (2013), Deb (2013)

CHAPTER 6

EXECUTIVE MANAGEMENT
The Doers

Sound corporate governance cannot exist without an active
CEO...committed to shareholders and their representatives
on the board.

—JOHN G. SMALE[1]

I

Interface with the Board

As noted earlier, executive management is responsible not only for assisting the board in its policy formulation role but also for ensuring that board-approved policies are implemented effectively and efficiently. Unlike the board that meets and deliberates at infrequent intervals, executive management is a full time ongoing activity that translates intent into action and thence to achievement. And yet, the executive is subordinate to the board, looking for, and helping to make policy, operating within the prescribed framework, and reporting back on performance. This interface between the board and the executive can be a complex affair, depending upon mutual understanding, trust and respect for the respective roles in the overall governance structure of the corporation.

CEO AND THE BOARD

Although there may be some merit in the perception that modern day CEOs are lionized to a surreal larger-than-life extent, there is no denying the fact that the leadership role of that position determines the course of progress and success of the corporation. Representing as they do the third critical component in the governance structure (besides shareholders and the board), the CEOs' importance in ensuring good governance in a corporation can never be overestimated. Former General Motors Chairman John Smale asserted, 'The responsibility for strengthening the board's oversight and advisory roles and the extent to which the board will be successful in fulfilling these duties still rest with one person—and that is the company's CEO.'[2] Some key aspects of a CEO's interface with the board and the directors individually are covered in the following discussion.

ACCEPTING THE BOARD AS THE BOSS

Theoretically and statutorily the suzerainty of the board over the company and its management is well established. But that does not guarantee that the CEO as the head of the operating dimensions of the company (with all the associated authority and the assured following) necessarily accepts the hierarchically superior positioning of the board in the corporation's governance structure. Nothing succeeds like success and the CEO understandably becomes the beneficiary of such success. For him or her to accept that the board is the boss is easier said than done. Explaining this phenomenon in the US, Millstein[3] recounts the strong performance US corporations in the post-war years with little competition from other countries. 'This lulled boards into doing little other than following senior management; ...handpicked [as they were] by the CEO from among friends, business associates and fellow country-club members, boards became less of a decision making-body and more of a social circle.' With boards thus willingly taking a back seat, the natural fallout was the ascendency of the CEO as the man (or woman) of consequence; by default, board primacy, neither demanded nor conceded, was the unfortunate casualty. Combining the positions of board chair and company CEO, with its potential for role confusion, further exacerbated this situation.

The problem is even more severe in countries like India with their predominance of family and concentrated ownership structures. The *de facto* supremacy of the promoter-CEO will rarely, if ever, be challenged. In either case, whether it is the dominant owner or a strongly performing professional CEO, the ultimate losers are the absentee shareholders and ironically, the CEOs themselves since they fail to benefit from the constructive inputs from the outside directors.

Kenneth Lay, the then-CEO of Enron, is quoted as saying in April 1999,

'What a CEO really expects from a board is good advice and counsel, both of which will make the company stronger and more successful; support for those investments and decisions that serve the interests of the company and its stakeholders; and warnings in those cases in which investments and decisions are not beneficial to the company and its stakeholders.'

Enron's board at that time had been described as a five-star board with a galaxy of directors with enviable credentials. Despite that and the unexceptional comments of Lay, Enron had to file for bankruptcy three years later. It would appear that Lay did not walk his talk and failed to take his board seriously, denying himself and his shareholders the benefit of their wisdom and counsel. On its part, the Enron board, in retrospect, appeared to have acquiesced with him and preferred to be led by, rather than lead the executive. To quote Nell Minow, the celebrated author and corporate governance activist, 'The key to assessing a board [and the CEO] is to look at what it actually does do' and not to be carried away by lofty expressions of what they ought to do.[4]

There are some developments, at least in the relatively well developed markets, that point to the beginning of a trend towards curtailing the unbridled power of the CEO to choose board members. The CEO would certainly be consulted but the decision to invite people on to the board is increasingly being taken by independent nomination committees. It will be quite some time perhaps before Indian boards reach that stage. A tentative beginning has been attempted in the Companies Act 2013 with the requirement of a mandatory nomination committee, but not its total independence.

None of this is to minimize the importance or the influence of the CEO in leading the company's operations towards delivering required results. Execution is of course the key to success, as we note later. And full responsibility for that along with required authority rests squarely with the CEO.

SOUNDING THE BOARD AS AN ADVISOR

Lonely at the top is an oft-quoted cliché but nowhere else is it more valid than when a CEO is making up his mind on some important strategic or operational issue. His executive team can of course be helpful to a point beyond which it may likely not venture to be seen as being overly critical or negative about a proposal credited to the CEO. The board is the ideal sounding board for such occasions—with the domain and experiential expertise the directors bring to the table, they would be the right choice for the CEO to seek advice from. Such consultations may take several forms. The CEO might table the proposal at a full board meeting and open it up for discussion. Alternatively, he might consider talking to the appropriate directors off-line seeking their views. Another forum for such discussions can be social occasions prior to the formal board meetings, over dinner or breakfast or even during breaks in the meetings themselves. As Stephen Kaufman, former CEO and non-executive board chair postulates, 'The one criterion that is important…is that the style [of discussion should] be conducive to real, open dialogue at some time and in some way.'[5] These are the occasions when directors are likely to be less formal than in a structured meeting and more relaxed to share their views freely.

It is often felt (and said) that CEOs with their resources and connections could easily hire consultants to advise them. Directors can, and ought to fit that bill and with a great difference—they and the CEO have a shared objective that is the good of the company and the interests of the shareholders, morally and legally. Successful and pragmatic CEOs never forget this rich source of support and counsel that is always freely available to them.

INFORMING THE BOARD

In governance discourse, a great deal of emphasis is laid on disclosure and information reporting to shareholders at large; similarly communications internally to the employees and externally to customers and other stakeholders have also received much attention. It is equally critical to ensure that the board is *informed* fully, frankly and promptly of all relevant facts and developments bearing upon matters requiring board concurrence or approval or decisions. An ill-informed or inadequately briefed board can hardly be expected to come out with quality decisions that would promote the interests of the company and its shareholders. What information needs to be provided to the board is always a subjective decision. The CEO representing the executive is the best judge to make a call, ensuring a balance between under-provision and over-loading of information. In effect, the executive's duty is to give the board what they need to know—in great detail if necessary—to execute oversight and counselling role, nothing more, nothing less. In this task, the CEO will be well advised to liaise with and obtain concurrence of the board chair since in the ultimate analysis it is the chair's call. Fraudulent holding back of information or deliberate misrepresentations in communications by the executive to the board should be distinguished from innocent inadequacies due to errors of judgement on the part of the CEO in deciding what information was appropriate for submission to the board. The latter can be corrected by supplementing the information during discussions especially if a vigilant board were to seek those additional inputs. But a successful CEO would preempt such information deficit situations arising at all.

CEOs should also remind themselves from time to time that outside directors meet infrequently during the year, maybe five or six times in case of Indian companies. Although engagement in between meetings is encouraged, there will be limits to how much meaningful time and effort outside directors could realistically devote. It is useful to provide a brief update at every meeting to bring directors to speed on company matters and developments.

ACCEPTING BOARD EXECUTIVE SESSIONS

The usefulness of outside directors meeting in executive sessions without the CEO or other management being present has already been discussed from a board perspective. How do CEOs respond to such meetings? Clearly, there would be many, especially promoter CEOs, who may not be comfortable with the idea of *their* company affairs being discussed without *them* being present. Partly this can be attributed to their fierce identification with their company but mostly this can also be a fall out of basic insecurity as to whether their communications to the board were being challenged or contradicted by others in the company. But there are also instances where CEOs have enthusiastically welcomed and encouraged such discussions; and cases where initially worried CEOs have come round to accepting such sessions as value adding.

A particularly striking example of the former category was the case of Union Bank of India, a top-ranking listed public sector bank: its Chairman and Managing Director, Leeladhar (who later served as a deputy governor of the Reserve Bank of India, the country's central banker) unhesitatingly accepted and endorsed the idea after a board presentation on good corporate governance.

ENCOURAGING BOARD EXPOSURE TO SENIOR EXECUTIVES

Behind every successful company and its CEO, there is a supporting management team. While the board would naturally be concerned with the succession of the CEO, development and career planning of the second and even third level reports is critical for the long term survival and prosperity of the company. The CEO should be actively involved in this process and share the strengths and weaknesses in the management support team with the board. One of the ways of developing senior managers is to expose them to board scrutiny and processes. Top management should be invited to attend board meetings entirely or in part (barring of course during confidential discussions) and to make presentations and answer queries from the directors.

The added advantage of this practice is two fold—the executives get a first hand feel of how the board approaches their issues and the directors get to assess for themselves the depth of management in the organization.

II

Strategy Formulation and Performance

A major area of contention in the governance discourse is the turf war between the role of the board and the executive on matters concerning corporate strategy. Clearly the board as the final arbiter in a company has the responsibility and the authority, to review, challenge, and approve strategy but equally, it is the prerogative of the executive to initiate and formulate strategy for board discussion and endorsement. But it is the CEO, with his or her team, who has to develop strategies in line with the purpose of the corporation and present them for board concurrence. Thereafter, it is the CEO's call to implement such approved strategies effectively and efficiently. In this task, the importance and contribution of the supporting staff and front line managers can never be overestimated, although it is not unusual to assign credit to the CEO for every success. A rare recognition of the team effort involved in successful corporate performance is offered by an Emerson Electric axiom: 'What leaders accomplish is the result of what other people do.'[6]

Exhibit 6.1: Strategy formulation and implementation Cycle

Phase	Objective	Activities / Initiatives
I	Formulate Strategies	• Top Management discussion on strategic issues • Challenges to assumptions to be addressed satisfactorily • Strategy formulation for board approval

II	Obtain Board Concurrence	<ul><li>Circulate strategy proposals to directors</li><li>If necessary sound out directors with domain expertise</li><li>Present proposals to the board, address questions satisfactorily</li><li>Obtain approval with or without modifications</li></ul>
III	Implement Approved Strategy	<ul><li>Communicate strategy to implementers with clarity</li><li>Attend to operational details and delegate responsibilities</li><li>Recognize challenges in communicating to multi-cultural, multi-linguistic and multi-geographic audiences</li></ul>
IV	Monitor and Evaluate Performance	<ul><li>Internally review implementation progress and results periodically</li><li>In multi-layered, multi-locational implementation, structure pyramidal reviews, reaching to the top in stages</li><li>Offer course corrections as necessary</li><li>Evaluate performance critically and prepare for board presentation</li></ul>
V	Report to Board	<ul><li>Present to board for performance review</li><li>Obtain feedback, course corrections, etc. for further action</li></ul>

A robust process of strategy formulation, implementation, and performance is key corporate success. Often, entrepreneurs and iconic CEOs are known to generate great ideas inspirationally but much of their success in practice is dependent upon how cost and time effectively their ideas can be translated into scalable performance.

Exhibit 6.1 sets out the five phases of the strategy formulation and implementation cycle. In particular, the executive may find the following experiential guidelines helpful

- Especially in case of major strategic initiatives, detailed preparatory work will be key in developing a robust strategic proposal. Internal debate on assumptions, freedom and indeed encouragement to challenge, and options to consider alternative approaches are all hallmarks of a robustly founded strategy proposal

- Board approval, after presentation and due debate, is a necessary part of any strategic initiative unless it is part of an already approved overall strategy

- Even the most well thought out strategies may fail to yield desired results if not clearly communicated to the rank and file charged with their implementation on the ground. Jack Welsh's dictum, 'communicate, and then communicate again' sums up the challenges involved in effective communication

- Periodical review of performance is an essential part of the cycle to assess the success or failure of decided strategies on the ground—'where the rubber meets the road'—as well as also in identifying and implementing any course corrections based on such experience. Reviews at the base operating levels, going up to divisional, subsidiary or associate, country or region levels, and finally at corporate levels at the top are a must in case of major strategic initiatives

- Finally, the outcomes of the initiatives will need to be presented to the board for their information, any course corrections and other feedback, for further course of actions

STRATEGIES UNLIMITED

Although one generally talks about strategy in a composite connotation, in practice it embraces a bundle of sub-strategies covering various aspects of the business and its diverse ramifications. Some of these are now briefly explored, particularly bearing upon on the role of the executive in formulating and implementing them. The focus here is on issues directly concerned with the shareholders, the board, and the executive, all at different levels of ownership and control layering; and also to an extent on issues bearing upon other stakeholders as well the corporate interface with public policy. Clearly, the listing is not exhaustive and both the content and context would vary in individual circumstances.

Corporation Strategies

This group largely comprises strategies adopted by promoters and corporate groups in respect of structuring their controlled businesses in a variety of ownership patterns. The overarching purpose would usually be to exercise maximum control over enterprise assets and resources consistent with minimal risk to the ultimate controllers. Risk mitigation strategies would include considerations relating to business risks (more risky ventures would ideally be sited in entities with lower ownership stakes), country or political risks (especially in case of multinationals that would wish to minimize their ownership stakes consistent with their ability to control the overseas subsidiary or associate), currency and taxation risks (with profits and cash surpluses being moved out of high taxation and weak currency jurisdictions), and environmental risks (with older, unsafe or inefficient technologies being deployed in developing and underdeveloped countries with poor environmental laws and poorer or corrupt enforcement records), and so on. The executive role in formulating these strategies and implementing them to the maximum advantage of the ultimate controllers is usually confined to the top executive managements of such corporations under the directions of their boards. In this process many of them may, and in fact do, enroll the top executive managements of the host country for its local knowledge and for facilitating local approval processes. As we have seen earlier, the local executives' primary responsibility is to the local entity and its shareholders; so long as their contribution to these corporation strategies of their parents are not inimical to the interests of the local company and its shareholders and other stakeholders, the situation can be a win-win for both the parent and the child, but that is easier expected than actually achieved [Case summary 6.1: Holcim, Ambuja Cements and ACC].

Growth Strategies

Growth is achieved by expanding and extending the market footprint of a company with regard to its geographical spread, product or service range, or a combination of both. While growth can be planned organically within the company, often it is relatively easier to achieve growth objectives faster by acquiring an existing business either in a friendly or a hostile bid. Many multinationals entering another host country adopt this strategy, if not by outright acquisition, by partnering with local established businesses, and over a period buying the local partners out if possible. In countries like India, where distribution logistics and networks may take time and effort, partners with such established structures offer a quick-fix solution so that together the joint venture (with or without local outside shareholder participation) can 'hit the ground running' and drastically cut time to market. In proposing any merger or acquisition of another business or company, the executive of the acquiring company must satisfy itself on the strategic fit of the target candidate with its own objectives. Such inorganic growth does usually bring in numerous other advantages, among them new or enhanced market access, cultivated customer base, enhanced production capacity, continuing regulatory permissions, assured input sources, skilled human resources, proprietary technologies, and so on. Often, acquisitions also dilute competition significantly, with consequent benefits on both the pricing and marketing cost dimensions. All these benefits, of course, come at a price and the acquiring entity must assure itself that despite the (often apparently unreasonable) premium paid for such acquisitions, the synergies would be so much better utilised that the combined entity's shareholder value maximization performance will not be impaired on a long-term basis [**Case summary 6.2: Tata Motors and Jaguar Land Rover**].

Parenting Strategies

The moment a company ceases to be a single location, single product entity, as an inescapable corollary a central controlling outfit comes in to being, variously called corporate office, head office, headquarters, central functions and so on. Often these central units are seen, particularly by business units which believe they alone were actually creating value for the corporation, as value guzzling functions contributing little to the business efforts of creating value. Following this logic, many corporations (GE in the US for example) set out aggressively to reduce corporate staff and decentralize most of the central functions to business units themselves. This was of course in direct contrast to the earlier strongly-held belief (for example at ICI in the UK) that central functions were an indispensable part of the overall command structure with all strategic directions and financial controls being initiated and their implementation by business units being monitored for reporting to top management and boards of their respective companies.

Despite such negative impressions, the fact remains that a coordinating agency (akin to the human body's central nervous system) as a repository of corporate-wide knowledge and driver of business performance of the composite corporate entity has its benefits, if the inherent tendency to proliferate and feed on itself can be effectively contained. That such an activity at the centre carried out by the CEO and his immediate advisors can add value by interventions and contributions has been established beyond doubt. Equally of course, corporate history is replete with value-destroying strategies handed down by central functions for example the bifurcation in 1993 of ICI into Zeneca (comprising pharmaceuticals and specialty chemicals) and residual ICI (retaining bulk chemicals) that possibly triggered the downward slide of UK's corporate jewel that ICI once was.

Boarding Strategies

There is yet another area of strategizing that relates to matters involving selection and appointment of board members. As seen earlier, populating the board with requisite expertise is the function of the board itself through its nomination committee but seldom do boards totally exclude or ignore the preferences and suggestions of the CEO while deciding upon the 'slate' of directors. In case of promoter controlled companies boards seem to have little say in who from the controlling family or group may get on to the board, either as executives or non-executives.

As important as having the right numbers and people on the board is, often it is equally critical to executive management (and to promoter groups) to decide as well on whom not to have on the board. This phenomenon can be observed in companies controlled by feuding family factions and warring joint promoters [**Case summary 6.3: Yes Bank**]. Easing out co-promoters, discarded siblings or cousins, and inconvenient co-directors is an age old practice, not limited to family groups alone.

III

Risk, Internal Control, and Assurance

Businesses normally expect to continue and grow indefinitely until such time the market for their products and services shrink and eventually disappear, unless the business itself is based on a finite timeframe such as in case of extractive industries like mining. The executive's task is to protect and enhance the business on what is known as the 'going concern' basis, where barring unforeseen circumstances, the enterprise continues to survive and prosper. The objective of the board and the executive is to protect the company from internal and external risks through structured mechanisms of risk identification and mitigation, and aided by internal control systems and regular assurance feedback processes.

RISK AND ITS MANAGEMENT

Business inherently is subject to a variety of risks, partly from the general and political ambience and more importantly, from its own vulnerabilities to 'attacks' on its survival, by factors such as technological obsolescence, competitive forces, cost disadvantages, and so on. In addition, there are also risks of loss of the company's tangible and intangible assets. There are risks arising from inadequate and even total non-compliance of legislative and regulatory mandates. And perhaps most importantly, from the viewpoint of the executive, there can be risks of contests for management control by hostile bidders if the company is perceived to be not effectively managed in the interests of shareholders at large.

The task of executive management is to ensure that all risks that can adversely impact its continued survival are timely identified and cost-effectively managed. Inherently, many of the risks do not lend themselves to easy identification but that challenge also presents an opportunity to far-seeing managements to differentiate themselves from others not so well endowed.

The second stage in the risk management process involves the impact of the risk event should it happen on the company's viability. Impact itself is a function of two components: the probability of the event happening, and the extent of its financial or other effect on the company. Most companies would totally ignore identified risks if they score low both on probability and adverse impact; and certainly protect themselves if both scores were high. The other two quadrants in the matrix, low probability-high impact and high probability-low impact would possibly be addressed with reference to the costs of risk mitigation arrangements.

At a corporate level, companies also seek to diversify risk by an appropriate mix of high-medium-low businesses in their portfolio if that were possible. Also, companies could choose to address risk in several ways: they can exit the risky investment if covering risk is far too expensive, they can share or pass on risk to a willing third party (such as an insurer wholly or on a part-bear and part-insure basis), they can hedge risks at a cost (as in currency or commodity hedging), or accept the risk as part of the business where the risk-adjusted rewards are deemed acceptable or even attractive (such as in portfolio investments by foreign institutional investors or in doing business in a country with high political risk), and so on. At all times though, it will be a calculated call balancing the probable adverse impact and the costs of acceptance, mitigation or exit.

The other key consideration is to be well within the acceptable risk criteria prescribed by the board. If there are opportunities for attractive risk-adjusted rewards, the right course for the executive would be to draw the board's attention and seek/ obtain their concurrence to such deviations on a temporary or more permanent basis. Not doing so may be not only injurious to the corporation but also lead to potential fiduciary breach litigation [**Case summary 6.4: Lehman Bros**].

INTERNAL CONTROL AND ASSURANCE

The executive is tasked with the responsibility of carrying out the operations of the business in such a manner to create value in line with the policies and strategies laid down by the board. In the discharge of this responsibility, there are two key dimensions: protecting creatable and created wealth and protecting wealth-creating assets, both tangible and intangible. Among the responsibilities of the board, as noted earlier, these are included as part of its oversight obligations. It is the executive, though, that has to install and operate the necessary systems of internal control to achieve these objectives and provide necessary assurance to the board.

Among the various control models or frameworks that have been developed in the last two decades and more, the COSO framework from the US has received wide support and acceptance. Individual audit firms in India rely upon their international affiliations, where available, for updating some of the techniques they adopt for such evaluations. Many Indian firms engaged in Sarbanes-Oxley compliance work for the subsidiaries and outsourced work of parent companies listed in the US do apply the COSO model for verifying internal control adequacy.

The executive should be particularly wary of the efficacy of internal control mechanisms across the organization which is vulnerable to managerial override. What this means is that while the control measures may well be in place, it is possible that local managers with their line authority seek to override such controls to achieve their limited local objectives (as for example in splitting payments to keep individual amounts within authorized limits). Many of these may be detected during routine audit checks but equally they may also escape such detection since audits will be done generally on test check basis. Top management has to rely on good gatekeeping systems where accounting staff do not yield to such breaches in the control systems and maintain the integrity of the overall control mechanisms. The professional integrity and independence of such staff should be encouraged and respected if full benefits are to be realized from the control framework.

INTERNAL AUDIT

A major instrument of surveillance and assurance to the executive and the board audit committee is an independent, competent and proactive internal audit function in the company. This is probably one of the most underestimated and under-utilised functions in companies, often considered too routine and largely obstructionist. Barring a few notable exceptions, this function likely exists in many Indian corporations essentially because of a statutory requirement.

What is Internal Audit?

A generally accepted modern definition of internal auditing positions it as 'an independent, objective assurance and consulting activity designed to add value and improve an organization's operations', and is considered as helping the 'organization accomplish its objectives by bringing a systematic, disciplined approach to evaluate and improve the effectiveness of risk management, control and governance processes.' The function is no longer confined to 'within the organization', and depending upon cost and expertise factors, especially in relation to the size of the organization, can be outsourced to competent agencies. The role is no longer just appraisal; it has moved up the scale to 'assurance' and now includes 'consulting services' in relation to the assurance function, again a step further up the value chain of internal audit contribution.

The function's objectivity and independence must be ensured at all times so that unbiased and fully professional feedback is available to the CEO and top management as well as to the board and the audit committee. This can be facilitated by the following measures.

- The appointment and continuance of the chief of audit (or the firm, if externally done) must be the responsibility of the audit committee, which should also determine both the scope of audit work and the remuneration

- The audit firm or the in-house chief of audit should report to the audit committee and have an opportunity to meet the committee members without any executive management or directors being present; similarly, the CEO should have a one-on-one session with the audit head without any audited department or division heads being present so that free and open communication of concerns and other sensitive issues can be communicated to the CEO

Value Addition by Internal Audit

A key ingredient of internal audit is its potential to add value to the organization. There is no value-add if the internal audit function in a company were merely to duplicate external audit tasks, even on an extended scale. Value addition will arise when the function reviews all operations according to a risk-based plan approved by the board audit committee and recommends better management practices that would lead to operational improvements. These initiatives could be taken by the internal audit function on its own under the guidance of the audit committee. While conventional auditing activities such as protecting company assets and procedural compliances will continue to be an ongoing part of the function, its value-adding potential would be considerably strengthened when it is used in addressing risk identification and management issues faced by the company. Due to the wide scope of the function and its continuity, it gains an accumulated fund of knowledge and insights concerning the company's operations, its culture and appetite for control, and even staff competencies over a period of time. When this knowledge base is constructively applied to the problems of the company and their possible resolution, this can be a strong comfort factor for the CEO and the company board, as it enables reporting on control effectiveness on an ongoing basis as opposed to statutory audits that are usually confined to an after-the-event reporting based on historical data.

The board and the audit committee can significantly contribute to strengthening the image of the company's internal audit function, with concomitant benefits accruing to themselves and executive management. An audit report or an assurance consultant could at best flag deviant behaviour and control failures in the organization. If the board, its audit committee and top management fail to take due note of the warning signals and initiate remedial action, the control system itself can do little to stem the rot. The CEO and the board audit committee should make adequate time to deal with control and systems related issues; such detailed attention will also be a signal to executive management and the organizational rank and file, that the CEO, the board and its committees take control matters seriously—a message that can only strengthen the respect for, and improve the prospects of compliance with, laid down processes and rules of conduct of business.

Case summary 6.1: Holcim, Ambuja Cements and ACC

Holcim, founded in Switzerland in 1912 and with a 2012 sales revenue of 21 billion Swiss Francs, is one the world's leading suppliers of cement and aggregates as well as further activities such as ready-mixed concrete and asphalt including services. Its global footprint covers some seventy countries where it has a majority or minority presence. In India, Holcim operates through two (listed and publicly traded) majority held companies, Ambuja Cements (50.59 percent), with a 2013 market capitalization of Rs 29300 crores) and ACC (50.30 percent), with a 2013 market capitalization of Rs 23200 crores). For various tax and other regulatory reasons,

---

Holcim's investments in the two subsidiaries were partly routed through a Mauritius-based, wholly owned subsidiary, Holcim India which held 9.77 percent in Ambuja and 50.01 percent in ACC. In 2013, Holcim planned a restructuring of its India operations that would simplify its Indian investment structures and also bring about greater synergies in operations and performance of both the companies. Given that ACC and Ambuja had their own history and culture besides strong brands and distribution capabilities, the plan was not to forego their independent identities but work towards greater collaboration and coordination for mutual benefit.

As part of this plan, Ambuja announced in July 2013 its intention to acquire 24 percent of Holcim India, and follow it up with acquisition of the remaining 76 percent in Holcim India by issue of fresh Ambuja shares at a swap rate determined by two independent valuers and certified as fair by a merchant banker, as required by Indian regulations. The 'appointed' effective date for the merger scheme was 1 April, 2013, subject to various shareholder and regulatory clearances and approvals. Holcim India's only assets were its holdings in Ambuja and ACC, and based on their respective market prices, the valuations and swap rates were considered reasonable from the viewpoint of Ambuja's shareholders. When completed, Holcim India would cease to exist, its Ambuja holdings would be cancelled, and the resultant holdings of Holcim in Ambuja would be 61.39 percent and in ACC would be same as before at 50.30 percent , with the only change that its holdings of 50.01 percent would be through Ambuja instead of Holcim India.

This transaction, according to Holcim CEO Bernard Fontana, was 'expected to generate synergy benefits of Rs 9,000 million (USD 150 million) per annum. ...will be realized in a phased manner over two years, will be shared by both companies equally through supply chain, shared services and fixed costs optimization.'

What was left unsaid was that the parent would also benefit from a cash inflow of Rs 3500 crores from Ambuja, besides tax advantages on the transaction.

This of course was the most contentious issue in the transaction, from the perspective of Ambuja's 191000 shareholders who held the remaining 49.99 percent of Ambuja's equity. Their principal concern would be the rationale and reasonableness of the controlling shareholders, Holcim, appropriating for itself Rs 3500 crore of Ambuja's cash in this process, when a much simpler and more direct option would have been to let Ambuja buy its 51.01 percent stake in ACC by a share swap issue of additional Ambuja shres to the holding company. All Ambuja had to do was to acquire 100 percent of Holcim India at the same agreed valuation in return for equivalent Ambuja shares value in Ambuja. Of course, in this alternative Ambuja's minority shareholders would have suffered a little more dilution of their holding compared to the company's proposals but that may have been more acceptable since Rs 3,500 crore would not have flown out of Ambuja's coffers. Not a small sum considering that amount represented almost the entire cash surplus with the company at that time and would have been handy in part-funding its expansion plans (as articulated by the company) involving over Rs 10,000 crore over the next two to three years.

In all this protracted deal arrangements, what was the role of the board, especially of the independent directors while considering and approving the proposals? Was there enough timely communication to Ambuja board members? Media reports seemed to indicate that may not have been the case, with some outside directors also confirming, anonymously, they had no such information until the board meeting; in response to queries based on market speculation, Holcim itself had denied there were any such proposals under their consideration to bring their two subsidiaries together, just three weeks prior to the board decision.

For Holcim in Switzerland, overburdened by heavy debt, the proposed scheme was indeed most ideal. It gave it access to a sizeable chunk of cash, the transaction was tax-efficient since the investments were routed through Mauritius which had an extremely pass-through investor friendly regime and tax treaty with India, and it brought in the much needed rationalization of its two major cement investments in the country.

The minority shareholders including institutional investors could express their concern and dissent but will be overruled by the majority voting power of Holcim. Of course, the situation would be different if the Companies Act 2013 is brought into force by the time these proposals are processed, since it would have disenfranchised Holcim from voting on such resolutions as interested shareholders in a related party transaction. And yet, Holcim has still to navigate through various regulatory hurdles like approvals from the capital market regulator SEBI, the Foreign Investment Promotion Board, and the country's central bank, Reserve Bank of India already saddled with depleting foreign currency reserves in the wake of the economic downturn worldwide. Would all this help in protecting minority shareholders' interests?

Source: Web Sites Holcim, Ambuja, and Stakeholder Empowerment Services

Case summary 6.2: Tata Motors and Jaguar Land Rover

Streamer media headlines on 9 August, 2013 'JLR keeps Tata Motors in the Black' would have been music to the ears for former chairman of Tata Motors, Ratan Tata, who passionately and almost single-handedly championed and drove the $2.3 billion acquisition of Jaguar Land Rover (JLR) completed on 2 June, 2008. Because there had been no dearth of critics in India and elsewhere who made no secret of their scepticism of the Tata buy. Ranging from Tata's commitment to continuity and doubts on Tata competence to succeed where Ford had failed, to the hostility on potential migration of manufacture to lower-cost India and doubts on the British acceptability of their marque brands being sold by an Indian company, questions at a round table for media reporters in Geneva on 4 March, 2008 on the sidelines of the famous annual motor show were direct and biting. Ratan Tata's soft-spoken responses, at once disarming and persuasive, would be an object lesson to speakers facing an unfriendly, if not positively hostile audience.

There are two parts to the Tata-JLR story, one each on either side. Tata Motors was an established, well-respected auto manufacturer, with significant presence both in cars and commercial trucks. While Tata trucks have been a prominent feature on Indian roads for ages, its entry into the passenger car business was relatively recent, only in the late nineteen nineties, with the introduction of the lower end *Indica* and the middle segment *Indigo*. In 2008, the ultra-small *Nano* was rolled out. These cars gradually began to establish themselves against stiff competition from the Japanese Suzuki which had an early mover advantage by several years. Although Tata Motors had a global footprint with facilities and sales outlets in several countries, its international image (along with the rest of the Indian car manufacturers) was that of a low cost car maker from a poor developing country known for its indifferent quality and safety standards.

On the other hand, JLR was British, although then owned by the American car major Ford, their cars were positioned as marque products with price tags in excess of £100,000, a connoisseur's preferred choice. Its place was at the top of this prestigious league in the company of the likes of BMW, Volvo and Mercedes. No matter its fortunes had been diving south for some years, to an extent that Ford (with its own problems) had to decide on putting JLR on the block. When it came to bidding, Tata Motors was the only car maker in the ring in the final stages (Mahindra and Mahindra having withdrawn after initial interest), besides a few other private equity bidders including one headed by a former Jaguar and Ford chief.

Tata's reputation as a responsible corporation is built over a century commencing from 1887 when Jamsetji Tata, Ratan's great grandfather, set up Tata Sons, which today is the group's parent entity (not holding company since it does not hold a majority stake in any of its close to one hundred group companies) housed in its unprepossessing headquarters building in Fort, Mumbai. Tata Sons is owned by a number of charitable trusts created by successive generations of the Tata clan, and to that extent most of the profits made by the company and distributed as dividends find their way to fund social and educational causes. The group's record of social work is well recognized and documented. So much so, after the Tata Motors presentations, Unite, JLR workers union, unhesitatingly announced Tata Motors was its preferred bidder; in the event, JLR management, after rounds of presentations and discussions also came to the same conclusion. Apart from the fact the Tata Motors bid matched the best offer price, their commitment to retain manufacturing in Britain, to support and grow the marque brands, and let the company retain it British pedigree and identity all helped to clinch the deal.

Was an acquisition like JLR part of a well thought out strategy of Tata Motors? Maybe, it wasn't. Responding to media questions in March 2008 at Geneva, Ratan Tata confirmed, 'We were not on the prowl to acquire another car company,' and, 'We were invited to bid and were pleased to be considered.' What did Tata Motors have to gain by the acquisition of such a high-end car company while its own positioning was way down on the scale? Clearly, there was nothing much in terms of technology, design, or components from JLR that Tata Motors could use with advantage, nor were there any such benefits to JLR from the parent. But this apparent deficiency was turned on its head and converted into an opportunity to let JLR be run by its own people without any impositions from the parent, a practice that was successful in producing committed results even while generating respect and endearment at JLR towards its owners. But as Ravi Kant, Tata Motors Managing Director is quoted as saying, 'In the companies we acquire, we keep management independent—but accountable. 'Hands off' is not the same thing as 'left alone'; it does not mean we are not involved. We challenge and critique—and ask hard questions, especially where there is a need for finance. We understand our responsibility. Once a plan is finalized we see that it is delivered.'

The first years were indeed difficult, compounded by the economic downturn following the global financial meltdown. Billions were required to keep the design and development effort going even as others were cutting down. Tata helped with funding locally and from overseas even under tight market conditions (helped by its 'safe and solid' financial branding that attracted the financial community to lap up its equity offerings), despite media pessimism in the UK on the company's prospects. This strategy handsomely paid off when economies began to rebound, and JLR was there ready to cash in.

Five years down the line, JLR is prospering. Revenues have moved up from £4.45 bn in 2008–09 to £12.52 bn in 2011–12; profit before tax from negative £376 mn to positive £1.5 bn; volumes have moved up from 286,880 to 357,773, recovering from a dip to 196,226 in 2009 due to the global downturn following the financial meltdown. In the £100,000+ Premium brand league, it is ranked sixth on the basis of 2012 sales, behind BMW, Audi, Mercedes, Lexus and Volvo.

The impact of Tata strategy, first in winning the battle for owning JLR and then in guiding and nurturing the company through the tough times that followed, was beginning to unravel; in the first fiscal quarter ended 30 June 2013, the parent on a stand-alone basis reported a profit of Rs 703 crore against Rs 205 crore in corresponding quarter in 2012. But this would not have been the case without the JLR difference: included in the parent's 2013 figures were dividends from JLR of Rs 1421 crores, shoring up and off-setting a weak domestic performance. This is perhaps a successful exception to the time-tested wisdom that more mergers and acquisitions fail than succeed!

Based on media reports, company web sites, Witzel (2010), and Hutton (2013)

Case summary 6.3: Yes Bank

It was a tragic and untimely demise during the 26/11 terrorist attacks in Mumbai that visited Ashok Kapur, the joint promoter of Yes Bank along with Rana Kapoor, a new generation bank that was soon to figure among the fastest growing banks in India. Both were closely related; they also had years of banking experience. Ashok had spent close to three decades with Grindlays Bank and held positions such as General Manager—Institutional Banking and managing director of Grindlays Merchant Bank of Nigeria. Other banking assignments included stints with ABN Amro as an executive vice president and regional manager at Singapore and country head for India, and later as managing director of Rabo

India in partnership with Rabo Bank of Netherlands, before setting up and joining Yes Bank as its non-executive chairman in 2003.

Rana Kapoor also had a pedigreed career in banking before co-promoting and joining Yes Bank as its CEO and managing director in 2003. He served as general manager and country head of ANZ Grindlays Bank (1996–98) and prior to that spent 15 years with Bank of America in several senior positions and winning awards and accolades. A more appropriately qualified and experienced pair of professionals to promote and operate a bank to world class standards will indeed be hard to find.

Each promoter held 26.125 percent of the equity with Rabo Bank holding 20 percent of the initial equity capital. Much of the rest of equity was funded by three private equity players and a few other professional managers in the bank. A third promoter, Harkirat Singh soon opted out abruptly before the bank had begun its business. In 2006 the bank was taken public with an IPO, soon after followed by some private placements; as a result the promoters' holdings came down. Meantime, Rabo Bank also exited the company.

Board composition was an issue specifically addressed in the Articles of Association of the company. Indian promoters together had the right to recommend three directors and also the right to propose the first three independent directors. Besides, they could also recommend the chairman and the managing director of the bank. Ashok and Rana were to be the chairman and the managing director respectively. Regulatory requirements however require these appointments could only be made with the approval of Reserve Bank of India; although company charters could not override regulatory or legislative mandates, these provisions were obviously intended to govern the rights between the promoters and together between them and the company.

After the unfortunate demise of Ashok in 2008, Rana felt he was the only surviving promoter and all the rights under these arrangements vested in him to be exercised at his discretion. Madhu Kapur, Ashok's widow, however had other ideas and wanted her daughter, Shagun Gogia to be appointed as a director on the bank's board, as a matter of promoter's right. The bank board rejected the request (likely at the behest of Rana) on the ground that she did not meet the 'fit and proper' criteria for bank directors laid down by the Reserve Bank of India. Whether or not this was a correct call on the part of the board is open to debate; if that was the only reservation, maybe the board could have appointed her and left it to the central bank to decide on her suitability for the position. But clearly there was more to the rejection than was put out in public domain. It would also have implied that Ashok's family, after his death, was entitled to be classified as promoters and inherit all the rights of promoters in terms of the company's Articles. That was what Madhu wanted to have established, and clearly Rana did not.

Ashok's family had also nurtured a grievance that Ashok's contribution to the formation and subsequent success of the bank had not been given the rightful credit due. Rana had allegedly sidelined Ashok's family even to the extent that its shareholdings were removed from the 'promoters' classification in company disclosures. Frustrated, Madhu took the matter to court seeking redress, and the matter is now *sub judice*.

The principal issue in this battle is whether any contractual rights of a 'promoter' survive after his or her death; in essence, whether such rights are 'property' that can be inherited by successors. If the judicial view is affirmative, then Madhu and her family will inherit the rights agreed to between the original promoters and the company. If the court's decision goes against such inheritance, it might queer the position of many other business families. Most of the present day shareholders in the private sector family controlled corporations are actually second and third generation inheritors and their shareholdings are all categorized as 'promoter' holdings for regulatory purposes. In that case, only first generation promoters would qualify as such; to protect any contractual rights of the promoters opposite their companies, they may have to incorporate themselves and hold their stakes in the name of their wholly owned private companies or trusts, as many promoters perhaps already do.

While this drama for a slice of control-related benefits is being played out, the company and its shareholders are suffering erosion of value; losses on a company-wide basis have been estimated at some Rs 2,000 crore. Shouldn't the independent directors on the board step in and resolve these issues quickly in the interests of the company and its absentee shareholders? Do or don't the regulators (in this case both the Reserve Bank of India and Securities and Exchange Board of India) have any right or obligation to intervene? Will the aggrieved shareholders have any legal recourse for their value losses against the board under the 'class action' provisions of the Companies Act 2013?

There was also another dimension impacting the company and its shareholders—under such circumstances a potential hostile takeover is not an unlikely threat, especially given the low stakes held by the (present) controlling promoter, something the incumbent executive cannot afford to overlook.

Source: Media reports and bank web site

Case summary 6.4: Lehman Bros

At 1.45 a.m. on 15 September, 2008, Lehman Brothers Holdings (Lehman), the fourth largest investment bank in the US filed for Chapter 11 protection, in what was then the largest ever bankruptcy in US history. The bankruptcy Judge, James Peck, for the Southern District of New York who was hearing the case commented, 'Lehman Brothers became a victim. In effect, the only true icon to fall in the tsunami that has befallen the credit markets. And it saddens me.' He was probably reflecting the sentiment of millions of Americans who had been touched by the century and a half plus old institution that had been part of the American dream. But then, the question, to which of course there are no easy answers, is why was that tragedy allowed to happen?

Human greed has been cited as the major reason for the misfortunes the global financial sector inflicted not only upon themselves but also on the rest of the population. Untold misery has been the lot of peoples and countries, in varying degrees, and five years since, most of them still struggling to get back to a measure of normalcy. Granted that 'performance' based executive compensation had led to enormously large pay packages and that motivation could have been an important contributory to what happened especially in the financial world, shouldn't there have been enough countervailing checks and balances in the system to mitigate if not totally eliminate such self-destructing activities of the corporate sector? After all, as has been witnessed, the consequences of such irresponsible actions are not limited to those who perpetrated them but passed on as externalities to the society as a whole and all the other stakeholders.

Running any business is a risky proposition, the extent of risk varying under different circumstances; and this is particularly so in the banking and other financial intermediation businesses where by definition firms operate on high financial gearing ratios. In the US, the Glass-Steagal Act had pegged the banks' borrowings to no more than twelve times their equity; but investment banks had approached the capital markets regulator, Securities and Exchange Commission in 2004 to seek relaxation of these salutary restrictions and indeed obtained the limits changed such they could borrow up to 40 times their equity funds. With that kind of leveraging, Wall Street firms did produce spectacular results (on which their compensation was based!) so long as the financing strategy worked; when it failed, this was also an invitation to disaster.

Lehman maintained approximately $700 bn of assets on a capital base of $25 bn. As noted Professor Luigi Zingales testified to a House Committee on Oversight and Reform in October 2008, with that kind of leverage, 'a mere 3.3 percent drop in the value of assets wipes out the entire value of equity and makes the company insolvent.' This was the price that Lehman had to pay when their mortgages and their derivative instruments turned toxic because of the inherent sub-prime values they were built upon. Some of the risks that (in retrospect) were not sufficiently well managed were the following

- To begin with, as noted above, Lehman operated at very high financing leverage levels, hovering over 40:1, an obvious financing risk management should have been aware of
- The mismatch in the timeframes between their assets and liabilities—their assets were essentially longer term mortgages while their liabilities were predominantly short term borrowings, routinely rolled over but highly risky if not renewed

In this strategy, Lehman funded itself every day through the *repo* markets and borrowed tens and hundreds of billions of dollars from counter parties to open for business. This was a trust-and-confidence based method of financing where assets are 'sold' to raise funds on the promise of 'purchasing' them back to repay, with an interest component included.

Lehman management was 'excessively' risk-attracted in return theoretically for higher rewards. Thus for example, when toxicity of sub-prime mortgaged instruments drove other competitors to wind down their exposure, Lehman actually went ahead and further increased their exposures in the hope of making more money!

To mislead others, lenders in particular, Lehman began to window-dress their financials regularly. Instead of showing *repo* position at quarter-ends as borrowings (which would have highlighted their highly leveraged position), Lehman used an accounting method under which the securities pledged were shown as 'sold' so that both the assets and their corresponding liabilities were taken off the balance sheet, and when they were redeemed early in the following quarter, showed them as 'purchased' to get them back in to the inventory! While this ruse was perhaps successful to a large extent opposite outsiders, the quantum of such manipulation began to grow so much that the management eventually were deceiving themselves in to a false sense of complacency they were comfortable with. As of January 2008, for example, the disclosed *repo* liability was $25 bn while the actual number was in excess of 450 bn.

The tragedy was that top management was indeed well aware of these unacceptable risk exposures far in excess of the board approved risk appetite caps, but not only did not comply with those policies but on the other hand positively massaged financial numbers and misled people both within and without.

When there was a low-key attempt to whistle-blow on these irregularities, the independent auditors to whom it was addressed not only did not take it seriously but later in fact tried to 'correct' their internal audit notes to pretend they were not aware of any such effort. The board was thus also kept out of it. The whistle-blowing executive, a senior vice president in the finance function, on the contrary, found himself dismissed from his job!

The board oversight of risk management and especially its compliance was also poor. Despite some of the best experts in the field on its board, Lehman's outside directors neither had the time nor the inclination to monitor management more closely than they did; nor did it appear they had enough internal control systems to detect and report to them any serious breach of laid down policies. If they did, it was not evident in their reaction or corrective measures.

High executive compensation packages, especially when predominantly tied to 'performance', are an invitation to risk related initiatives that boards and top management should be conscious of. Lehman failure is a perfect illustration of this potentially lethal virus.

Source: Lehman Bankruptcy Examiner's Report, Valukas (2010)

CHAPTER 7

CORPORATE REPUTATION
Ethics, Values, and Citizenship

I am Prosperity and I live where character abides and so
do righteousness, truth and strength.

—THE MAHABHARATA[1]

I

Building Reputations

Important as the pursuit of profit is for business corporations and their boards to provide an attractive return to their shareholders, all their efforts may come to naught if they did not ensure their continued business reputations through high levels of operational integrity, ethical behaviour, social responsibility, and societal acceptability. In other words, if they were not to adopt and follow a value framework that would enable them to be perceived and respected as a good corporate citizen. This value framework is to corporations what systems software is to a computer. The key to sustainable corporate success is in winning the acceptance and admiration of all relevant stakeholders, even as the corporation must strive to optimize economic profits and profitability. The normative Indian approach to corporate citizenship and social responsiveness, both in tradition and modern practice is one of recognition of the need to win the approbation of society and all contributing stakeholders in the value creation chain

Corporate reputation is built over a period of time, mostly through hard work on the ground, and facilitated by appropriate dissemination of information to the society at large. It is founded on a set of values that form the core beliefs of the corporation. It is the result of initiatives on several fronts, including corporate social responsibility, business ethics, integrity and trust, corporate giving, transparent communication, and good citizenship. There are quite a few guidelines and reference frames available to assist the corporation, such as the Caux Round Table Principles, the Global Compact, the Sullivan Principles, and in India, the Tata Code of Business Conduct, besides a host of principles handed down in the scriptures from time immemorial. Numerous methodologies of structuring, measuring and reporting on these initiatives are available in the Balanced Scorecard approach, Triple Bottom Line approach, London Benchmark Group approach, Global Reporting Initiative approach, and so on, while assurance of compliance and implementation can be ascertained through various rating, certification and other independent audit procedures. Exhibit 7.1 sets out a schematic model of the seven pillars that serve as the foundations of Corporate Reputation, offering a conceptual framework for discussion and adoption in practice.

Exhibit 7.1: Seven Pillars of Corporate Reputation

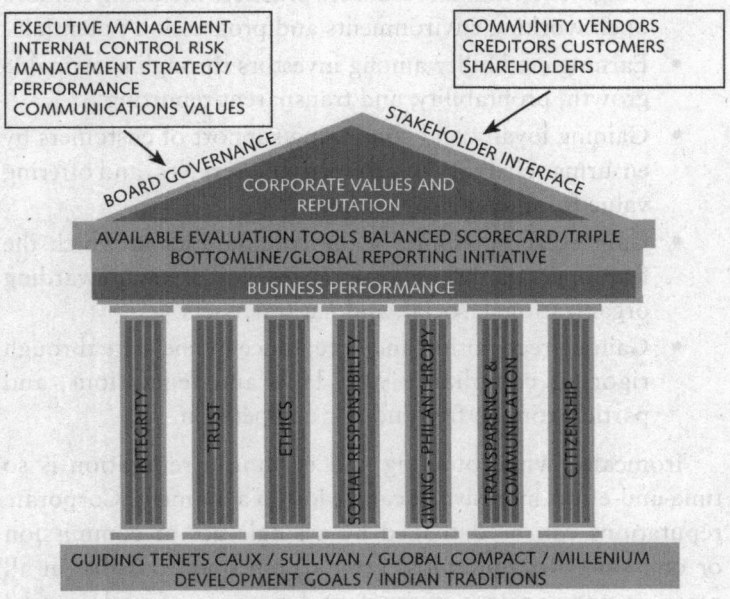

EXECUTIVE MANAGEMENT
INTERNAL CONTROL RISK
MANAGEMENT STRATEGY/
PERFORMANCE
COMMUNICATIONS VALUES

COMMUNITY VENDORS
CREDITORS CUSTOMERS
SHAREHOLDERS

BOARD GOVERNANCE

STAKEHOLDER INTERFACE

CORPORATE VALUES AND REPUTATION

AVAILABLE EVALUATION TOOLS BALANCED SCORECARD/TRIPLE BOTTOMLINE/GLOBAL REPORTING INITIATIVE

BUSINESS PERFORMANCE

INTEGRITY

TRUST

ETHICS

SOCIAL RESPONSIBILITY

GIVING – PHILANTHROPY

TRANSPARENCY & COMMUNICATION

CITIZENSHIP

GUIDING TENETS CAUX / SULLIVAN / GLOBAL COMPACT / MILLENIUM DEVELOPMENT GOALS / INDIAN TRADITIONS

CORPORATE REPUTATION

Reputation then, whether it is of an individual or a corporation, is based on an external assessment (or perception) on how the outside world views the entity, undoubtedly based on its lineage, track record, composition and its credibility of actions matching words. It is an intangible asset, defined as 'that portion of the excess market value which can be attributed to the perception of a firm as a responsible domestic and global corporate citizen.'[2] The components of reputational capital are the following business practices that enhance firm reputation in the view of its concerned stakeholders.

- Earning the trust and admiration of employees through enlightened human resources practices including fair and open working environments and progression potential
- Earning credibility among investors through sustainable growth, profitability, and transparent reporting
- Gaining loyalty and continuing support of customers by ensuring reliability of products and services, and offering value for money propositions
- Gaining acceptability of the communities in which the firm operates through responsible initiatives stewarding organizational, social, and natural assets
- Gaining recognition and acceptance by the state through rigorous compliance with laws and regulations, and participating in free and fair competition

Ironically, while building and earning a reputation is so time-and-effort intensive, it can be lost in a moment. Corporate reputations can be damaged by a single act of commission or omission. Regaining lost ground, not quite possible in all cases, is once again a monumental exercise of undoing the damage through appropriate disaster recovery measures.

Boards, directors and executive management should be ever so conscious of this Damocles' sword of reputation loss hanging over their heads, and have systems in place to pre-empt them. Should such a situation arise, they should be forearmed with necessary damage control and loss containment measures to be pressed into swift and decisive action at short notice. Johnson and Johnson's handling of the Tylenol disaster that hit them in the nineteen eighties is an instance of successful containment of the ill effects to its reputation. [**Case summary 7.1: Tylenol Disaster Management at Johnson & Johnson**]. Indian business has had its share of both fatal and lethal damage due to loss of reputation. In recent times, Tata Finance went through catastrophic convulsions due to loss of reputation arising from its managing director allegedly engaging in deals that smacked of self-dealing. The company was fortunately salvaged by the timely intervention of the Tata Group and the injection of considerable funds to get the distraught company back on its feet. Another case where the company was not so fortunate was the Global Trust bank, one of the new generation private sector banks, which suffered major loss of reputation on account of self-dealing, non-permissible and recklessly speculative lending, and poor board oversight. In the event, the promoters were disgraced and lost management control, and the bank ceased to have an independent identity, having had to be merged with the Oriental Bank of Commerce in a salvage operation under the auspices of the Reserve Bank of India. These instances highlight the efforts and problems involved in building reputations and protecting them on a continuous basis. The watchword is that past reputation is no guarantee for its continuation in future, unless it is protected and built upon each day.

Reputation is a subtle but powerful differentiator that offers tangible benefits flowing down to the financial bottom line. These benefits manifest themselves in many ways: lower employee costs and higher employee productivity due to better quality recruitment and retention, better profits due to the premium customers are willing to pay for the perceived value of the firm's goods and services, preferred vendor relationships resulting in better grade suppliers, their assured delivery and quality and their innovations facilitating better quality of firms' own products and services, better business and partnership potential with local and foreign collaborators, improved shareholder and creditor loyalty leading to lower cost of funding, and so on.

It is however a double-edged sword. Positive reputation enhances corporate performance through enabling and promoting greater acceptability and patronage by all stakeholders including the shareholders. Negative reputation impairs corporate performance through stakeholder deprecation and rejection of the firm and its products, services and even employment.

BUILDING REPUTATIONS: A FOUR DIMENSIONAL APPROACH[3]

Inherent in the reputation building process are four dimensions, respectively dealing with products and services, stakeholders, financiers, and geographical footprints.

Product/Service Reputation

In this dimension the inherent value of the product or service is the focus. The key components at this level are the functionality of the offering, its perceived cost-benefit equation for the customer, its quality, back-up support and service, and often, its emotional or aesthetic appeal. Does the customer accept the product or service offered as most appropriate for the intended application or adoption? Does he or she perceive the price of the product or service as being equal to or less than the value received? Where appropriate, is the post-sales support prompt, adequate and cost-effective? Is the product or service attractively and appropriately packaged? To borrow a phrase from Sir Humphrey, the master bureaucrat in the BBC serial *Yes, Prime Minister*, 'Is it something Harrods would sell?'[4] Is there, in other words, an appropriate *emotional surplus*[5] in the minds of customers?

Stakeholder Recognition

In this second dimension, broader business reputation emerges when a cross-section of relevant stakeholders are taken into account, including customers. Suppliers and vendors are key not only to promote better operational capabilities but also inbuilding reputation; obtaining a 'preferred customer' rating from a vendor ensures winning half the value chain battle even before production and operations begin. Prompt settlement of dues, clear and transparent purchasing specifications and approval processes, and treatment of vendors as partners in the value creation activity, are all measures that ensure such acceptance and recognition. Employees, especially in human resource-centric businesses pose a unique challenge to corporations in matters of recruitment and retention. Which explains why, such companies strive to get into listings of the most admired companies and best places to work in! Reputation as a good employer is the key to survival in such businesses.

Corporate reputations can also benefit from good leadership personnel and practices. While executive leadership is the visible face of a corporation in terms of media attention and market interface, the company's board as its ultimate decision-making body is a key institution that can impact the company's reputation, positively or negatively. The personal reputation of board members rubs off on the company's own reputation, and this is possibly one of the major reasons why respected, celebrated, trustworthy and successful individuals are in great demand for board positions. Similar is the case with parentage. Progeny inherit the reputation, good or bad, of the parents and corporations are no exception. Companies belonging to a particular family or domestic or multinational group have the advantage of basking in the parents' glory, but will have to work very hard indeed to maintain that position. Subsidiaries and affiliates of international companies, concomitantly also expose themselves to the risk of often undeserved erosion of reputation should the parent or a sibling elsewhere in the world be exposed to some disastrous event or development. Equally, the parent also has the onerous responsibility of ensuring its subsidiaries or affiliates do not bring disrepute to it or the group companies elsewhere. This calls for continuing vigilance by the boards and the concerned executives on both sides.

Credibility in Financial Markets

The third dimension covers the world of financiers and investors. A company's ability to establish a strong financial reputation is critical to its cost-effective fund-raising capabilities to finance its operations. This reputation is built upon strong financials, prompt debt servicing, good governance and executive management, and transparent communication and reporting.

Societal Reputation

The fourth dimension relates to how societies respond to perceived corporate behaviour. The choice to buy a product or pay for a service is often as much psycho-social as a financial or need based decision. Consequently, it can be influenced by environment and social concerns as well as economic factors. Product acceptability is often a reflection of the national or global media's response to a corporation's reaction to social and environmental issues. Multinationals in particular, have to be sensitive to the importance of regional and local societal reputation. 'Being global and acting local' is an exhortation which is worth its weight in gold when it comes to matters of assessing and addressing reputational issues specific to different markets and geographies in this global village.

As corporations become more globally spread out, their business strategies and risk containment capabilities get stretched and become major issues in reputation management. The likely reactions of local communities need to be proactively assessed and appropriate measures devised to deal with the issues in a mutually satisfactory manner. Not doing so or not reacting to any adverse developments in a timely and sensitive manner will sooner or later be grievously injurious to the reputation of the corporation.

Overall, reputation is a vital ingredient of success or failure that corporations can ill afford to ignore. The good fragrance of jasmine and the foul smell of rotting fish both share something in common—neither needs an announcement of its presence! So also is the case with good and bad corporate reputations.

II

Business Ethics and Values

Ethics has been traced, etymologically, to 'the Greek word *ethos*, meaning character or custom'[6]; it has also been described as the problem of good and evil, which we speak of as 'the ethical problem.' Throughout history, the confrontation has been between good and evil, between right and wrong, between inclusiveness and selfishness. Both in terms of corporate reputation and societal tolerance, company behaviour has come under intense scrutiny and in several instances has also led to regulatory mandates to contain such abuse. The inordinate delays in the dispensation of justice and punishment of the guilty, though, have diluted the deterrent impact of such regulation.

An appreciation of how ethics theory awareness can assist corporate governance practitioners, both at the board level and in executive management. Exhibit 7.2 sets out a schematic classification of various ethical approaches, as a backgrounder. Broadly, these theories are grouped as deontological or teleological, with a third classification covering some of the others. A comprehensive discussion on ethics in general is beyond

Exhibit 7-2: A Schematic of Major Ethics Theories

Major Ethics Theories

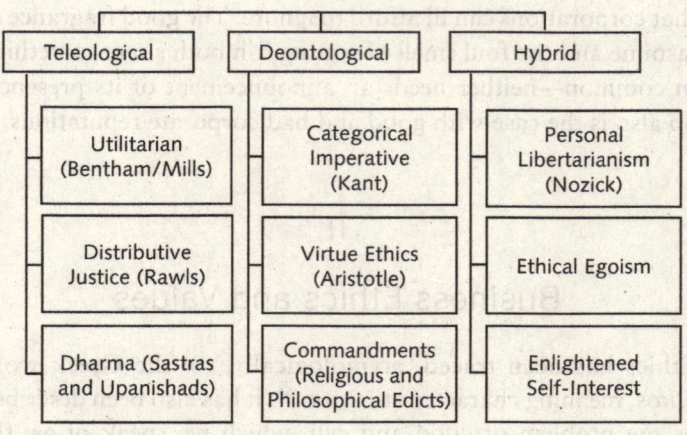

the scope of this book but a brief description of key ethical tenets would be of value in corporate decision making.

Deontological Theories

These are based on prescribed or ordained rules or principles that govern decisions and seek to question whether they were *right*, and explore how such 'rightness' can be discovered. Deontology has traditionally meant referring to a set of principles, defined rights, duties or obligations. In a business sense it is associated with considering the rules and regulations that have been previously identified as appropriate and following a set of processes which adhere to those principles, rules or regulations. Hence an organization which emphasizes a deontological approach to 'right' behaviour is likely to becontrol oriented and internally focussed, such as for example, a security force, a hospital, a prison or a bank. It will have a clear, well defined understanding of its principles and is able to determine 'ethical' behaviour by referring to how those principles are to be upheld—respectively, protecting society, making people well, confining and reforming prisoners, managing depositors' funds prudently, and so on. Many of these principles would be codified in structured and detailed manual of instructions, legislative or regulatory mandates. At operational levels, they are not open to questioning but only for implicit obedience and compliance, often on pain of punishment in case of breach.

The sources of deontological benchmarks are many— they could be religious, scriptural or traditional (like the Ten Commandments in Christianity, the Vedic admonitions to tell the truth and to follow the righteous path in the Hindu tradition), or legislative and regulatory imposed by the State or its delegates (like maximum permissible emission levels, or foreign ownership levels in certain sensitive business sectors, ultimately in public interest based on ethical criteria of peoples' health and national security respectively). In the latter category, there can be a policy debate on whether the prescriptions are reasonable or not but the decisions once taken are binding on the people for strict compliance.

Virtue Ethics

Virtue ethics, theoretically structured and articulated by Aristotle, are often associated with personal ethics, those that are most commonly identified with individual decision-making and behaviour. As such they are commonly framed in terms of personal values and morality—the aspects of personality or character that drive one to behave in a 'virtuous' way. Aristotle called them *habits* one should cultivate to be worthy of the title of 'citizen', the habits people adopted which would lead to the notion of a good life being led by all.[7] Principally, these were enumerated as: courage, self-control, generosity, magnificence, high-mindedness, gentleness, friendliness, truthfulness, wittiness, and modesty.[8]

TELEOLOGICAL THEORIES

Teleology is the form of ethics which determines the morality of decisions by measuring probable outcomes, or consequences. It is a term derived from two Greek words, *telos* meaning 'purpose or end' and *logos* meaning 'word.' In the ethics arena, it translates into evaluating personal or organizational decisions in terms of their potential to achieve the best possible overall result or outcome. It is often seen in terms of the individual—the best outcome for 'me', ethical egoism, ('what is best for me') or the 'other', albeit another individual, altruism, ('what is best for other(s)') or the group, utilitarianism ('what is best for all of us').

Utilitarianism is an approach postulated by John Stuart Mill (and Jeremy Bentham before him) who suggested that an ethical action is one which produces 'the greatest good for the greatest number.' It is considered a strong theory essentially because it is liberal (it appeals to no prescribed dictum or authority in resolving differences), and because it is able to describe and relate to much of the human decision-making processes. Its primary weakness of course is that it overlooks the impact on individuals, since measurements are on aggregates of good and bad results. Consequently, some individuals may suffer great injury while most others may benefit only modestly.

Some of these concerns are addressed by another approach referred to as *distributive justice*, based on the concept of fairness, developed by John Rawls.[9] Ethical decisions under this approach are those where goods and services are distributed equally, which in turn calls for determination of fairness criteria. Rawls suggested that the distribution system be devised without removing our *veil of ignorance* as to our status in society, whether one is rich or poor, educated or illiterate, backward or advanced, and so on. Theoretically, Rawls contended that this approach, would lead to more equitable decisions based on fairness. Many of our contemporary debates on *inclusive* development and growth have to do with these concepts of equity, fair play and justice.

Applied to corporate situations, the utilitarian approach can be useful in decisions where for the larger good of the company or its shareholders or its workforce, some may suffer. Such 'tough' decisions may involve laying off people, shutting down operations that are not value-contributing, outsourcing operations to more cost-effective locations, etc. The concomitant of such decisions is to explore ways and means of mitigating to the extent possible the ill effects on those adversely impacted by fair compensation, rehabilitation or other succour. Similarly, the principles of distributive justice may be relevant in matters relating particularly executive compensation. For example, when profit dependent bonuses are granted, are they equitably shared? Or, does the CEO garner a lion's share of the grants and leaves little or nothing to his team which may have contributed largely to those profits? In discussions on extortionary CEO pay packages, when comparisons are made between ratios of pay increases of the average employee and the CEO, we can see linkages to the underlying *injustice* in slicing the value-added cake among the total employee population.

AN INDIAN APPROACH TO ETHICS

Indian ethical thought derives from two distinct sources: First, despite some external façade of enlightened atheism in some sections of the population, a significant part of Indian society is religious and god-fearing in different degrees; and almost all religions practised in India propagate righteous behaviour as a virtue to be sought in private life as well as in business conduct.[10] Second, as a nation struggling to overcome its pervasive-and-oppressive poverty, a substantial proportion of those who have managed to break out and climb the ladder towards relative prosperity have lingering memories of their own families' struggles and the values they imbided in the process that encourage in them a measure of empathy and a desire to be as ethical and socially responsible as they can. Often labelled *middle class morality*, these experientially internalized evaluations of right and wrong tend to get reflected in their behavioural manifestation. Nobel Laureate Amartya Sen, commenting on the ethical underpinnings of Indian jurisprudence, relates the two concepts of *niti* and *nyaya* respectively to organizational propriety and behavioural correctness and to realized justice;

the role of institutions, rules and organization need to be judged in the broader and more inclusive perspective of *nyaya* linked with the reality of the actual outcomes.[11] In a business context, these can be compared to having codes, procedural rules and prescription on the one hand, and on the other, ensuring due compliance and surveillance so that intended benefits do accrue in practice. There is little value in having volumes of *niti* (like stringent laws) without the benefits being realized (as happens when they are not enforced in a timely manner).

Ethical Implications for Business

In the ultimate analysis, ethics is the art and science of human conduct and behaviour, the systematized principles on which humans should act between and among themselves, as well as towards their natural environmental surroundings. The primary objective is to bring about happiness by establishing harmonious relations 'between members of a family; between families that make a community; between the communities that make up a nation; between nations that make up humanity; between humanity and the other inhabitants of the earth and those of other worlds of the system. The great circle goes on spreading outwards indefinitely, and including larger and larger areas within its circumference. ...The ultimate object of morality, of ethics, of the science of conduct, is to bring about universal happiness and welfare, by uniting the separated selves with each other and with the supreme self.'[12] Corporations as collections of individuals thus derive their responsibility and obligation through ethical conduct to make the world a better place to live in now, and in the future.

ETHICS, VALUES, AND REPUTATION

Values are the governing principles held inviolable in intent and practice. They represent a set of 'commandments' that are to be embedded in the various decisions and practices of corporations. Values are 'the organization's essential and enduring tenets—a small set of general guiding principles, not to be compromised for short-term financial gain or expediency.'[13] While such beliefs must always have existed in business operations, in recent years, several corporations have begun to articulate explicitly their values and beliefs. This is perhaps to demonstrate their commitment to these principles, or in the context of the growing size and geographical diversity of modern corporations, to lay down how they expect and require their employees to conduct the business, and for the information of their stakeholders including customers and vendors.

'Values,' according to James Champy, 'are the link between emotion and behaviour, the connection between what we feel and what we do. Values instruct our feelings so that we don't always have to pause and think before we act on them.'[14]

In the Indian context, values have a deeper meaning and purport. They encompass not only the end objectives that the corporation desires to achieve, but also the means of achieving or delivering those commitments. This concept of ends not justifying foul means has been ingrained in the Indian *psyche* from time immemorial, and repeatedly reinforced by various religious and visionary pronouncements. Gandhi, the architect of Indian independence, averred, 'What I should be concerned about is the means and when I am sure of the purity of the means, faith is enough to lead me.'[15] And there does not seem to be any divergence of opinion even between communist thinkers and capitalist practitioners. For example, Karl Marx is quoted as saying, 'An end which necessitates unholy means is not a holy end,'[16] and in the twentieth century industrial economy, J.R.D. Tata is quoted as saying, 'No success or achievement in material terms is worthwhile unless it serves the needs or interests of the country and its people and is achieved by fair and honest means.'[17]

Accepting this primacy of ethical means over material ends is only the first half of the battle; the more difficult part is to ensure its truthful compliance in practice. In an unequal world of competitive business, compounded by elements not only not averse to but positively looking for illegal gratifications, abiding strictly by the self-imposed ethical rules can be challenging.[18] Successfully resisting such pressures even in the face of potential business loss is the sign of ethical leadership. Temporary hardships there may be, sacrifices to be made quite often perhaps, but over time people learn not to expect any such illicit favours from leadership companies with a reputation for ethical standards. Former long-time chairman J.R.D. Tata epitomized both the conviction and the costs of being ethical:

> 'What would have happened if our philosophy was like that of some other companies which do not stop at any means to attain their ends. I have often thought of that and I have come to the conclusion that if we were like other groups, we would be twice as big as they are today. What we have sacrificed is a 100 percent growth, but we wouldn't want it any other way.'[19]

The reputational legacy that such business leaders leave behind is far greater and enduring and more than make up for the transient losses they may entail. The group saw that in their Jaguar Land Rover acquisition in the UK.

III

Social Responsibility and Philanthropy

In broad terms, corporate social responsibility is about aligning business operations with social values, taking into account the interests of various stakeholders in devising and implementing the company's policies and processes. In spirit therefore, the concept goes beyond just compliance with legislative and regulatory requirements, towards doing what is considered good and desirable from the viewpoint of societal expectations.

Corporate views on social responsibility have changed dramatically for the better since the early and middle decades of the twentieth century. A much more widespread and far stronger acknowledgement and acceptance of corporate social responsibility is evident now. Illustratively,the European Commission defined CSR as a concept whereby companies integrate social and environmental concerns in their business operations and in their interaction with their stakeholders on a voluntary basis, while the World Business Council on sustainable development defined it as, the commitment of business to contribute to sustainable economic development, working with employees, their families, the local community and society at large to improve their quality of life.

Industrialist Dave Packard is quoted as saying, 'I think many people assume, wrongly, that a company exists simply to make money. While this is an important result of a company's existence, we have to go deeper and find the real reasons for our being. As we investigate this, we inevitably come to the conclusion that a group of people get together and exist as an institution that we call a company so that they are able to accomplish something collectively that they could not accomplish separately—they make a contribution to society, a phrase which sounds trite but is fundamental.'[20] In a speech at the Johannesburg World Summit for Sustainable Development in 2002, the then UN Secretary General, Kofi Annan told the assembled business leaders, 'I hope corporations understand that the world is not asking them to do something different from their normal business; rather, it is asking them to do their normal business differently.'[21] That probably sums up the current thrust of the business-centric CSR drive to promote achieving corporate profit ends through legitimate and socially acceptable means, partly laid down in the law of the land and partly prescribed by best practice expectations.

CSR AND SUSTAINABILITY

Especially in the context of business impact on the environment, the social responsibility concepts have been extended to include sustainable development without unduly impairing the earth's natural resources. The mission is to enhance economic productivity of goods and services required by society without permanently destroying natural resources, many of them non-renewable. Sustainable development is one 'that meets the needs of the present without compromising the ability of future generations to meet their own needs.'[22]

Corporations and Their Triple Effect on Society

Corporations need to reconfirm and reiterate to themselves that they operate within a society, with its sanction and authority, and ultimately for its common good, not just for themselves or their shareholders, employees and managers alone. Without this understanding, there will be no social cohesion between and among government, business and society. When there is complete understanding and appreciation of these imperatives, the country, and business as a sub-set, will thrive.

Business impacts society in three dimensions. First, the economic dimension, where the corporation has to ensure the best input-output ratios in relation to the monetary and other resources it uses, and is most commonly reflected by its financial and economic profitability. In the second dimension its impact is on the environment, on matters relating to pollution and emission controls, product life cycle strategies, energy conservation, climate change, and so on. And finally, the third dimension deals with its social impact, in terms of employment generation and equal opportunities, inclusive development, community regeneration and other such societal issues. While for-profit corporations would usually be well tuned in to the first economic dimension, in respect of the other two dimensions, businesses can address the specific issues relevant to them in one of the following ways—they can totally deny such an issue exists and do nothing, they can comply with the minimum required by law, or decide to tackle the problem when it surfaces, or proactively examine what needs to be done, and implement the measures that are considered necessary. In each of these alternatives, the corporation will indeed be auto-selecting its character. This would equate respectively with burying one's head underground and wishing away the problem, crossing the bridge when coming to it, just complying with the bare minimum legal requirements for the time being, or assuming a leadership role and tackling the issues in anticipation. Those that adopt the fourth option are usually the ones that gain leadership status in their respective industries, geographies or intellectual domains.

Walking the CSR Talk

A key requirement in effectively adopting CSR and TBL principles in business is to ensure their internalization in organizational decision making and operational processes. Without this, CSR and TBL are likely to remain standalone initiatives without getting absorbed in organizational cultures. Following are some ground level examples of how such embedding could be implemented.

On Social Issues

This can be done for example by announcing a policy on equal opportunity employment and ensuring that these are in fact provided. If the organization has a whistle-blower policy, it must ensure that genuine non-frivolous whistle-blowers are not victimised or discriminated against. Employee volunteers must be encouraged to participate and contribute to socially responsible initiatives not only on their own but also on company time, within certain business-centred guidelines.

Workmen safety is another issue where serious lapses occur between proclaimed policies and actual practices. Use of hazardous technology or material, economising on safety-related requirements, and cutting back on routine but essential safety check-ups in airlines sector, for instance, are commonly observed deficiencies that jeopardize safety of both the workforce and the customers.

One of the most important elements of true commitment to CSR practices is to ensure their observance in outsourced entities as well. Given that such outsourcing of various activities has become a way of life in modern-day business operations, either for cost or competency reasons, corporations have an obligation to see that CSR-friendly practices are observed in the contract units as rigorously as they are applied within the company. The relevance of extending this obligation has been recognised for a long time, but its application and enforcement are increasingly gaining ground. The Sarbanes-Oxley legislation in the US extending corporations' responsibility on certain matters to outsourced units beyond their political borders is just a reinforcing manifestation of the moral and legal compulsions that had always been implicitly presumed but rarely addressed.

Leadership companies may also preferentially rate their vendors wherever possible on the basis of whether their CSR practices measure up to certain basic minimum prescriptions (such as perhaps not employing child labour or sweat-shop practices).

On Environmental Issues

In manufacturing industries especially, companies should ensure that they not only comply with but improve upon emission and pollution control regulations. It is not an acceptable rationalization that the gutters and canals where pollutants are discharged are worse in quality than the treated effluents discharged by the factory. The leader should lead by example, not hide behind defensive excuses.

In a land of consistent energy shortfalls, ensuring effective energy management is a key social response. This applies not only to the energy usage or wastage within the company but also to the energy efficiency of its products and services. Likewise, while designing products and services, companies may like to invest in technologies that facilitate recycling and optimally utilise the resources consumed in providing the product or service.

On Economic Issues

On the economic front, creating wealth or productive surplus, whether in the private or the public sectors, is the ordained obligation of every business. Eliminating wastage, enhancing efficiency, and making every rupee invested or spent worthwhile in terms of its return, are all a company's societal obligation to ensure the business produces enough surplus through its operations, societal resources are well employed and utilised.

CORPORATE PHILANTHROPY

A common perception among business executives and entrepreneurs is that all corporate social responsibility requires is philanthropy, or just writing out cheques for what they perceive as deserving causes. There are thousands of businesses, small and large, that even today keep a fractional percentage of their sales revenue each day for charity, and for them it is their way of discharging their responsibility to society. Building temples and setting up religious and educational foundations are of the same variety, only the scale is larger. Important and welcome as these initiatives are, they are but one small component of a responsible organization.

Giving

At a personal, individual level, giving has been considered a very desirable trait and human virtue in almost all religious faiths. In Hindu scriptures, *Daana* (charity or largesse) was extolled right from *Vedic* times through to more recent times. 'He who gives liberally, goes straight to the gods; on the high ridge of heaven he stands exalted,' assures the *Rig Veda*. The Buddhist *Dhammapada* echoes the same message: 'Verily, misers go not to the celestial realms. Fools do not indeed praise liberality. The wise man rejoices in giving, and thereby becomes happy thereafter,' and again, 'One should give even from a scanty store to him who asks.' Jainism proclaims, 'Charity—to be moved at the sight of the thirsty, the hungry and the miserable, and to offer relief to them out of pity—is the spring of virtue.' Judaism and Christianity ordain, 'For the poor will never cease out of the land; therefore I command you, you shall open wide your hand to your brother, to the needy and to the poor, in the land.' Islam, likewise, exhorts: 'Let him who believes in Allah and the Last Day be generous to his neighbour, and let him who believes in Allah and the Last Day be generous to his guest.'[23] *Thiru Kural,* for example, postulates, 'Those who know duty well never neglect giving, even in their own unprosperous season,' and again, 'He who understands the duty of giving truly lives, all others shall be counted among the dead,' but cautions, 'Giving to the poor is true charity. All other giving expects some return.'[24] Giving has been sanctified and eulogized beyond compare in every age and in every clime. As Kalidasa similes in *Raghu Vamsam,*[25] it is a sign of the great to acquire wealth only to distribute it to the needy and deserving, even as the sun draws water and moisture from the oceans only to return them in the form of copious rains on a welcoming earth.

Having thus universally extolled and encouraged charity, some texts[26] also go on to categorize such charity into three types—gifts to those with no expectations of any return or gain, purely on the basis that they ought to be given, at the right place and time and to worthy recipients; gifts given for the sake of receiving in return, or with a view to fruit, or grudgingly; and those given at unfit places and time, and to unworthy recipients, disrespectfully and contemptuously. Of these, the first is the most welcome and suitable; the second is just acceptable, while the third has no particular value. These injunctions, although centuries-old, are quite relevant even now.

There are questions that arise with regard to corporate philanthropy that need discussion.

- While the merits of individual philanthropy are undoubted, is the corporate form of business an appropriate vehicle for similar charitable activities?
- Is there a business case for corporate philanthropy?
- How best are such activities to be structured?

SHOULD CORPORATIONS GIVE?

There is a school of thought that does not take too kindly to corporate philanthropy due to its potential for misuse; for example.

- All too often, it was seen as reflecting the personal whims and fancies of those in high authority, who could use other people's money for personal aggrandisement. Stephanie Strom[27] alludes to several US examples of CEOs usurping credit and fame for themselves with donations out of company coffers, having institutions named after them, or being invited to join prestigious third sector boards and trustees. At the senior corporate level, when cultural institutions invite someone on their board, it's very clear they expect that person to come with the resources of the company behind him. Inherently, there is nothing wrong if such actions are credited to the company and are perceived as being beneficial to the company's interests; in practice, it may not always be so straightforward or clear
- A theory-based argument against corporations engaging in philanthropy is that it does not align with the company's obligations to shareholders of maximizing their returns

from business, unless of course it had been authorised by them either through the company's charter documents or by specific resolutions. Exceptions are possible if it can be argued that such activities were actually in the business interests of the company and hence in tune with wealth-maximization objectives. [**Case summary 7.2: Two Faces of Corporate Philanthropy**]

- The iconic Warren Buffett put it quite simply, while writing to his shareholders: 'Just as I wouldn't want you to implement your personal judgments by writing checks on my bank account for charities of your choice, I feel it inappropriate to write checks on your corporate 'bank account' for charities of my choice.'[28] Corporations in general do not have the freedom to apply shareholders' money to non-business related philanthropy without their concurrence. There is however the concept of materiality that Indian law takes in to account with regard to such philanthropic activities of corporations. Shareholders' approval is required only if such contributions in any year exceed 5 percent of the average profits of the company during the preceding three years[29]

- Obviously, there are advantages in routing charitable donations through corporations. Barring big ticket donations from high net worth personalities, individual contributions are unlikely to be large and hence both cost-and-effort inefficient in mobilization. On the other hand, because of their size, corporations are much better placed to offer substantial contributions in a relatively cost-efficient manner. This may still be a preferred option if appropriate approvals and processes are taken care of.

BUSINESS CASE FOR CORPORATE PHILANTHROPY

Corporations have both the reason and the potential to achieve tremendous impact on social problems, especially those that are directly related to their businesses. Viewed from this perspective, philanthropy of this type will fall under the second category of giving discussed earlier, where it is done with an eye on return.

- Porter and Kramer[30] point out, 'The success of companies and the health of their communities inextricably depend on each other: Companies depend on stable social conditions and an educated, healthy and well housed workforce, while societies depend on businesses to generate the income that supports an adequate standard of living. Unlike other kinds of charitable donors, companies can leverage their expertise, employees and influence to achieve productive social change.' There is thus a strong case to integrate their philanthropic activities with well thought out and executed strategies that would support business even as they effectively promote social change

- Porter and Kramer also extend their contextual philanthropy approach applicable to a nation's competitive advantage.[31] It is in this competitive context that corporations have to perform and grow. A leadership company could transform such challenges to great opportunities by building necessary contextual philanthropic initiatives to overcome some of these problems, while at the same time ensuring that their own competitiveness is improved by the end results. For example, investment in educational and research facilities to augment available resources through grants, in-house training, sabbaticals, and so on, could help the corporation turn these so-called problems to their own competitive advantage. Corporations could thus convert a host country 'problem' in to a philanthropic opportunity for themselves. In the same category fall initiatives such as running a primary school or a basic health centre in a factory location which would not only be welcomed by local communities but may lead to less absenteeism and late coming because the workmen otherwise had to go a long distance to the nearest town where such facilities were available

- Corporations can use philanthropy towards contributing and sustaining a corporation's reputation. The absence, as in most Indian cases, of a transparent and democratic decision-making process, may lead to a measure of stakeholder, especially employee, cynicism but even this gets somewhat mitigated by the overall forgiving Indian attitude that overlooks deficiencies and perceives only the goodness of the eventual decision

STRUCTURING CORPORATE PHILANTHROPY

The next issue is how a corporation's philanthropic activities ought to be structured. Principally, should they be done in-house or through a separate dedicated Foundation route? Both have their advantages and weaknesses; many companies opt for a combination approach depending upon their circumstances.

Philanthropy management generally requires different skills compared to companies' business management requirements. Very few companies would wish to add more head count for this purpose unless the requirements of managing the initiatives are so closely aligned to their own businesses that they could be beneficially addressed from within. Otherwise, it might be better to entrust that job to experts in the field, who can devote the time, have the necessary managerial skills, and the passionate dedication and commitment to create an effective impact from their spending. This is probably the reason that Warren Buffett, when deciding to donate some 85 percent of his $43 billion wealth, chose to entrust that significant sum to the Bill and Melinda Gates Foundation, with its competencies and track record of performance in the field.

In India, at an individual level, we have the Wipro chief, Azim Premji, seting up with his own personal funds a Foundation named after himself to carry out his mandate of improving primary education in the country. Examples of companies choosing the Foundation route are the Aditya Birla group, Mahindra and Mahindra, and Infosys, just to mention a few. Given the widespread prevalence of family control of Indian corporations, it is not surprising that many of the foundations set up by their companies are named after their family members, although in case of contributions from the company, often a substantial part of the corpus also belongs to the absentee shareholders.

The Tatas have established an enviable record in philanthropy in giving off their personal wealth to various laudable causes of their choice. The pioneering Tata patriarch, Jamsetji Tata whose vision was for 'India [to] take its place among the advanced countries of the world', that required excellent higher education, left half of his not-inconsiderable wealth to the Indian Institute of Science at Bangalore, started in 1911. Sir Dorab Tata's substantial trust helped to found the Tata Memorial Hospital, Tata Institute of Social Sciences, the Tata Institute of Fundamental Research, and the National Centre for Performing Arts, all prestigious world class institutions. The National Institute of Advanced Studies in Bangalore was sponsored by the JRD Tata Trust. Many of these trusts together hold some two thirds of the equity of Tata Sons, the group's parent company, and the dividends they receive from their investments get recycled back to supporting various social causes.[32]

Many other business houses and families have developed their own models to create and manage their philanthropic activities. The key is the underlying belief that that individuals and businesses ought to 'give' with reverence, modesty and liberally,[33] in other words with dedication and conviction, not just to comply with some regulation or to keep up with peers. Whichever way and in whatever manner it is done, there is little doubt that philanthropy projects, promotes and protects corporate reputation and is an inseparable concomitant to sustained growth and prosperity.

Case summary 7.1: Tylenol Disaster Management at Johnson & Johnson

In 1982 and again in 1986 TYLENOL, a product of McNeil Consumer & Specialty Pharmaceuticals subsidiary was altered by unknown individuals who placed deadly cyanide in the capsule form of the product. The result was the death of seven people in 1982. The product was voluntarily recalled and Johnson & Johnson took a $100 million charge against earnings. No one was ever convicted of the tampering and subsequent deaths. In 1986, as a result of the second tampering incident and another fatality, the decision was made to discontinue the sale of TYLENOL in capsule form, and subsequently the caplet form of TYLENOL was introduced. Johnson & Johnson received much praise for its quick and honest handling of the crisis. The company reintroduced TYLENOL in pioneering tamper-evident packaging, eventually regaining its leading share of the analgesic market.

Source: Johnson & Johnson website

Case summary 7.2: Two Faces of US Corporate Philanthropy

The following judgement extracts illustrate the judicial application of the Agency theory of corporate governance to corporate philanthropy in the US. In the first case, Henry Ford felt stockholders had made enough money and ceased an annual special dividend, arguing he needed the money for capacity expansion, and wished to reduce prices since times were tough. Dodge brothers who held 10 percent of the equity sued Ford. In the second instance, the dispute was with regard to a donation to Princeton University which was questioned as not being in the interest of shareholders.

Ford vs Dodge (1919) (On price reduction of cars to enlarge the market)

Majority Opinion by Justice J Ostrander

'He [Henry Ford] has to some extent the attitude towards shareholders of one who has disposed and distributed to them large gains and that they should be content to take what he chooses to give. His testimony creates the impression, also that he thinks the Ford Motor Company has made too much money, has had too large profits, and that although large profits might still be earned, a sharing of them with the public by reducing the price of the output of the company, ought to be undertaken. ... There should be no confusion (of which there is evidence) of the duties which Mr Ford conceives that he and the stockholders owe to protesting minority stockholders. A business corporation is organised and carried on primarily for the profit of the stockholders. The powers of the directors are to be employed for that end. The discretion of directors is to be exercised in the choice of means to

---

attain that end and does not extend to a change in the end itself, to the reduction of profits or to the non-distribution of profits among stockholders in order to devote them to other purposes."

A.P. Smith Manufacturing Co. vs Barlow (1953) (On donation to Princeton University)

Judge Stein

'I [the judge] cannot conceive of any greater benefit to corporations in this country than to build, and continue to build, respect for and adherence to a system of free enterprise and democratic government, the serious impairment of either of which may well spell the destruction of all corporate enterprise. Nothing that aids or promotes the growth and service of the American university of college in respect of the matter here discussed can possibly be anything short of direct benefit to every corporation in the land. The college-trained men and women are a ready reservoir from which industry may draw to satisfy its need for scientific or executive talent. It is no answer to say that a company is not as benefited unless such need is immediate. A long-range view must be taken of the matter. A small company today might be under no imperative requirement to engage the services of a research chemist or other scientist, but its growth in a few years may be such that it must have available an ample pool from which it may obtain the needed service.'

Source: Bowie and Duska (1990, pp. 24–25)

EPILOGUE
Making the Difference

As our desire, so is our will
As our will, so are our acts
As we act, so we become

—BRIHADARANYAKA UPANISHAD[1]

I

Changing Profile of Corporate Boards and Directors

Incorporated companies and chartered entities have been around for several centuries, along with their boards and directors. In their own way, they have largely been successful although several have been failures for a variety of reasons. It is therefore a pertinent issue to raise what is the need for directors now and in future to 'make the difference'. A simple response would be that one should strive for excellence through improvement in any field of work, directorships not excluded. But there is more to the imperatives of making a difference as we shall presently see. The business environment has been (and will continue to be) changing rapidly and being satisfied with status quo is a sure invitation to distress and failure. With their fiduciary duties to shareholders particularly, directors cannot afford to let that happen to their companies.

Composition of corporate boards in the pre-independence era was a fairly simple affair. Most of the businesses were owned and/or controlled by British and Indian managing agencies and families who had promoted them and taken them public. Boards were relatively small, their members were usually the promoters themselves or senior executives from the groups, and meetings, if actually held, were generally to comply with legal requirements. If any outsiders were invited to the boards, it was essentially to use their connections and influence to further the interests of the companies. The profile of the directors in such an environment was largely executive or ownership-based; the former carried their management mindset to the board while for the latter their own entrepreneurial objectives were the only concern.

The company legislation in 1956 and the decades that followed saw some material changes in the role and obligations of corporate boards: for one thing, the concept of managing agencies was being jettisoned, and each company was to be governed and managed by its own board and executive managements. 'Groups' were looked down upon as unholy collections of business-people and companies pursuing policies not necessarily in public interest; this was further bolstered by the rigours of anti-monopolies legislation and constraints on foreign ownership and control of businesses considered non-core by the State. Business houses, used to centralised control of their business empires, still managed to do so in reality even while in form complying with the legal requirements.[2] But even such radical reforms in corporate law did not by themselves translate in to any significant changes in the profile of corporate boards. Hindustan Lever, for example,continued its practice of having virtually the whole of its board comprising of senior executives from within or at best from its parent or other global siblings until regulations mandated otherwise at the dawn of the new millennium. There was thus no perceptible change in the profiles of directors on company boards during the second half of the twentieth century.

There was one material change, however, during this period that had a bearing on board composition. India was industrializing in a hurry post-Independence and there was plenty of funding made available to accelerate this process by largely government owned development banks and investment institutions. As part of the conditionalties governing these funding arrangements (whether by way of debt or equity participation), assisted companies were required to 'broad-base and professionalize' their boards with induction of outside directors, in addition to these institutions nominating their representatives on such boards. That usually meant larger-sized boards and induction of non-family directors. But in practice the 'executive or owner' mindset did not materially change since such additions were largely from the same kind of people only; instead of the company's, these were executives of institutions or owners of other businesses!

The twenty-first century ushered in regulations that called for substantial proportions of boards of listed companies to consist of 'independent' directors. As we have noted elsewhere, this also did not make too much of a dent in the ownership-executive make-up of the boards since barring a few notable exceptions, these independent directors too were more often than not chosen from incumbent executive ranks elsewhere and were prone to continue in the same manner as before. But what has had a dramatic impact in recent years is the realization of directorial responsibilities enforceable by legislation and prosecution (Satyam was an eye opener to many independent directors) and increasingly stringent legislative and regulatory regimes that are not only bringing India in line with, but in several cases even excelling international best practices. The Companies Act 2013, SEBI regulations and stock exchange listing conditions are all aimed at making corporate boards more accountable to shareholders and responsible to other stakeholders under pain of punishment for breaching the mandates. Compounding this situation further are developments that expose corporations to contests for control in case of sub-optimal performance or unacceptable governance risks to absentee shareholders. Institutional investors, whether domestic or foreign, under pressure to deliver value to their own constituents, are already showing signs of activism not imaginable in the earlier decades and the scope for litigation against companies and their directors, already observed, are likely to get further boost as more stringent legal regimes take root. On top of all these, absentee shareholders (including institutional investors who had earlier been indifferent to below-par governance risks in their investee-companies on either cost or materiality considerations) now have the benefit of proxy advisory firms which research and recommend approval or disapproval of contentious resolutions brought forward by companies at their members' meetings; and a new breed of investigative financial journalists lose no time in exposing governance weaknesses and likely fiduciary failures, to the great embarrassment of company boards, executives and promoters. This is a heady concoction with potentially grave reputational damage and litigation threats. Business as before is therefore not a viable option to the incumbent and future directors of corporations.

The required profile and action agenda of a company director in the twenty first century would thus be completely different from what it was even a few years earlier. From an inward-looking, hierarchy-circumscribed, or filially-subdued individual to an outwardly-focussed, independent, contributing member of a corporate board, it seems not very unlike the ascent of man, in a metaphorical sense! Every company director, incumbent or aspiring, executive or independent, will have to accept in full measure this metamorphosis in the required profile if he or she expects to be successful and value-adding. What worked quite well even a decade ago is unlikely to be considered adequate in the current more evolved and still evolving environment.

11

Towards Successful Board Membership

In setting one's own aspirational standards of board performance, it would be useful to view them under the three dimensions of board role, contributing, counselling, and controlling, fine tuned to the competencies of the individual. For example, it may be unreasonable to expect a first-time director to perform at the same levels as a more board-experienced colleague, an outstanding marketing person at the same high level to perform on the control dimension as would a qualified and experienced finance and accounting professional. There will be exceptional people with multi-disciplinary competencies and they should set their performance standards at a higher threshold. These few successful directors should set themselves as role models to their colleagues on the boards they serve and even beyond; and the rest with plans to scale the heights of success in this rarefied atmosphere should instinctively observe and adapt the qualities they see as potential contributories to their own personal improvement. There are no limits to such experiential learning—and the hunger for such learning is what would distinguish a potential board leader from the also-rans.

WHAT CHANGES ARE REQUIRED?

Here is an illustrative checklist of improvements that may be necessary to confront and cope with the realities of the evolving environment where for the foreseeable future corporate ownership will continue to be predominantly concentrated in the hands of the promoting family groups, multinationals and the State. These may be broadly categorized under three heads— those that overlook the fundamentals of corporate directorships, those that exaggerate the so called weaknesses, and those that undermine strengths.

A. Revisiting Fundamentals

1. Directorship as a position of Trust

Contrary to popular perceptions, board memberships are not wholly cushy jobs that have all the perquisites of power and opulence with no accountability strings attached. Whether or not the absentee shareholders actively influence the election of a director to their board is in many ways an irrelevant issue— the reality is that when one's appointment is approved at a members' meeting, he inherits the responsibility for looking after the interests of all such shareholders whether they voted in favour or against, or not at all. In this, the position of a company director is not dissimilar to that of an elected member of parliament, who is accountable to the entire constituency of people, not just only to those who voted to elect him or her. While this has always been the position, many directors of the past era have tended wittingly or otherwise to gloss over this and felt more obligated to the promoters or executive management being seen as responsible for bringing them on to their boards. With increasing shareholder activism, institutional investing, and shareholder awareness of their power, leadership directors could no longer afford to ignore this fundamental trusteeship obligation that has to be their guiding light in discharging their obligations.

2. Absentee Shareholder Protection Paramount

While granting that total mistrust of promoters and the executive cannot be a sound basis for cohesive board functioning, directors do not have the option of compromising the interests of absentee shareholders by being negligent on this count. Enlightened promoter groups and executive management by themselves also should eschew such deleterious efforts (which were passé before) in future in their own interests as well; directors cannot take that for granted in their deliberations. The Satyam, Enron, and Lehman episodes among others, should serve as a constant reminder to directors never to let their guard down, even while not necessarily adopting a confrontational approach. The guiding maxim should be trust but verify!

B. Converting Weaknesses into Strengths

3. On Being Outnumbered

A common attitudinal trait of independent directors is a general feeling of helplessness even on decisions where they are not comfortable; this arises primarily from the fact that promoter and executive directors including non-independent non-executive directors add up to a larger number. Even if, as in a few companies, independent directors are in a majority, they may feel this helplessness since if the matter goes to the shareholders' meeting, such resolutions may be carried because of their relatively higher proportion of voting power; consequently, they may decide not to oppose and create bad blood in an otherwise congenial board room ambience. This was a real issue of frustration until now but with the enactment of the Companies Act 2013, at least in respect of related party transactions this would not be the case since 'interested parties' may not exercise their votes on such resolutions. This is a hard won gain after years of advocacy and should help independent directors to act entirely based on their judgement in the interests of all shareholders.

4. 'They Know Best'

It is true that the external directors, with all due respect to their experience and wisdom, can never hope to match, let alone beat the executive management in business-specific expertise. But they bring an invaluable external perspective based on their own experience which may not always be matched by executive management. The idea would be to leverage mutual strengths, not to score brownie points. It is a well-established fact that committed executive management welcomes such value-adding inputs from its external directors.

Outside directors also tend to take a detached view rationalising the lack of such knowledge as due to their being part-timers without access to day to day operational issues. Many CEOs tend to overcome this knowledge gap first by a proper induction programme and later on through periodical short updates on developments affecting the company so that external directors do not feel left out in the cold until the following board meeting.

Often, such directors may also be inclined to genuinely believe that what the promoters are proposing must be good for the company and all its shareholders since they have longer term family interests in mind and could not do otherwise. This may largely be the case but in any event human nature dictates that self-interest take precedence over others' interests. Directors cannot afford to take chances with other shareholders' interests. Every effort is to be made to get acquainted with the business of the company and its operational structures (not the details) so that there could be an intelligent appreciation of proposals coming up for decision. The approach should be to challenge assumptions underlying proposals, not to doubt or discredit management but to ensure the strategies and other initiatives proposed are based on robust grounding.

C. Building on Strengths

5. Not just Advisors but Controllers as Well

Many old-school directors have been led to believe, and in fact actually have believed too, that their job was to function exclusively as advisors and consultants to promoters and executive management. Opening opportunity doors through their network influence, and discreetly sharing, often privileged, information they have had access to have been considered the hallmarks of a well thought of director. All this is of course true and value-adding to the company, but they should build on these strengths to exercise their control function responsibilities as well. Because of their value on these contributing and counselling roles, they would be in a position to command attention and compliance when commenting on the control issues and they should fully exploit this advantage for the benefit of all shareholders.

External directors are also a potential source for transfer of best practices from elsewhere, gleaned from their network contacts. No opportunity should be lost in doing so for the benefit of shareholders. Even more importantly, the observed skill sets from network contacts can help directors to build on their own directorial skills to enhance their performance.

6. Communicating to Colleagues

Nowhere else are persuasive communication skills more in demand than in the board room. Here hierarchies don't operate (except perhaps in case of executive directors who, even in the board room may not be able to shed their subordinate status to the CEO); bringing colleague directors to one's viewpoint is wholly dependent on how purposeful are the persuasion efforts.[3] Whether by training or observation, directors need to acquire these skills as essential and invaluable tools in their armoury for success.

7. Preparation

Finally, a successful performance at any meeting is the result of comprehensive preparation, and board and committee meetings are no exception. In the relatively relaxed ambience of the past, non-executive directors could hope to, and actually also succeed in shooting from the hip without too much of prior preparation. Notwithstanding their global rankings, no great player in any sport could do away with proper preparation before a game, why should a director attending a board or committee meeting be any different? For sure, experience and deep understanding of a subject would stand a director in good stead in impromptu handling of any issues going his way but through such performances do not always bring out the potential in full measure.

As noted earlier, overall board performance is a team effort with each player contributing with his or her own expertise. Given the usually heavy content of importance that these meetings are required to address in a relatively short time, one will not have the luxury of using valuable contact time at meetings spent on reading or searching for questions to ask or answers to respond with. At least on agenda items in areas of one's own domain expertise, the director should prepare in advance and be ready to meaningfully contribute during the meeting.

These then are some of the items conscientious directors aiming to achieve excellence in their performance might wish to give some thought to.

III

Fulfilling a Mission

We conclude this brief journey in to the realms of corporate directorship with a final self-probing question: why did we choose to become a corporate director? In case of executive directors, the answer may lie in reaching the summit of the organizational pyramid with a sense of exhilaration and achievement. Becoming a director is a sign of having 'arrived' and the initial feeling is bound to be heady. But that represents only the executive part of the director's job. As well as being a reward for executive performance (within the company or elsewhere), this 'achievement' has a concomitant 'promise' as well for delivering value in future. In addition, becoming a director brings in an additional dimension of trusteeship to an extent that may not have been apparent at an executive level.

In case of non-executive, the question is even more poignant: why would anyone want to take on a non-executive directorship of a company without any executive authority but plenty of fiduciary obligations and oversight responsibilities? Additional earnings (which can certainly be attractive in most cases, and especially when one has wound up an active executive career or professional practice) and a feeling of importance at being invited to a board may well be a key reason. But given the trusteeship role that these directorships involve and the legal liabilities that these entail, many of the directors may wonder if the monetary compensation they receive was commensurate enough to the risks and responsibilities they have to shoulder.[4] If people did and do continue in their positions, it could only mean either they thought the risk-reward equation was fair in their case, or they were conscious of a more important driver that encouraged them to continue, a feeling that they were there to protect the interests of millions of absentee shareholders who had risked their savings with their companies and had reposed their trust in them to take care of their interests. Those who were influenced to stay on wholly of partly by this latter thought ought to be considered real leadership directors worth emulation.

Decades ago, Adrian Cadbury, the pioneer of modern corporate governance in the UK and widely followed by many other countries including India, suggested 'governance by exit' was not a commendable option; rather, it would be more desirable for the shareholders, the company and the country, for directors to stay on and correct the aberrations in the governance of their companies.

Where would these 'good' or 'role model' directors find their success? Perhaps in the fulfilment of their mission to serve the interests of absentee shareholders, perhaps also in growing the publicly traded segment of business leading to further investments, further innovations and further employment, all leading to the betterment of the people in general and companies' stakeholders including shareholders in particular.

In concluding this brief exhortation to increase the tribe of good, conscientious, and successful directors for the future, it is appropriate to recall the insightful words of Peter Drucker written in 1946 in the US context:

> 'What we look for in analysing [American] society is ... the institution which sets the standard for the way of life and the mode of living of our citizens; which leads, moulds, and directs; which determines our perspective on our society; around which crystallizes our social problems and to what we look for their solution... And this ... in our society today is the large corporation.'[5]

And that corporation as an instrument of business as well as a purveyor of social wellbeing is vulnerable to abuse because in many ways, its design and purpose may often tempt it towards passing on to society the costs of its operation it does not wish to absorb. Monks characterizes the corporation as 'an externalizing machine, in the same way that a shark is a killing machine...'[6] which is detrimental to the very communities it seeks to serve. To keep it away from such devious misadventures through its supervisory functions over the errant executive is the job of its board of directors, however much difficult or frustrating that task might be. Exiting the board when the going gets difficult is not the sign of a leader, since it denies him the opportunity to fight from within and eliminate or mitigate the adverse impact in the larger interests of the shareholders and the corporation itself.

There are several outstanding examples of corporations and directors who have already travelled down this less chosen road to personal and corporate glory. The task ahead is to get more to follow and emulate these illustrious role models.

ACKNOWLEDGEMENTS

I am humbled by a deep sense of overwhelming gratitude to a number of institutions and people as I begin to record my sincere acknowledgements to those who have contributed to my learning which I have tried to reflect and share with readers in this short book.

The idea of writing this volume was initiated by Professor Samir Barua, then the director of the Indian Institute of Management Ahmedabad. He has been a source of constant encouragement and support throughout, and has freely given his time going through earlier drafts of this book and suggesting invaluable improvements, besides also writing the foreword; to him I owe a great debt of gratitude.

I have used material from some of the cases authored jointly, and I acknowledge with gratitude my co-authors' contribution and support; in particular: Samir Barua, Subramanian Raghunath, and Sundararajan Selvaganapathy. I would also like to acknowledge the initial work and research support provided by several of my students and associates in the preparation of the full teaching cases from where many of these summaries have been made.

I acknowledge the support provided by Random House in getting this book to its publication. Milee Ashwarya and especially my editor, Radhika Marwah, have been wonderfully creative and supportive in structuring the book and rendering it reader friendly.

Finally, I acknowledge with gratitude the unfailing encouragement and support I have received from my wife, Jamuna (despite her own serious health problems), my son and daughter-in-law, Madhu and Rashmi, and the mature understanding I have been favoured with by Anannya, my six-year-old granddaughter, even when her birthright demands on her grandfather's time were not fully met!

Any remaining deficiencies in the book are, of course, my sole responsibility which I fully accept.

NOTES

INTRODUCTION

1. Drucker (1946, pp. 13-14)

GOVERNING THE CORPORATION

1. Origo, Iris (1957, 1992, p. 110), *The Merchant of Prato: Daily Life in a Medieval Italian City*, Penguin, London
2. *Do Foreigners Invest Less in Poorly Governed Firms?* Leuz, Christian, Karl V. Lins, Francis E. Warnock (2006), Working Paper 12222, National Bureau of Economic Research. The study used US investments in foreign countries as a proxy for foreign investments in general
3. *Karnataka Development Report 2005*, (2006), Government of Karnataka, Bangalore
4. *Report on the Observance of Standards and Codes, Corporate Governance Country Assessment— India* (2004), World Bank, p. 1. Annex C of this Report sets out some statistics and observations on enforcement of shareholder rights, Annex pp. 1-5
5. Mill (1859, p. 4)
6. Joshi (2002, p. 38)
7. Micklethwait and Woolridge (2003, pp. 7-9)

8. 1776, pp. 780-818
9. An Act limiting the liability of all members of joint stock companies was passed by parliament. Such companies had to add the word 'limited' added to their name, and also include in their 'deed of settlement' (roughly equivalent to the modern day 'Memorandum of Association') a statement that the company's liability was 'limited'
10. 2004, p. 13
11. Unlike in India and many other countries including the UK, company legislation in the US is a State prerogative; there is thus no uniform federal corporate legislation though capital markets regulation is centralized in the Securities Exchange Commission and some of the reactive initiatives like the Sarbanes Oxley and Dodd Frank statutes are federal laws
12. Of the Managing Agency system, the Bhabha Committee had commented '...[H]istory, geography and economics all combined to create a system which, in some of its distinctive features, still retains its unique character' (Nigam 1958), (Bhabha 1952)
13. Section 10 (1) of the Companies Act 2013
14. The *Arthashastra*, (edited and translated) Rangarajan, L.N. (1992), Penguin Books India, based on the authoritative work, *The Kautilya Arthasastra*, Kangle, R.P. in three parts, (1960, 1963 and 1965 respectively) University of Bombay

SHAREHOLDERS

1. As of 31 December, 2012, there were 12,89,229 companies on the Register; of these 8,72,957 were at work: 8,06,666 private companies, and 66,291 public companies. Of these latter, 5000+ companies were listed on stock exchanges (Ministry of Company Affairs Annual Report 2012-13, pp. 21-22)
2. Illustratively, this is what happened in Satyam Computers when shareholders revolted and rejected the promoters' plans

to merge two of their other companies in infrastructure and real estate segments, a clear case of tunnelling, transferring cash from away from Satyam

3. Companies Act 2013, Section 2 (69)
4. Bainbridge (2005); Bebchuk (2005), 2006; Gelter (2012); Lipton (2007); Strine (2006)
5. Berle (1931, 1932); Weiner (1964)
6. This important provision in the Companies Act 2013 was first recommended in 1999 by a Government Committee on Corporate Excellence and has taken more than a decade to find its place in the statute book
7. These may include a desire to move up to a wholly-owned status when local regulations permit, or when activism of a small absentee shareholder population is seen to be an irritant, or even when regulatory costs and requirements of continuing listed status are considered to be incommensurate with the benefits. Taking a company private overall offers greater freedom and privacy to companies that see it as a preferred option when feasible
8. These advantages may be diluted and circumscribed if the company is large
9. Berle and Means (1932)
10. Weinstein (2012, p. 15)
11. Section 2 (28) of the Companies Act 2013
12. Section 186 (1) of Companies Act 2013 (with some relaxations for overseas acquisitions by Indian companies)
13. A shareholders' agreement is an instrument that sets out the understanding between partners in joint control of a corporation, with or without the presence of other absentee shareholders, on matters such as board composition and processes, product and market footprint, technology transfer and sub-licensing, capital and dividend policies, brand names usage, appointments of CEO and CFO, exit pricing, and so on. Generally, provisions of these agreements have to be incorporated in the Articles of Association of the companies to

be legally binding on them. Material provisions bearing upon absentee shareholders' interests are also required to be disclosed in any public offering of shares by the company

14. SEC Press Release 2013-65 dated 22 April, 2013 and NPA dated 18 April, 2013 http://www.sec.gov/news/press/2013/2013-65.htm
15. OECD (2004, III.F.1, p. 37)
16. FRC 2012 b
17. Market regulator SEBI is considering regulatory interventions concerning disclosure of institutional investors' policies on corporate governance, voting and voting records, material conflicts of interest, and so on. See SEBI's Consultation paper in January 2013 (pp. 32-35)
18. DCA (2000, para 2.86)
19. pp. 13-14
20. OECD (2005, pp. 33-34)
21. DCA (2000, para 2.86)

BOARDS AND DIRECTORS

1. Galbraith (2004, p. 58)
2. SEBI (2000), TSE (1994, 4.6(3)), GS (2012, Art. 1, 5.1.2), for example
3. Cicero, *De Senectute*, translation. Cited in Cadbury (2002)
4. Corporate history is replete with such purposeful interventions (General Motors, IBM) and sadly, also with examples where the rod was spared with disastrous consequences to the companies and their boards (Enron, WorldCom). A rare Indian example is Tata Finance where the board was caught unawares and had to dismiss its CEO for alleged fraud and self-dealing
5. Arrow 1974, pp. 68-70
6. Bainbridge (2002)
7. Strine (2006).
8. Blair and Stout (1999)

Notes

9. Section 179 (1) of the Companies Act 2013

10. Chapter XVI of the Companies Act 2013 deals with prevention of oppression and mismanagement. 'Eligible' members are: not less than one hundred members of the company or not less than one-tenth of the total number of its members, whichever is less, or any member or members holding not less than one tenth of the issued share capital of the company Section 244 (1) (a)

11. There can be exceptions to this general rule, when there is a breakdown in executive performance, or the board has lost confidence in the leadership and delivery capability of the chief executive, or there are other extraordinary circumstances or development which the board feels cannot be left to the executive for handling. Also, when the *Cyclical Theory* of confidence followed by its erosion and later by its restoration begins to apply

12. *Yesha supteshu jagarti* is how the Sun is described in *Aditya Hrudayam*, an invocation to the Sun God in poet-saint *Valmiki*'s famous Indian epic *Srimadramayanam*. Roughly translated, it refers to one who is wide awake and alert when the rest are asleep. The metaphor relates to the Sun always shining twenty-four hours every day while half the world in its shadow at any time restfully sleeps and is hence not vigilant

13. Bastiat (1850, p.6)

14. Section 149 (4) of Companies Act 2013

15. Listing Agreement Clause 49

16. Illustratively, in Hindustan Lever (as it then was called), Unilever's Indian affiliate, which customarily had virtually the entire board comprising of executive directors (during the pre-clause 49 days), the single strong and respected non-executive director, Mr M. Narasimham (former Reserve Bank Governor, and Union Finance Secretary), could and did make significant contributions to board decisions and processes, and his views could not be, and were not, lightly taken or brushed aside.

Source: Mr M.K. Sharma, former Vice Chairman, Hindustan Unilever Ltd, Quoted with kind permission

17. *Satyagraha* is a Sanskrit word difficult to translate into English. Freely, it denotes, 'holding to the truth' in every situation, no matter how fierce the storm (Easwaran 2003, p. 53)

18. Tandon (2005, pp. 6, 115); Bhartrihari's *Atha Nitishatakam*, a collection of verses on human behaviour in a civilised society, on polity, prudence and wisdom. Barthrihari was a poet-king during the first century AD and ruled in Ujjain, now part of the central Indian state of Madhya Pradesh

19. Technically, the board recommends and the shareholders approve and elect the directors at their annual general meetings; given the voting equations and the poor attendance and by and large indifferent participation of absentee shareholders including institutional shareholders, such elections turn out to be mere formalities. How this issue is to be tackled, especially with regard to institutional shareholders' responsibilities, is a separate matter that is addressed elsewhere in this chapter

20. GC (2012, Art 1)

21. Muth and Donaldson (1998, p. 6)

22. Galbraith (1973, p. 138) Galbraith defines *techno-structure* as the large group in corporations covering the most senior officials down to the levels where it interfaces with white and blue collar workforce, embracing all who bring specialised knowledge, talent or experience to group decision-making, those he calls the guiding intelligence, the brain of the enterprise. He distinguishes this group from the traditional *management* comprising the higher echelons of boards, presidents, and so on; for our discussion, there is little to exclude this elite group from the applicability of the stewardship approach

23. Pfeffer and Salancik (1978)

24. Spencer Stuart (2013, p. 12)

25. FRC (2012, B.1)

26. Section 149 (4), Companies Act 2013

27. Forbes and Milliken (1999, pp. 489, 494-95), Davies Report (2011)
28. Cadbury (2002), Tyson Report (2003), Davies Report (2011)
29. Mill (1859, p. 116, Loc. 3382)
30. Section 203 (1) dealing with this matter allows combining the two positions if a Company's Articles of Association permit and also where a company has multiple businesses with separate CEOs. In practice, these provisions are unlikely to usher in any major shift in the current trends unless there is acceptance of the beneficial spin-offs for the investors by separating the two positions
31. UK Code (2012, A.4.1 and A.4.2)

BOARD COMMITTEES

1. Ranganathananda (2001, I. 4-34, pp. 463-64)
2. For example, where the audit committee decisions or recommendations are not accepted by the full board, the directors' annual report to the shareholders is required to disclose them and the reasons for non- acceptance (Section 177 (8) of the Companies Act 2013)
3. Landefeld, *et al* (2008, pp. 2-3)
4. The Companies Act 2013—Section 178 (1) combines remuneration and nomination in a single committee although international practice suggests their separate constitution
5. ABA (2010, pp. 1015-16)
6. *Statement of the New York Stock Exchange on Audit Committee Policy,* (1977), New York Stock Exchange, p. 1
7. FRC (2012, C.3.1)
8. Section 177 (1) and (2) of the Companies Act 2013
9. In practice, this may not be as delicate or difficult as it may apparently seem. Largely, enforcement depends upon the stature and reputation of the Committee Chair and his/her communication skills involving a judicious mixture of politeness

and firmness. Also, these precedents have to be established right from the beginning of a Committee Chair's tenure; any subsequent effort is likely to be less well received

10. Defined in Section 203 (1) as the Managing Director, or Manager and in their absence, a Wholetime Director, a Chief Financial Officer and a Company Secretary

11. Section 203 (2) of the Companies Act 2013 mandates appointment of the CFO to be approved by the board but the chief of internal audit and assurance is not yet covered by such a requirement

12. Section 205 (1)(a)

13. Section 177 of the Companies Act and Clause 49 of the Listing Agreement

14. The case of Enron in the US is typical: despite a five star board and an audit committee to match, the effectiveness of their performance left much to be desired, eventually leading to the demise of what was once the darling of the stock markets

15. Spira (1999, pp. 231-260)

16. Section 178

17. Section 178 (1)

18. This section draws upon earlier work (together with S K Barua and D Karthik, 2013-C

19. Bebchuk *et al* (2002, p. 10)

20. Extortionist pay levels especially in the financial services sector that were observed during the investigations following the global financial meltdown in 2008-09 are a case in point

21. This assumption has been questioned and described as a self-serving myth; illustratively, Marko Tervio (2007) argues that it is a case of scarcity of opportunities at the top rather than scarcity of talent

22. Regulatory mandates on disclosure of use of compensation consultants are a recognition of the undue impact of this practice on escalating executive pay in the US

23. Wesbach (2005, p.5)
24. Rule 405 under the Securities Act of 1933
25. Sections 152 (6) (c) and (d) of the Companies Act; the three longest serving among the directors (other than those not subject to such retirement) are the ones that will retire by rotation each year
26. Section 178 (5) and (6)
27. Companies with a net worth of at least five hundred crores, or turnover of at least one thousand hundred crores, or profits of at least five crores are covered by this requirement—Section 135 (1)
28. Schedule VII of the Companies Act enumerates the activities that would qualify for this purpose. These are: eradicating extreme hunger and poverty; promotion of education; promoting gender equality and empowering women; reducing child mortality and improving maternal health; combating human immunodeficiency virus, acquired immune deficiency syndrome, malaria and other diseases; ensuring environmental sustainability; employment enhancing vocational skills; social business projects; contribution to the Prime Minister's National Relief Fund or any other fund set up by the Central Government or the State Governments for socio-economic development and relief and funds for the welfare of the Scheduled Castes, the Scheduled Tribes, other backward classes, minorities and women; and such other as may be prescribed

BOARD EFFECTIVENESS

1. Vivekananda (1997, p. 224)
2. Useem (1995)
3. Brandeis (1914)
4. The Companies Act 2013, Section 2 (76) defines a related party comprehensively to include a director or his relative, a key managerial personnel or his relative, a firm or a private

company in which the director or manager is a respectively a partner, or a member or director, a public company in which the director or manager is a director or holds, along with his relatives, 2 percent or more of it equity, or a person or a corporate body's board, managing director or manager, whose instructions, advice or directions of the director or manager

5. Bentham, Jeremy, in Bozovic (ed) (1995), pp. 29-95. In brief, this design for prisons permitted the jailor or jail-inspector a vantage position from where he could see all prisoners and thus have effective surveillance on their activities

6. Gallhofer and Haslam (1993), pp. 320-330, citing Bahmueller, C F (1981)

7. Gallhofer and Haslam (1993), p. 322

8. Berle and Means, (1932), p. 279

9. TSE (1994), Paragraph 4.6 (4)

10. SEBI (1999), Paragraphs 2.8 and 2.10

11. Luke, 6:31

12. Section 178 (2)

EXECUTIVE MANAGEMENT

1. Smale (2003, p. 93)

2. Smale (2003, p. 93). Smale was the non-executive chair of General Motors for three years from 1992 after retiring from Procter and Gamble serving as its CEO during the last nine of his forty years there, and played a stellar role during the turnaround phase when General Motors moved from a $11 million loss each day towards regaining market share and returning to profitability

3. Millstein (2003, p. 146)

4. Minow (2003, p. 133)

5. Kaufman (2003, p. 127)

6. Knight, Charles F with Davis Dyer, (2005), p. 53. Knight was a long time CEO and board chair of Emerson Electric

7. Competition laws and regulations in various countries seek to mitigate any unduly adverse impact on the competitive scenario; also, in an international context, national governments seek to shield businesses in their domain from seemingly unfair incursions into their viability from overseas. Benefits arising from acquisition are therefore limited to the extent where break points may be invoked in the form of such regulatory interventions

8. Tata Steel's acquisition of Corus, Jet Airways' acquisition of Sahara Airlines, Mittal Steel's acquisition of Arcelor, Kingfisher's acquisition of low-cost carrier Air Deccan, and Vodafone's acquisition of Hutchison Telecom, all during 2005-07, are examples of the apparently high acquisition costs, but obviously in the opinion of their executives and their boards, such costs were justified in a long-term cost-benefit equation. In retrospect, Jet and Kingfisher suffered huge losses (the latter in virtual extinction), Vodafone landed in huge tax demands, and Arcelor Mittal is just about surviving although, to be fair, all these companies were also hit by unforeseen recessionary trends following the global financial meltdown in 2008-09

9. Goold, et al (1994) documents in detail their research-based findings on parenting advantage and their value creating potential

10. COSO (1992)

11. IIA (2001)

12. ECIIA (2000)

CORPORATE REPUTATION

1. C.V. Vaidya (1907, 2011, p. 165)
2. Petrick and Quinn (2000, 23, p. 15)
3. Balasubramanian and Kimber (2000, pp. 67-75)
4. Lynn and Jay (1989, 1997, p. 80)

Notes

5. A concept developed by Shombit Sengupta, the branding and transformation expert, to mean 'the end delivery which surpasses customer and consumer expectation', and 'the summit of subliminal attachment between the product and customer life cycle'. Source: Company website http://www.shininguniverse.com. Also, Thirunarayana, *et al* (2001, pp. 31-46)
6. Solomon (1984), McGraw-Hill, p. 3, in Shaw (2003, p. 4)
7. McKeon, Richard (2001, pp. 927-1112)
8. Mintz (1996) in Hartman (2002, p. 8)
9. Rawls (1971)
10. Hinduism offers numerous texts and scriptures (the four ancient *vedas* accompanied by a large number of *upanishads*, the two major epics, the Ramayana and the Mahabharata incorporating the famous Bhagavad Gita, and later day Thiru Kural, among many others) that lay down normative behavioural requirements for its people. Quite similar are the teachings of Zoroastrianism, where 'good thoughts, good words, and good deeds form the ethical foundation upon which righteousness rests and the basis upon which the entire structure of the system of the Mazdayasnian philosophy is reared' (Dhalla 1994, p. 49). For an illuminating summary of modern approaches to business ethics based on various other religions, see Mele (2006) in Epstein and Hanson (2006, pp. 11-43)
11. Sen (2009, p. 20)
12. Besant and Das (2000, pp. 167-68)
13. Collins and Porras (2002, p. 73)
14. Champy (1995, p. 77)
15. Chander, (ed) (1947-1985, p. 129)
16. Damodaran, in Biswas, (1969)
17. Lala (2004, p. 277), quoting JRD Tata, in a letter dated 13 September 1965, to K.C. Bhansali, a school teacher in Calcutta
18. Das (2009) refers to numerous instances in the *Mahabharata* of the problems confronted, often unsuccessfully, in following the ordained righteous path

284

19. Lala (2004, pp. 201-02)
20. *What is a Business For?* Handy, Charles (2002), Harvard Business Review, December, p. 54, quoting Dave Packard, Co-Founder of Hewlett Packard Company in 1939
21. *Towards the Age of Corporate Responsibility? Emerging Challenges for the Business World*, Wilenius, Markku (2004), Elsevier, Futures 37 (2005, p. 133)
22. WCED (1987)
23. Wilson, Andrew (1991). Quotations are from the *Rig Veda* (1.125.5) [622], from Buddhism, *Dhammapada*, 177 and 224 [623 and 699], from Jainism, *Kunakunda, Pancastikaya* 137 [697], from Judaism and Christianity, *Deuteronomy,* 15.7-11 [698], and from Islam, *Forty Hadith of an-Nawawi,* 15 [700]. Page numbers in the book are in square parentheses
24. Subramuniayaswami (2000), respectively verse numbers 218, 214, [p. 95], and 221 [p. 99]
25. Devadhar (2004, II-p. 76), Kalidasa of King Vikramaditya's court in the first century BC is arguably the earliest and most famous Sanskrit poet and playwright in the Indian tradition, in the same league as Homer, Virgil, and Shakespeare
26. Ranganathananda (2001, III, pp. 229-234), Verses XVII-20, 21, 22
27. Strom (2002)
28. Buffett (1989, pp. 52-3)
29. Section 181 of the Companies Act 2013
30. Porter and Kramer in Epstein and Hanson (2006, p. 190)
31. Porter and Kramer (1990), describe four contextual criteria (factor conditions, demand conditions, strategic competitive and rivalry environment, and related and supporting industries) constituting a National Diamond that determines the competitive advantage of country or region
32. Lala (2004, pp. 253-265)
33. Sastry (1993, pp. 162-64, I.xi.8)

EPILOGUE

1. Easwaran (1996, IV.iv.5)
2. This was usually structured, for example, through inter-company services agreements which would carefully avoid provision of any 'management' services and by distributing staff in centralized functions placed on the payroll of different companies even while working together as a single unit at corporate headquarters
3. A similar scenario exists in discussions among jurors in a criminal case: there is no hierarchy, each one based on the briefings and evidence available will have to reach an informed conclusion and the only way to get a measure of unanimity is through talking to persuade. The Hollywood film, *Twelve Angry Men*, offers an excellent dramatization of such a case
4. This was clearly brought out by the number of the independent directors who either resigned from their board positions or very seriously evaluated doing so after the Satyam episode
5. Drucker (1946, p. 6)
6. Bakan (2004, p. 70)

REFERENCES AND SELECT BIBLIOGRAPHY

Allen, James (1902,2006), *As a Man Thinketh*, Sterling Publishers, New Delhi

Al-Mudhaki, Jawaher and P L Joshi (2004), The Role and Functions of Audit Committees in the Indian Corporate Governance: Empirical Findings, International Journal of Auditing, vol. 8, pp. 33–47

American Bar Association (2010-11), *Corporate Director's Guidebook*, Sixth Edition, Committee on Company Laws, ABA Section of Business Law, The Business Lawyer, vol. 66, 2010-11

Anderson, Sarah (2007), *Executive Pay Debate Raging in Europe and the United States*, Foreign Policy in Focus, Washington DC, August 29

Argenti, Paul A and Janis Forman, (2003) The Power of Corporate Communication, Tata McGraw-Hill, New Delhi

Arrow, Kenneth J (1974), *The Limits of Organization*, W W Norton & Company

Bahar, Rashid and Luc Thevenoz (2006), *Conflicts of Interest: Disclosure, Incentives, and the Market*, in Thevenoz L and R Bahar (2006)

Bahmueller, C F (1981), *The National Charity Company: Jeremy Bentham's Silent Revolution*, University of California Press

Bainbridge, Stephen M, (2002), *A Critique of the NYSE's Director Independence Listing Standards*, University of California, Los Angeles School of Law Research Paper no. 02-15

Bakan, Joel (2004), *The Corporation: The Pathological Pursuit of Profit and Power*, Constable, London

Bakan, Joel (2004), *The Corporation – The Pathological Pursuit of Profit and Power*, Constable & Robinson, London [This entry is already in the References list but needs correction to modify publishers' name]

Balasubramanian N (2009), *Addressing Some Inherent Challenges to Good Corporate Governance*, The Indian Journal of Industrial Relations: A Review of Economic and Social Development, Shri Ram Centre for Industrial Relations and Human Resources, New Delhi. Volume 44, No. 44, April

Balasubramanian N (2010), *Corporate Governance and Stewardship: Emerging Role and Responsibilities of Corporate Boards and Directors*, Tata McGraw Hill, New Delhi

Balasubramanian N (2011), *A Case Book on Corporate Governance and Stewardship*, Tata McGraw Hill, New Delhi

Balasubramanian N (2013), *Gender Equality, Inclusivity and Corporate Governance in India*, Journal of Human Values, 19-1, Management Centre for Human Values, Indian Institute of Management Calcutta–April

Balasubramanian N and Anand Ramaswamy (2013), *Ownership Trends in Corporate India- Major Listed Companies: 2000-2011*, Working Paper No. 419, IIMB Centre for Corporate Governance and Citizenship, Indian Institute of Management Bangalore. Also at http://ssrn.com/abstract=2303684, and Indian Institute of Management Ahmedabad Working Paper 2013-10-03

Balasubramanian N and David Kimber (2000), *Corporate Governance, Reputation and Competitive Credibility*, IIMB Management Review, June, pp. 67-75

Balasubramanian N Rejie George (2012), *Corporate governance and the Indian institutional context: Emerging mechanisms and challenges*, IIMB Management Review 24, 215-233 Elsevier

Balasubramanian N, Samir Kumar Barua and D Karthik (2013), *Corporate Governance Issues in Executive Compensation: The Indian Experience—2008-2012*, IIMB-NSE Research Paper No. 426, Centre for Corporate Governance and Citizenship, Indian Institute of Management Bangalore; National Stock Exchange of India Centre for Excellence in Corporate Governance, Mumbai

Balasubramanian N., Barua, S., Bhagvatula, S., and George, R. (2011). *Coping with corporate cholesterol: Board interlocks and their impact on corporate governance: The Indian experience*, IIMB Centre for Corporate Governance and Citizenship Working Paper No. 342, Indian Institute of Management Bangalore. Also at Indian Institute of Management Ahmedabad Working Paper No. 2011-06-01, and at http://ssrn.com/abstract=1857430

Balasubramanian N., Bernard S Black, and Vikramaditya S Khanna (2010). *The relation between firm-level corporate governance and market value: a case study of India*, Emerging Markets Review, 11, 319-340

Balasubramanian, N (1993), Corporate Financial Policies and Shareholder Returns, Himalaya Publishing, New Delhi

Balasubramanian, N (2011 a), Corporate Ethics and Governance in an Inclusive Growth Framework, Indian Journal of Industrial Relations–A Review of Economic and Social Development, Vol. 46, N0. 4, pp. 571-593, April, Shri Ram Centre for Industrial Relations and Human Resources, New Delhi

Balasubramanian, N (2011 b), Glass Ceilings and Oak-Paneled Walls: Women on Corporate Boards, Prime Database Directory 2011, New Delhi; also at http://ssrn.com/abstract=1933651

Bastiat, Frederick (1850), *The Law*, Kindle Edition, Amazon, New York

References and Select Bibliography

Bebchuk Lucian A, Jesse M. Fried and David I. Walker (2002), *Managerial Power And Rent Extraction In The Design Of Executive Compensation*, Working Paper 9068, National Bureau Of Economic Research, Cambridge MA., (http://www.nber.org/papers/w9068)

Bebchuk Lucian and Yaniv Grinstein (2005), *The Growth of Executive Pay*, Oxford Review of Economic Policy, vol. 21, pp. 283–303

Bentham Jeremy (1995), *Panopticon or The Inspection House*, in *The Panopticon Writings*

Berle Adolph A (1931),*Corporate Powers as Powers in Trust*, Harvard Law Review, 44:1049-1074

Berle Adolph A and Gardiner Means (1932-1991), *The Modern Corporation and Private Property*, New Edition, Transaction Publishers, Brunswick and London

Besant Annie and Bhagvan Das (2000), *Sanathana Dharma–An Advanced Text Book of Hindu Religion and Ethics*, The Theosophical Publishing House, Chennai

Bhabha C H (1952), *Report of the Company Law (Bhabha) Committee*, Department of Company Law Administration, Government of India, New Delhi

Bharat-Ram, Vinay (2011), *From the Brink of Bankruptcy–The DCM Story*, Penguin-Viking, New Delhi

Biswas S C (1969), (ed), *Gandhi–Theory and Practice*, Indian Institute of Advanced Study, Simla

Blair Margaret M (1995), *Ownership and Control: Rethinking Corporate Governance for the Twenty-First Century*, The Brookings Institution, Washington DC

Blair Margaret M and Lynn Stout (1999), *A Team Production Theory of Corporate Law*, Virginia Law Review, Vol 85, No 2

Bossidy Larry and Ram Charan, with Charles Burck (2002), *Execution: The Discipline of Getting Things Done*, Random House, London

Bowie Norman E and Ronald F Duska (1990), *The Moral Responsibilities of Business*, Prentice-Hall

Bozovic Miriam (ed) at http://www.cartome.org/panopticon2.htm

Brandeis Louis D (1914), *Other People's Money and How the Bankers Use It*, Seven Treasures Publications, E-Book Kindle Edition, (2009), Amazon, New York

BRT (2012), *Principles of Corporate Governance*, Business Roundtable, Washington DC

Buffett Warren (1989), *Annual Report*, Berkshire Hathaway, http://www.berkshirehathaway.com

Buffett Warren (1996) *An Owner's Manual,* , Berkshire Hathaway, Principle 12; athttp://www.berkshirehathaway.com

C V Vaidya (1907, 2011), *Epic India – as depicted in The Mahabharata and The Ramayana*, Asian Educational Services, New Delhi

Cadbury Adrian (1992), *Report of the (Cadbury) Committee on The Financial Aspects of Corporate Governance* (1992), Gee Publishing, London

Cadbury Adrian (2002), *Corporate Governance and Chairmanship: A Personal View*, Oxford University Press

Campbell David (1993), *Why Regulate the Modern Corporation? The Failure of 'Market Failure'*, in *Corporate Control and Accountability,* JosephMcCahery, et al, (ed. 1993), Oxford University Press

Campos Roel C (2007), *Speech by SEC Commissioner: Remarks Before the 2007 Summit on Executive Compensation*, New York, US Securities and Exchange Commission, http://www.sec.gov/news/speech/2007/spch012307rcc.htm

Carroll Archie B (1979), *A Three-Dimensional Conceptual Model of Corporate Performance*, Academy of Management Review, vol. 4, no. 4

Cary Dennis C and Marie-Caroline Von Weichs (ed) (2003), *How to Run a Company*, Crown Business, New York

Champy James (1995), *Reengineering Management*, Harper Collins

Chander Jag Parvesh (ed) (1947), *Teachings of Mahatma Gandhi*, Indian Printing Press, Lahore; reprinted in *Enlightened Citizenship* (1985), Ramakrishna Mission, New Delhi

Chandrashekar S and K. Muralidharan (2012), *Networks of Power and Influence- Board Interlocks in India 1995-2007—An Empirical Investigation*, Working Paper No. 374, Indian Institute of Management Bangalore

Chaturvedi Badrinath (2006), *The Mahabharata: An Inquiry in the Human Condition*, Orient Longman.

Christie Michael (2003), *The Director's Fiduciary Duty Not to Compete*, The Modern Law Review, vol. 55, no. 4

CII-IiAS (2012), *Institutional Investors—Driving Force for Good Governance-A Survey*, Confederation of Indian Industry, New Delhi

Coady A and C Sampford (eds) (1993), *Business, Ethics and the Law*, Foundation Press

Coffee Jr John C (2006), *Gatekeepers: The Professions and Corporate Governance*, Oxford University Press

Collins James C and Jerry L Porras (2002), *Built to Last*, Harper Collins Publishers

COSO (1992), *Internal Control—Integrated Framework*, Committee of Sponsoring Organizations of the Treadway Commission, American Institute of Certified Public Accountants, New York

Dallas Lynne L (2002), *The New Managerialism and Diversity on Corporate Boards of Directors*, University of San Diego School of Law, Public Law and Legal Theory Working Paper 38

Dalley Paula J (2004), *The Misguided Doctrine of Stockholder Fiduciary Duties*, Hofstra Law Review, vol. 33:175, pp. 175–222

Das Gurcharan (2009), *The Difficulty of Being Good: On The Subtle Art of Dharma*, Allen Lane–Penguin

Davies Keith (1975), *Five Propositions for Social Responsibility*, Business Horizons, 18 June, The Foundation for the School of Business at Indiana University

References and Select Bibliography

DCA (2000), Report on Corporate Excellence on a Sustained Basis to Sharpen India's Global Competitive Edge and to Further Develop Corporate Culture in the Country (2000), Government of India, (then) Department of Company Affairs, 20 November

Deb Sandipan (2013), *Fallen Angel: The Making and Unmaking of Rajat Gupta*, Rupa, New Delhi

Devadhar C R (2004), *Works of Kalidasa*, Vol. II, Motilal Banarasidass

Dhalla Maneckji Nusservanji (1994), *Mazda's Ministering Angels*, in *History of Zoroastrianism*, The K R Cama Oriental Institute, Mumbai

Dodd E M (1932), *For Whom are Corporate Managers Trustees*, Harvard Law Review, 45: 1145-1163

Drucker Peter F (1946), *Concept of the Corporation*, Transaction Publishers (New 1994 Edition)

Dunlavy Colleen A (2004), *Citizens to Plutocrats: Nineteenth-Century Shareholder Voting Rights and Theories of the Corporation*, in Kenneth Lipartito and Gavid B Sicilia (eds), *Constructing Corporate America: History, Politics, Culture*, Oxford University Press

Easterbrook Frank H and Daniel R Fischel (1991), *The Economic Structure of Corporate Law*, Harvard University Press, Cambridge

Easwaran Eknath (2003), *Gandhi–The Man*, Jaico Publishing

Easwaran, Eknath (1996), *The Upanishads*, Chapter IV, Section iv, Verse 5, Penguin

ECIIA (2000), *Internal Control and Internal Auditing: Guidance for Directors, Managers and Auditors*, European Confederation of Institutes of Internal Auditing, Antwerp, Belgium

Epstein Marc J, and Kirk O Hanson, (2006), (ed) *Accountable Corporation, Vol. 2: Business Ethics*, Praeger

Epstein Marc J, and Kirk O Hanson, (2006), (ed) *Accountable Corporation, Vol. 3: Corporate Social Responsibility*, Business Ethics, Praeger

Feldman Mark L and Michael F Spratt (1999), *Five Frogs on a Log*, PricewaterhouseCoopers, Harper Collins, New York

Fombrun Charles J and Cees B M Van Riel (2004), *Fame & Fortune: How Successful Companies Build Winning Reputations*, Financial Times-Prentice Hall

Fondas N. and S. Sassalos (2000), 'A Different Voice in the Boardroom: How the Presence of Women Directors Affects Board. Influence over Management,' Global Focus, 12: 13-22

Forbes Daniel and Frances Milliken(1999), *Cognition and Corporate Governance: Understanding Boards of Directors as Strategic Decision-Making Groups,Academy of Management Review*, Vol. 24(3)

FRC (2012 a), The UK Corporate Governance Code, Financial Reporting Council, London

FRC (2012 b), *The UK Stewardship Code* Financial Reporting Council, London

Freeman R Edward (1998), *A Stakeholder Theory of the Modern Corporation*, in Max B E Clarkson (ed), *The Corporation and Its Stakeholders: Classic and Contemporary Readings*, University of Toronto Press, Toronto

Friedman Milton (1962), *Monopoly and Social Responsibility* in *Capitalism and Freedom, Chicago University Press,* Chicago

Fukuyama, Francis (2011), *The Origins of Political Order*, Farrar, Straus and Giroux, New York

Gabor, Andrea (2000), *The Capitalist Philosophers*, Crown Business- Random House, New York

Galbraith John Kenneth (1973), *The New Industrial State*, Oxford and IBH Publishing

Galbraith, John Kenneth (2004), *The Economics of Innocent Fraud – Truth of our time*, Houghton Mifflin Company, Boston

Gallhofer Sonja and Jim Haslam (1993*), Approaching Corporate Accountability*, Accounting and Business Research, vol 23, no. 91A

Ganguli Kisari Mohan (2000), *The Mahabharata*, Munshiram Manoharlal Publishers, New Delhi. English translation from the Sanskrit original

GC (2012), *German Corporate Governance Code*, Government Commission, Federal Republic of Germany, Bonn

Gerstner Jr. (2002). *Who Says Elephants Can't Dance?* Harper Collins, New York

Goodman Ted (ed) (1999), *The Forbes Book of Business Quotations*. Konemann, Cologne

Goodstein Jerry, Kanak Gautam and Warren Boeker (1994), *The Effects of Board Size and Diversity on Strategic Change*, *Strategic Management Journal*, Vol. 15

Goold Michael, Andrew Campbell and Marcus Alexander (1994), *Corporate-Level Strategy–Creating Value in the Multibusiness Company*, John Wiley, New York

Grabosky P and A Sutton (1991), (ED), *Stains on a White Collar: Fourteen Studies in Corporate Crime or Corporate Harm*, Federation Press, Sydney

Gunningham N. (1989), *Asbestos Mining at Baryulgil: a case of corporate neglect?* in, Grabosky and Sutton (1991)

H&S (2009), *Boards in Turbulent Times 2009*, Heidrick & Struggles International, Inc

Haigh Gideon (2006), Asbestos House: The Secret History of James Hardie Industries, Scribe, Carlton North, Victoria, Australia

Hamdani Assaf (2003), *Gatekeeper Liability*, South California Law Review, 53

Handy Charles (2002), *What is a Business For?* Harvard Business Review, December

Hartman Laura P (2002), *Perspectives in Business Ethics*, Tata McGraw-Hill

Hawkins David F (1986), *Corporate Financial Disclosure: 1900–1933*, Garland Publishing

Hecker Jr. Edwin W (2006), *Fiduciary Duties in Business Entities*, Kansas Law Review, vol. 54, p. 977–980

Huntington Samuel P (1968), *Political Order in Changing Societies*, Yale University, 2009 Indian Edition, Adarsh Books, New Delhi

Hutton Ray (2013), *Jewels in the Crown: How Tata of India Transformed Britain's Jaguar Land Rover*, Elliot and Thompson, London

IIA (2001), *Standards for the Professional Practice of Internal Auditing*, The Institute of Internal Auditors, Altamonte Springs, Florida

IoDSA (2009), *King Code of Governance Southern Africa* an the *King Code of Governance Principles (King III)*, Institute of Directors in Southern Africa, Parklands, Johannesburg

JCGC (2001), *Revised Corporate Governance Principles*, Japan Corporate Governance Committee, Tokyo

Joshi Divya (ed) (2002), *Gandhi on Villages*, Gandhi Book Centre, Bombay Sarvodaya Mandal, Bombay

K Damodaran (1969) *Ends and Means*, in Biswas, (1969)

Kaufman Stephen P (2003), *The Board as Consultants*, in Carey and Weichs (2003)

Keys Tracey S and Thomas W. Malnight (2012), *Corporate Clout Distributed: The Influence of the World's Largest 100 Economic Entities*, Global Trends, June, Strategy Dynamics Global Limited. http://www.globaltrends.com/

Kimber David and Fran Siemensma (2008), Biaguel, Unpublished Case Study, Indian Institute of Management Bangalore

Knight Charles F with Davis Dyer, (2005), *Performance without Compromise*, Harvard Business School Press

Koh Pearlie (2003), *Once a Director, Always a Fiduciary?* Cambridge Law Journal, 62(2)

Konrad A M, V W Kramer and S Erkut (2008), *Critical mass: The Impact of Three or More Women on Corporate Boards*, Organizational Dynamics, Volume 37, Issue 2 (April-June)

Kraakman Reinier (1986), *Gatekeepers: The Anatomy of Third-Party Enforcement Strategy*, 2 Journal of Law, Economics and Organization, 53

Kubarek Joseph P (2006), *Shaping Board and Committee Calendars*, The Corporate Board, September/October

Lala R M (2004), *The Creation of Wealth*, Penguin India

Lewi, John E (2003), (Ed) *The New Rights of Man*, Robinson, London

Lynn Jonathan and Antony Jay (1989), *The Grand Design,* in *Yes, Prime Minister: The Diaries of the Right Hon. James Hacker,* BBC Books, India Book House 1997 edition

MCA (2012), *Report of the (Adi Godrej) Committee constituted by MCA to formulate aPolicy Document on Corporate Governance*, Ministry of Corporate Affairs, Government of India, New Delhi

McDonald Hamish (1998), *The Polyester Prince: The Rise of Dhirubhai Ambani*, Allen and Unwin, St Leonards, New South Wales

McKeon Richard (1941), *The Basic Works of Aristotle*, (ed), Random House, New York; 2001 Modern Library Paperback Edition, New York

Mele Domenec (2006), *Religious Foundations of Business Ethics*, in Epstein andHanson, (2006)

Micklethwait John and Adrian Wooldridge (2003), *The Company—A Short History of a Revolutionary Idea*, 2005 PB edition, The Modern Library-Random House, New York

Mill John Stuart (1859), *On Liberty*, J W Parker & Son, London, Kindle Edition, Amazon, New York

Mill, John Stuart (1869), *The Subjection of Women*, Kindle Edition, Amazon, New York

Miller Paul B W and Paul R Bahnson (2005*), The Seven Deadly Sins of Financial Reporting* in *Quality Financial Reporting*, Tata McGraw-Hill

Millstein Ira (2003), *Reforming the Corporate Governance Process*, in Carey and Weichs (2003)

Minow Nell (2003), *Keeping Management in Check*, in Carey and Weichs (2003)

Mintz Steven (1996), *Aristotelian Virtue and Business Ethics Education*, Journal of Business Ethics 15, no. 8, pp. 827–38

Morck Randall K, Michael Percy, Gloria Y. Tian, and Bernard Yeung (2007), *The Rise and Fall of the Widely Held Firm; A History of Corporate Ownership in Canada*, in *A History of Corporate Governance around the World: Family Business Groups to Professional Managers*, ed. Randall K. Morck, University of Chicago Press

Mukherjee Siddhartha (2011), Emperor of All Maladies: A Biography of Cancer, Fourth Estate, London

Mukherjee, Siddartha (2011), *The Emperor of All Maladies – A Biography of Cancer*, Fourth Estate- Harper Collins, London

Muth Melind M, and Lex Donaldson (1998), *Stewardship Theory and Board Structure: A Contingency Approach*, Corporate Governance—Scholarly Research and Theory Papers, Vol. 6, No. 1, January, Blackwell

Newman, John H (1833), *Lead, kindly Light*, www.cyberhymnal.org/html/l/e/a/leadkind.htm

Nigam Raj K (1958), *Managing Agencies in India: Basic Facts*, Department of Company Law Administration, Government of India, New Delhi

Nunes, Paul and Tim Breene (2011), *Jumping the S-Curve: How to Beat the Growth Cycle, Get on Top, and Stay There*, Harvard Business Review Press, Boston

Obal Shelly and Julie Walsh (2005)(ed), *Corporate Governance in Canada*, Osler, Hoskin & Harcourt

OECD (1998), *Corporate Governance: Improving Competitiveness and Access to Capital in Global Markets, A Report to the OECD by the Advisory Group on Corporate Governance,*

Organization for Economic Cooperation and Development, Paris

OECD (2001), *OECD Transfer Pricing Guidelines for Multinational Enterprises and Tax Administrations* Organization for Economic Cooperation and Development, Paris

OECD (2004), *OECD Principles of Corporate Governance*, Organization for Economic Cooperation and Development, Paris

OECD (2004), *OECD Principles of Corporate Governance*, Organization for Economic Cooperation and Development, Paris

OECD (2005), *OECD Guidelines on Corporate Governance of State Owned Enterprises*, Organization for Economic Cooperation and Development, Paris

OECD (2005-a), *Comparative Report on Corporate Governance of State Owned Enterprises: A Survey of OECD Countries, Organization for Economic Cooperation and Development, Paris*

OECD (2009), *Guide on Fighting Abusive Related Party Transactions in Asia*, Organization for Economic Cooperation and Development, Paris

OECD (2011-a), *OECD Guidelines for Multinational Enterprises*, Organization for Economic Cooperation and Development, Paris

OECD (2011-b), *The Role of Institutional Investors in Promoting Good Corporate Governance*, Organization for Economic Cooperation and Development, Paris

Origo Iris (1957), *The Merchant of Prato–The Daily Life in a Medieval Italian City*, Jonathan Cape, Penguin Edition (1992), London

Orwell, George (1945), *Animal Farm*, Secker & Warburg, London; 2012 Indian edition, Hachette, Gurgaon

Owens, Lily (ed) (1996), *The Marsh King's Daughter*, in *The Complete Han Christian Andersen Fairy Tales*, Gramercy-Random House, New York

Pande Santosh (2012), *Position and Rights of Minority Shareholders in Listed State owned Enterprises (SOEs)-experiences and lessons from India*, at www.ssrn.com/abstract=2149566

Paul Swraj (1998), *Beyond Boundaries: A Memoir*, Penguin, New Delhi

Petrick Joseph A and John F Quinn (2000), *The Integrity Capacity Construct and Moral Progress in Business*, Journal of Business Ethics, Vol. 23, p. 15

Pfeffer, Jeffrey, and Gerald R Salancik (1978), *The External Control of Organizations: A Resource Dependence Perspective*, Harper & Row

Porter Michael E and Mark R Kramer (1990), *Competitive Advantage of Nations*, The Free Press

Porter Michael E and Mark R Kramer (2006), *Corporate Philanthropy: Taking the High Ground*, in Epstein and Hanson (2006)

Radhabai Atmaram Sagoon, Bombay. 2001 edition–Asian Educational Services, New Delhi

Raghavan Anita (2013), *The Billionaire's Apprentice*, Hachette India, Gurgaon

Ranganathananda Swamy (2001), *The Universal Message of the Bhagavad Gita*, Volume III, Advaita Ashrama, Calcutta

Rangarajan L N (1992), *Kautilya's Arthashastra*, Penguin, New Delhi

Rawls John (1971), *A Theory of Justice*, Harvard University Press, Cambridge, MA

RBI (2005) The *Report of the (Satwalekar) Working Group on Conflicts of Interest in the Financial Sector*, Reserve Bank of India

Ruigrok Winfried, Simon Peck, Sabina Tacheva, Peder Greve and Yan Hu (2006), *The Determinants and Effects of Board Nomination Committees*, , Journal of Management and Governance, vol. 10, no. 2, pp. 119–148.

Sastry Alladi Mahadeva (1993), *The Taittiriya Upanishad*, Samata Books, Chennai

Sealy Ruth and Susan Vinnicombe (2012), *The Female FTSE Board Report 2012, Milestone or Millstone?* Cranfield International Centre for Women Leaders, Cranfield School of Management, Cranfield, Bedford

SEBI (1999), *Report of the [Kumar Mangalam Birla] Committee on Corporate Governance*, Securities and Exchange Board of India, Mumbai

SEBI (2013), *Consultative Paper on Review of Corporate Governance Norms in India*, Securities and Exchange Board of India, Mumbai

Sen Amartya (2009), *The Idea of Justice*, Allen Lane–Penguin

Sen Gupta N K (1974), *Corporate Management in India*, Vikas Publishing, New Delhi

Sharer Kevin (2003), *The Working Relationship Between a CEO and His Directors*, in Carey and Weichs (2003)

Shaw William H (2003), *Business Ethics*, Thomson Asia

Slater Robert (1999), Jack Welch and the GE Way, McGraw-Hill

Smale John G (2003), *The Board as the Boss: The Relationship Between the CEO and the Board*, in Carey and Weichs (2003)

Smith Adam (1776), *An Inquiry into the Nature and Causes of the Wealth of Nations*, 2000 Modern Library Edition, Random House, New York

Solomon Robert C (1984), *Morality and the Good Life*, McGraw-Hill

Solomon Robert C (1993), *Corporate Roles, Personal Virtues, Moral Mazes: An Aristotelian Approach to Virtue Ethics*, in (Coady and Sampford, 1993)

Spencer Stuart (2012-a), *Spencer Stuart Board Index- 2012 (US)*, Spencer Stuart, New York.

Spencer Stuart (2012-b), *UK Board Index- 2012–Current Board Trends and Practices at Major UK Companies*, Spencer Stuart, London

Spencer Stuart (2013), *India Board Index: Current Board Trends and Practices in the BSE 100*, Spencer Stuart, Mumbai

Spira Laura F (1999), *Ceremonies of Governance: Perspectives on the Role of the Audit Committee*, Journal of Management and Governance, vol. 3

Strine Jr Leo E,(2006), *Toward a True Corporate Republic: A Traditionalist Response to Bebchuk's Solution for Improving Corporate America*, Harvard Law Review, Vol. 119:1759

Strom Stephanie (2002), *In Charity, Where Does a C.E.O. End and a Company Start?* New York Times, September 22

Subramuniayaswami Satguru Sivaya (2000), *Thiru Valluvar's Thiru Kural*, Abhinav Publications

Supreme Court of India (1986), *AIR 1370, Life Insurance Corporation Of India vs Escorts Ltd. & Others*, on 19 December, 1985

Tandon Rajendra (2005), (Tr) Barthrihari's *Atha Nitishatakam*, Rupa & Co, New Delhi

Thevenoz L and R Bahar (eds.) (2006), Conflicts of Interest: Corporate Governance and Financial Market, Kluwer Law International

Thirunarayana N Mithileshwar Jha and YLR Murthy (2001), *Shombit Sengupta: Brands and the Art of Living*, Interview: IIMB Management Review, September, pp. 31–46

Thoreau, Henry David (1849, 2004), *Civil Disobedience*, Simon & Schuster, New York

Toynbee, Arnold and Jane Caplan (1972), *A Study of History*, Thames and Hudson, London

Tricker R I (2000), *The Evolution of the Company–How the Idea has Changed* , in *Corporate Governance*, Tricker, R I (ed) (2000), Ashgate Publishing, London

TSE (1994), *Where were the Directors? Guidelines for Improved Corporate Governance in Canada*, Toronto Stock Exchange, Toronto

TSE (2001), *Beyond Compliance: Building a Governance Culture*, Interim Report of the Joint [Saucier] Committee on Corporate Governance (2001), Toronto Stock Exchange, Toronto

Tyson, Laura D'Andrea (2003), *The Tyson Report on the Recruitment and Development of Non-executive Directors*, London Business School

UK (2006), Companies Act 2006, Government of the United Kingdom of Great Britain, London

UKG (2011), *Women on Boards 2011, The Davies Report*, Ministries of Business and Women, Government of the United Kingdom, London

UN (2012), *Guiding Principles on Business and Human Rights: Implementing the United Nations 'Protect, Respect and Remedy' Framework,* Office of the Special Representative of the Secretary General for Business and Human Rights, UN General Human Rights Council, Geneva. Available at http://www.ohchr.org/documents/issues/business/A.HRC.17.31.pdf

UN (2013), *Global Compact,* Principle 7, United Nations, New York

Useem Jerry (1995), *Managerial Duties and Business Law*, Harvard College

Vaidya C V (1907), *Epic India: India as Described in The Mahabharata and The Ramayana,*

Valukas Anton R (2010), *In Lehman Brothers Holdings Inc, et al, Report of the Examiner,* Volume 1, United States Bankruptcy Court, Southern District of New York

Vivekananda, Swami (1997), The Complete Works of Swami Vivekananda, Vol. 3, Advaita Ashrama, Kolkatta. p.224

WCED (1987), *Our Common Future: The (Bruntland) Report of the World Commission on Environment and Development,* Oxford University Press

Weinstein Olivier (2012), *Firm, Property and Governance: From Berle and Means to the Agency Theory, and Beyond,* Accounting, Economics, and Law, Vol 2 Iss. 2, Article 2

Whitney, John O and Tina Packer (2000), *Power Plays – Shakespeare's Lessons in Leadership and Management*, Simon & Schuster, New York

Wilenius Markku (2004), *Towards the Age of Corporate Responsibility? Emerging Challenges for the Business World*, Elsevier

Wilson, Andrew (ed) (1991), *World Scripture: A Comparative Anthology of Sacred Texts*, Motilal Banarasidass Publishers.

Witzel, Morgen (2010), *Tata: The Evolution of a Corporate Brand*, Penguin, New Delhi

A NOTE ON IIMA BUSINESS BOOKS

The IIM Ahmedabad Business Books series brings key issues in management and business to a general audience. With a wealth of information and illustrations from contemporary Indian business, these non-academic and user-friendly books from the faculty of IIM Ahmedabad are essential corporate reading.

www.iimabooks.com

OTHER BOOKS IN THIS SERIES

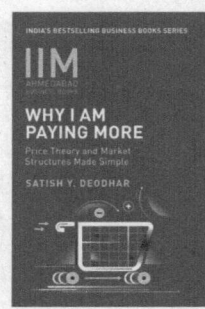

IIM
AHMEDABAD
BUSINESS BOOKS

STRATEGIES FOR GROWTH

Help Your Business Move Up the Ladder

ATANU GHOSH

IIM
AHMEDABAD
BUSINESS BOOKS

BUSINESS LAW FOR MANAGERS

Kaleidoscopic Tales

ANURAG K. AGARWAL

IIM
AHMEDABAD
BUSINESS BOOKS

DAY TO DAY ECONOMICS

SATISH Y. DEODHAR

IIM
AHMEDABAD
BUSINESS BOOKS

CONTRACT TERMS ARE COMMON SENSE

AKHILESHWAR PATHAK